Languages of the Caucasus

Editors: Diana Forker (Universität Jena), Nina Dobrushina (National Research University Higher School of Economics, Moscow), Timur Maisak (Institute of Linguistics at the Russian Academy of Sciences, Moscow), Oleg Belyaev (Lomonosov Moscow State University).

In this series:

1. Daniel, Michael, Nina Dobrushina & Dmitry Ganenkov (eds.). The Mehweb language: Essays on phonology, morphology and syntax.

2. Forker, Diana. A grammar of Sanzhi Dargwa.

3. Dolatian, Hossep, Afsheen Sharifzadeh & Bert Vaux. A grammar of Iranian Armenian: Parskahayeren or Iranahayeren.

ISSN (print): 2699-0148
ISSN (electronic): 2699-0156

A grammar of Iranian Armenian

Parskahayeren or Iranahayeren

Hossep Dolatian

Afsheen Sharifzadeh

Bert Vaux

language
science
press

Hossep Dolatian, Afsheen Sharifzadeh & Bert Vaux. 2023. *A grammar of Iranian Armenian: Parskahayeren or Iranahayeren* (Languages of the Caucasus 3). Berlin: Language Science Press.

This title can be downloaded at:
http://langsci-press.org/catalog/book/354
© 2023, Hossep Dolatian, Afsheen Sharifzadeh & Bert Vaux
Published under the Creative Commons Attribution 4.0 Licence (CC BY 4.0):
http://creativecommons.org/licenses/by/4.0/
ISBN: 978-3-96110-419-2 (Digital)
         978-3-98554-077-8 (Hardcover)

ISSN (print): 2699-0148
ISSN (electronic): 2699-0156
DOI: 10.5281/zenodo.8177018
Source code available from www.github.com/langsci/354
Errata: paperhive.org/documents/remote?type=langsci&id=354

Cover and concept of design: Ulrike Harbort
Proofreading: Amir Ghorbanpour, Diana M. Lewis, Elliott Pearl, Geoffrey Haig, Jean Nitzke, Jeroen van de Weijer, Mary Ann Walter, Maša Bešlin, Patricia Cabredo, Rebecca Madlener, Steven Kaye, Tom Bossuyt, Vladan Sutanovac, Yvonne Treis
Fonts: Libertinus, Arimo, DejaVu Sans Mono, Mardoto
Typesetting software: X⅃LATEX

Language Science Press
xHain
Grünberger Str. 16
10243 Berlin, Germany
http://langsci-press.org

Storage and cataloguing done by FU Berlin

Freie Universität Berlin

Contents

Contents

Acknowledgments

First and foremost, we thank the speakers of Iranian Armenian who shared their speech and culture with us.

Afsheen extends his heartfelt gratitude to his parents, Khalil and Simin Sharifzadeh, whose support allowed him to acquire his first Armenian primer as a teenager, and years later to journey freely throughout Persia and Armenia conducting fieldwork. Afsheen thanks his brother, Arya Sharifzadeh, who acted as a sounding board for sociological and linguistic discussions, and without whom his research on the Iranian Armenian dialect would not have happened. To Dr. Ina Baghdiantz-McCabe, a world expert on New Julfa who inspired his passion for Iranian Armenian topics, Afsheen says մի աշխարհ շնորհակալություն. Afsheen extends a special thanks to his dear friends Sevada, Tina and Lernik Yedgarian for their undying hospitality and becoming something of an adoptive Armenian family in Tehran, Yerevan, and Los Angeles.

Bert thanks Armen, Anna Gevorkyan, Ara Ghazarians, Arsineh Artounians Hovannisian, Bavrina Bigjahan, Hagop Hachikian, Narineh Hacopian, Anahit Keshishian, Armineh Mirzabegian, and Alla Petrosyan. He would especially like to thank Karine Megerdoomian for her extensive insights into Iranian Armenian lexis, syntax, and sociolinguistics over the years, and Richard Hovannisian for introducing him to many members of the Iranian Armenian community in the Los Angeles area over the years, which first made him aware of how distinctive and widespread the dialect is, and for organising the 2004 UCLA conference on Armenians in Iran that forced him to begin crystallizing his fieldwork on the dialect.

Hossep thanks Hannah Cox and Vartan Haghverdi for teaching him what Iranian Armenian is in the first place. Hossep also thanks Karine Megerdoomian for continuing fieldwork together.

Among Hossep's consultants, much of the material in this grammar wouldn't have been possible without Hossep's main consultant and language teacher, Nicole Khachikian. Hossep thanks her from the bottom of his heart for all the Zoom meetings. He thanks Arevik Torosyan for providing Eastern recordings, and for bearing with him over Facebook. Vahagn Petrosyan is owed special thanks for organizing the Eastern Armenian paradigms on Wiktionary in such a way that it was relatively easy to go about our morphology fieldwork. We thank the many Eastern speakers who helped us with elicitations and Eastern syntax: Mariam Asatryan, Harut Hayrapetyan, Katherine Hodgson, Victoria Khurshudyan.

We thank Beaina Amirian, James Barry, Maryam Ghiasian, Shushan Karapetian, Varand Nikolaian, Shakeh Amirian Petrossian, Hakimeh Rezayi, Claris Sarkissian, and Hamo Vassilian for help in tracking down Iranian Armenian sources.

We thank the comedians who wrote and acted out the sample text on Instagram:[1] Tiffany Alice, Ryan Ebrahamian, Helen Kalognomos, Loucineh Mardirossian, Shant Nazarian, and Gilbert Sinanian.

For discussion of various aspects of Armenian dialectology, we thank Nikita Bezrukov, Peter Cowe, Garoun Engström, Hagop Gulludjian, Tereza Hovhannisyan, Hrach Martirosyan, and Anooshik Melikian. For Turkic discussions, we thank Stephen Nichols and Jonathan North Washington.

For discussion of various aspects of Persian phonology and syntax, we thank Koorosh Ariyaee, Reza Falahati, Hamed Rahmani, Nima Sadat-Tehrani, and Scott Seyfarth. We especially thank Nazila Shafiei for syntax elicitations.

For discussion of the liquid deletion process, we thank Arto Anttila, Canaan Breiss, Larry Hyman, Mark Liberman, Kate Lindsey, Nicholas Rolle, Katherine Russell, Hannah Sande, and Shanti Ulfsbjorninn.

For discussions of the past perfective paradigms, we thank Sargis Avetyan, Matthew Carter, Borja Herce, Brian Joseph, Laura Kalin, Shuan Karim, and Jordan Kodner.

We thank Diana Forker, Felix Kopecky, and Sebastian Nordhoff for their patience and advice as we went through the publishing process. We owe a special thanks to our reviewers (Katherine Hodgson and Donald Stilo) and proofreaders for making this book better.

Finally, we thank the sender of the anonymized email in §1.3. If it wasn't for that email, Hossep would not have bothered to do any of the synthesis or replication work. For better or worse, this grammar was done out of resistance against linguistic discrimination.

---

[1]https://www.instagram.com/tv/COWtIvUn4KA/

Abbreviations

√	root	INS	instrumental
ABL	ablative	LOC	locative
ACC	accusative	LV	linking vowel
AGR	agreement	NEG	negation
AOR	aorist stem or suffix, regardless of whether it's used in the past perfective or in other contexts	NMLZ	nominalizer
		NOM	nominative
		NX	stem extender between irregular nouns or pronouns and oblique cases
ASP	aspect	OM	object marker (for Persian)
AUX	auxiliary verb or copula 'is'	ORD	ordinal
K	case	PASS	passive
CAUS	causative	PERF.CVB	perfective converb
CLF	classifier	PL	plural
CON	connective	POSS.1SG	first person possessive
CN.CVB	connegative converb suffix or converb form	POSS.2SG	second person possessive
		PRO	pronoun
DAT	dative	PROG	progressive (used for Persian)
DEF	definite	PROH	prohibitive
DET	determiner	PRS	present
FUT	synthetic future	PTCP	participle
FUT.CVB	future converb	PST	past
GEN	genitive	RPTCP	resultative participle
IMP	imperative	SG	singular
IMPF	imperfective	SIM.CVB	simultaneous converb
IMPF.CVB	imperfective converb	SBJV	subjunctive
INCH	inchoative	SPTCP	subject participle
IND	indicative (used for Western Armenian)	T	tense
		TH	theme vowel
INDF	indefinite	VX	meaningless suffix as a verbal stem-extender
INJ	interjection		
INF	infinitive		

1 Introduction

In this grammar, what we call Iranian Armenian is the koine variety of spoken Eastern Armenian that developed in Tehran, Iran over the last few centuries. It has a substantial community of speakers in California. This variety or lect is called 'Persian Armenian' [pɒɹskɒhɒjeɹen] or 'Iranian Armenian' [iɹɒnɒhɒ-jeɹen] by members of the community (romanized as 'Parksahayeren' and 'Irana-hayeren'). A speaker of this dialect (or a person descended from this community) is called a 'Persian Armenian' [pɒɹskɒhɒj] or 'Iranian Armenian' [iɹɒnɒhɒj] (ro-manized as 'Parskahay' and 'Iranahay'). The name is a compound of the term for Persian or Iranian, plus the compound linking vowel /-ɒ-/, and then the word for Armenian (Table 1.1).

Table 1.1: Name of the language and of the ethnic group

	Armenian	Persian Armenian	Iranian Armenian
Person	hɒj	pɒɹsk-ɒ-hɒj	iɹɒn-ɒ-hɒj
	հայ	պարսկահայ	իրանահայ
Language	hɒjeɹen	pɒɹsk-ɒ-hɒjeɹen	iɹɒn-ɒ-hɒjeɹen
	հայերէն	պարսկահայերէն	իրանահայերէն
Roots:		pɒɹsik 'Persian'	iɹɒn 'Iran'
		պարսիկ	իրան

Persian Armenian is the more conventional name for the language. It reflects the historic name for Persia used in the Armenian language, *Parskastan* Պարս-կաստան, which is still widely used by Armenians in Iran today, and the fact that the Armenian community and their dialects existed prior to the creation of the modern state of Iran. But in recent years, some circles within the community have shifted to preferring the term "Iranian Armenian." They feel that using the name "Persian Armenian" creates the wrong sense that either a) the Armenian variety is closely related genetically to the Persian language, or b) that these Ar-menians are ethnically Persian. Out of respect to this newer sentiment in the community, we use the English name "Iranian Armenian" (IA) in this grammar to refer to this dialect.

The present book is not a comprehensive grammar of the language. It occupies a gray zone between being a simple sketch vs. a sizable grammar. We try to clarify the basic aspects of the language, such as its phoneme inventory, noticeable morphophonological processes, various inflectional paradigms, and some peculiar aspects of its syntax. We likewise provide a sample text of Iranian Armenian speech (Chapter 8). Many aspects of this variety seem to be identical to Standard Eastern Armenian, so we tried to focus more on those aspects of Iranian Armenian which differ from that variety. Readers are encouraged to consult Dum-Tragut's (2009) reference grammar of Standard Eastern Armenian if needed.

The introduction provides a basic typological sketch of the language (§1.1). We then discuss the origin of the Iranian Armenian community and its demographics in §1.2. The community displays triglossia and we discuss the community's basic sociolinguistics in §1.3. We discuss how we carried out our fieldwork in §1.4 and our annotation system in §1.5.

At the time of writing this grammar, we have made recordings of some but not all of the examples in the grammar. We have created an online archive. We are currently holding it on GitHub, but we plan to transfer it to a more dedicated archive in the future.[1] The archive consists of the following items:

- some recorded elicitations

- original sound files that are used in the figures in the phonology chapter (Chapter 2)

- complete verb conjugation classes from the verb morphology chapter (Chapter 6)

- the sample text from Chapter 8

Elicitation records were made over either Zoom, Audacity, or text messaging services (Telegram and Facebook Messenger); the recording medium does have some effects on the acoustic signal (Sanker et al. 2021). The elicitations and sample text were transcribed with Praat TextGrids (Boersma 2001), and then broken up with Praat scripts (DiCanio 2020).

---

[1]https://github.com/jhdeov/iranian_armenian

1.1 Overview of Iranian Armenian

When providing a basic typological sketch of this variety, it is wise to first explain how Iranian Armenian relates to other Armenian varieties. Armenian is an independent branch of the Indo-European language family. Its earliest attested ancestor is Classical Armenian of the ~5th century. The modern varieties of Armenian are conventionally divided into two branches: Western and Eastern. There are two standardized dialects that are mutually intelligible after significant exposure: Standard Western Armenian (SWA) and Standard Eastern Armenian (SEA), which we sometimes call Standard Western and Standard Eastern. Both branches have dozens of extinct, endangered, or viable non-standard varieties (Adjarian 1909, Աճառեան 1911, Greppin & Khachaturian 1986, Vaux 1998b: §1.1, Baronian 2017, Dolatian submitted).

Geographically, the dividing line between the two branches roughly corresponds with the Turkey-Armenia border. Dialects that developed and were spoken in the Ottoman Empire are part of the Western group, while dialects that developed in the Persian and Russian Empires constitute the Eastern branch. Iranian Armenian is part of this Eastern branch. The variety likely developed from a common ancestor between Standard Eastern and Iranian Armenian. Whereas Standard Eastern (as spoken in Yerevan) is a more conservative descendant of this ancestor, Iranian Armenian has developed various innovations that we discuss in this grammar. Despite these innovations, speakers of Iranian Armenian report feeling that Iranian Armenian is a dialect of Standard Eastern.

In terms of its segmental and suprasegmental phonology, Iranian Armenian for the most part resembles Standard Eastern Armenian. Like Standard Eastern and unlike Standard Western, Iranian Armenian has a three-way laryngeal contrast for stops and affricates, e.g., /b, p, pʰ/ as in Table 1.2 (§2.1.1) (Hacopian 2003). It has a two-way rhotic contrast between a trill /r/ and a retroflex approximant /ɻ/ (§2.1.2). It has a relatively simple vowel inventory of /ɒ, e, i, o, u, ə/, and it includes /æ/ as a marginal phoneme, mostly for Iranian loanwords (§2.1.4).

Table 1.2: Illustrating the three-way laryngeal contrast in Standard Eastern and Iranian Armenian, but not Standard Western

	IA	SEA	SWA	
'word'	bɒr	bɑɾ	pʰɑɾ	բառ
'cheese'	pɒniɭ	pɑniɾ	bɑniɾ	պանիր
'elephant'	pʰiʁ	pʰiʁ	pʰiʁ	փիղ

In terms of differences, the Iranian Armenian segments /ɹ, ɒ/ correspond to Standard Eastern /r, ɑ/, while /æ/ does not exist in Standard Eastern. These differences are likely due to contact with Persian. A significant area of difference is in question intonation: Iranian Armenian has adopted the intonation patterns of Persian when forming questions (§2.2.3).

For morphophonology (Chapter 3), Iranian Armenian has grammaticalized as obligatory some processes that are optional or variable in Standard Eastern. These involve allomorphy of the definite article (§3.2.2), and a process of liquid deletion in periphrasis (§3.3). Liquid deletion is a type of phonosyntactic or syntax-sensitive phonological process (or arguably syntax-sensitive allomorphy). The liquid of the perfective converb suffix *-el* or *-eɹ* is deleted if the suffix does not precede the auxiliary.

For morphology, Iranian Armenian has agglutinative and suffixal inflection. There is no grammatical gender. Nouns inflect for case, number, and determiners (definite, possessive), with some residue of irregular inflection. Nominal morphology is largely the same in Standard Eastern and Iranian Armenian (Chapter 4).

For verbal morphology (Chapter 6), Iranian Armenian verbs are divided into different conjugation classes based on the type of theme vowel, presence of valency suffixes (causative, passive, inchoative), and any irregularities in inflection (root suppletion, affix allomorphy, etc.). Iranian Armenian uses synthetic inflection for some parts of the verbal paradigm, but it is largely periphrastic. Like Standard Eastern and unlike Standard Western, Iranian Armenian forms the present indicative by using a converb and an inflected auxiliary, while Standard Western uses a synthetic form instead (Table 1.3).

Table 1.3: Illustrating periphrastic vs. synthetic verbal inflection across the dialects

IA	siɹ-um	e-m	սիրում եմ
SEA	sir-um	e-m	սիրում եմ
	like-IMPF.CVB	AUX-1SG	
SWA	gə-sir-e-m		կը սիրեմ
	IND-like-TH-1SG		
	'I like.'		

Compared to Standard Eastern, Iranian Armenian has developed some significant changes in verbal inflection. The suffix /-m/ is a 1SG agreement marker for present verbs in Standard Eastern Armenian, but this suffix has been generalized to mark the 1SG for any possible tense in Iranian Armenian (§6.2.2). Compare the various tenses of 'to read' in Table 1.4. And in the past perfective or aorist, Iranian Armenian has developed extensive changes in what suffixes are used to mark the past and perfective/aorist morphemes (§6.4.1). In brief, Standard Eastern Armenian uses the morpheme template /-t͡sʰ-i/ for most verb classes, such as A-Class 'to read' and E-Class 'to sing', while it uses /-∅-ɑ/ for irregulars like 'to eat'. Note the presence of theme vowels before /-t͡sʰ-i/, and the absence of theme vowels before /-∅-ɑ/. In contrast, Iranian Armenian has generalized the /-∅-ɒ/ pattern and uses this template for many types of regular verb classes, such as 'they sang' but not 'they read'.

Table 1.4: Illustrating changes in verbal inflection across Standard Eastern and Iranian Armenian

Tense	Verb	SEA	IA	
Sbjv. Pres. 1SG	'to read'	kartʰ-a-m կարդամ	kɒɹtʰ-ɒ-m կարդամ	read-TH-1SG
Sbjv. Past 1SG	'to read'	kartʰ-aj-i-∅ կարդայի	kɒɹtʰ-ɒj-i-m կարդայիմ	read-TH-PST-1SG
Past Pfv. 3PL	'to read'	kartʰ-a-t͡sʰ-i-n կարդացին	kɒɹtʰ-ɒ-t͡sʰ-i-n կարդացին	read-TH-AOR-PST-3PL
Past Pfv. 3PL	'to sing'	jerkʰ-e-t͡sʰ-i-n երգեցին	jeɹkʰ-∅-∅-ɒ-n երգան	sing-TH-AOR-PST-3PL
Past Pfv. 3PL	'to eat'	ker-∅-∅-a-n կերան	keɹ-∅-∅-ɒ-n կերան	eat-TH-AOR-PST-3PL

In terms of syntax (Chapter 7), we have not been able to carry out an extensive study of Iranian Armenian. Based on intuitions of our speakers, it seems that Standard Eastern and Iranian Armenian have relatively few significant syntactic differences. Like Standard Eastern Armenian, Iranian Armenian is primarily an SOV language but with free word order. One important area of commonality is that the copula is a mobile auxiliary in Standard Eastern and Iranian Armenian but not in Standard Western (Kahnemuyipour & Megerdoomian 2011). The auxiliary is added to focused words in Standard Eastern and Iranian Armenian (Table 1.5).

Table 1.5: Mobile clitic in Standard Eastern and Iranian Armenian but not Standard Western

IA	**mɒɹjɒ-n**	ɒ	uɹɒχ	Մարիան ա ուրախ:
SEA	**marja-n**	e	uɾɑχ	Մարիան է ուրախ:
	Maria-DEF	AUX	happy	
SWA	**marja-n**	uɾɑχ	e	Մարիան ուրախ է:
	Maria-DEF	happy	AUX	
	'MARIA is happy.'			

There are some syntactic differences that we have noted. Due to contact with Persian, Iranian Armenian can use the second person possessive suffix *-t* to act as an object clitic. No such use is attested for the other persons. There are other minor innovations in relative clause formation, again mostly due to Persian contact.

In terms of its lexicon, we have not found any major differences between Standard Eastern and Iranian Armenian. Because of contact and sometimes bilingualism with Persian, Iranian Armenian speakers tell us that they often use Persian words for some concepts, such as for various plants or spices. The community has likewise borrowed some Persian phrases and turned them into Armenian phrases, i.e., calques.

For example, the following phrases in Table 1.6 are common phrases in Persian; they are syntactically complex predicates made up of a word and light verb.[2] Armenian speakers have adopted these phrases and just replaced the light verb with an Armenian equivalent. These phrases are known even by young members of the California diaspora who speak Iranian Armenian but not Persian.[3]

Unfortunately due to lack of time and resources, we haven't been able to carry out an extensive study of such phrases in Iranian Armenian. See Sharifzadeh (2015) and our sample text (Chapter 8) for more examples of calques and borrowed words.

Finally, Iranian Armenian is under-described as a language. To our knowledge, the only manuscript that even has data on this variety is Shakibi & Bonyadi (1995). This manuscript provides some sample paradigms, and a large glossary of Iranian Armenian. However, this document seems to actually describe a type of code switching or mixing between Iranian Armenian and Standard Eastern

---

[2]For the Persian borrowing [pʰæχʃ], NK felt that this word meant nothing outside of the context of the calqued phrase in Table 1.6. So we are not sure if this word should be translated as 'broadcast' or not.

[3]Persian IPA is taken from Wiktionary, verified by Koorosh Ariyaee.

Table 1.6: Calqued phrases from Persian to Iranian Armenian

	Persian			Iranian Armenian	
'to take a nap'	t͡ʃʰoɾt nap	zædæn hit	چرت زدن	t͡ʃʰoɾtʰ nap	χəpʰel hit
'to broadcast'	pʰæʃ broadcast	kærdæn do	پخش کردن	pʰæχʃ X	ɒnel do
'to shower'	duʃ shower	geɾeftæn catch	دوش گرفتن	duʃ shower	bərnel catch

Armenian. For example, that manuscript uses some Iranian Armenian features like the 1SG suffix *-m*, but it also uses more Standard Eastern Armenian features like using the Eastern style of marking the past perfective.[4] As we discuss later, Standard Eastern and Iranian Armenian are two registers of Armenian as spoken by the Iranian Armenian community in a type of diglossia.

1.2 Migration history and dialect classification

Armenians have had a long historical presence in Persia or Iran. We briefly review this history in order to later illustrate the sociolinguistic situation of the modern community.

Ethnic Armenians have been in contact with Persian or Iranian culture since antiquity, since at least the 6th century BCE (Dekmejian 1997: 421, Hovhannisian 2021: 1). Because of this historic contact, there has been extensive language contact between Armenian and Iranian languages, particularly Parthian and Middle Persian (Meyer 2017: §1). There have been villages or areas in modern-day Iran with historically large Armenian populations, especially in Northwest Iran or Iranian Azerbaijan such as Tabriz. These villages, towns, and districts developed their own dialects or Armenian varieties. These varieties differ significantly from Standard Eastern Armenian and from (Tehrani) Iranian Armenian.

An incomplete list of some area-specific varieties include Maku (Կատվայան 2018b), Maragha (Աճառյան 1926), New Julfa (Աճառյան 1940, Vaux in preparation),

---

[4]Shakibi & Bonyadi (1995) do not represent the three-way laryngeal contrast for stops and affricates. We suspect that this is because this manuscript seems to have developed without using linguistic sources on Armenian (which would state that there is such a distinction), and that the authors of this manuscript likely don't speak Armenian.

Salmast (Vaux 2022b), and Urmia/Khoy (Ասատրյան 1962). For an overview of these dialects, see Martirosyan (2019, 2018: 85). These dialects constitute the historical region of "Persian Armenia", called [parskahajkʰ] Պարկսահայք in Standard Eastern Armenian (Martirosyan submitted). For an overview of the migration patterns of these dialects, see Mesropyan (2022). For lists and historical overviews of past and present Armenian villages and districts, see Amurian & Kasheff (1986) and Ghougassian (2021). For in-depth historical and anthropological overviews of the Armenian community in Iran, see Cosroe Chaqueri (1998), Sanasarian (2000), and Barry (2017b, 2018). There is likewise recent work on language signage in Armenian-populated areas (Rezaei & Tadayyon 2018).

In terms of demographics, the ancestors of most modern Iranian Armenians entered Iran via mass migrations (Kouymjian 1997: 19, Hovhannisian 2021: 3). In the 1600s, Shah Abbas I of Persia forced the mass migration of ethnic Armenians from historical Eastern Armenia, especially from modern-day Nakhchivan or Nakhijevan (Նախիջեւան). The number of these Armenians is estimated as 400,000 being deported to Iran in 1604, of which 300,000 individuals survived by 1606 (Ghougassian 2021: 314). These Armenians then settled in different regions of Iran, especially in Tabriz and in the New Julfa quarter of Isfahan, which had been constructed specifically for their resettlement (Hovhannisian 2021: 9). Other areas where Armenians were settled in Safavid times included Peria (Fereydan), Chaharmahal, and Buurvari, while thereafter New Julfan trade networks gave rise to Armenian communities in other urban centers throughout Persia and as far as Astrakhan, India, Burma/Myanmar, and Java.

Over time, large numbers of Armenians then moved to Tehran sometime in the 19th and early 20th centuries, drawn by better prospects for wealth and social mobility. (Hovhannisian 2021: 6). Then in the mid to late 20th century, particularly around the time of the Islamic Revolution (1979), large numbers of Armenians emigrated from Tehran to elsewhere around the globe, especially to Los Angeles county in Southern California.

In terms of contemporary population size, it is difficult to get clear numbers (Iskandaryan 2019).[5] Some sources estimate that the Armenian population of Tehran reached a peak of 50,000 people in the late decades of the 20th century (Hovhannisian 2021: 6). The US government gives larger numbers. Curtis & Hooglund (2008: 101) estimate that the size of the Armenian population in Iran was around 350,000 in 1979 (prior to the revolution). Emigration then led to a population count of 300,000 in 2000. They report that 65% of the population lived in Tehran, around 195,000.

---

[5]To illustrate this, see the inconsistent population estimates on the Wikipedia page for Iranian Armenians: https://en.wikipedia.org/wiki/Iranian_Armenians

As for the Iranian Armenian diaspora, Iranian Armenians are a culturally significant subset of the Armenian population in California (Bakalian 2017). The US census lists 47,197 individuals in California who report themselves as Armenians born in Iran (United States Census Bureau 2015). For more in-depth socioeconomic, demographic, and anthropological studies of the California population, see Der-Martirosian (2021) and Fittante (2017, 2018, 2019).

Because of these complicated demographic changes, it is possible that modern Tehrani Iranian Armenian developed as an offshoot of Standard Eastern Armenian. The Tehrani variety had some degree of contact with the varieties of other Armenian villages in Iran over the centuries. Over time, as Armenians moved within Iran to Tehran, the Tehrani community levelled their speech to form modern-day Tehrani Iranian Armenian. This modern variety is what we refer to as Iranian Armenian. This is the variety that is spoken and acquired by Armenian children in Tehran, and in the large Iranian Armenian diaspora.

Because Iranian Armenian is a spoken vernacular, there are only scant records of it. Within Armenian philology, the earliest reference we have found for Tehrani Iranian Armenian is in the introduction chapter of Adjarian 1940 (Աճառ-յան 1940), which is a grammar of New Julfa Armenian (translated into English in Vaux in preparation). For that grammar, Adjarian collected data from native speakers on a visit to New Julfa in 1919. That variety is spoken primarily in the New Julfa district of Isfahan. He contrasts New Julfa Armenian with what he calls "Persian Armenian" or "Perso-Armenian" which he says is spoken in the northern regions of Iran, including Tehran. He doesn't provide any data on this dialect but he states that this Perso-Armenian lect is socially predominant and close to Yerevan Armenian. We suspect that what he calls Perso-Armenian is the direct ancestor of modern Tehrani Iranian Armenian.

Based on conventional dialectological work in Armenian (Աճառեան 1911), the ancestor of Standard Eastern Armenian is often assumed to be the dialect of Old Yerevan Armenian (Dolatian submitted), though the exact genetic relationship is complicated (Sayeed & Vaux 2017). Tehrani Iranian Armenian may have developed as a subdialect of 16th century Yerevan Armenian, or a koine that arose via mingling Yerevan and SEA with other migrant communities (like Julfa Armenians) and the pre-existing Armenian dialects of Iran (such as in Maragha, Khoy, and others). Based on migration patterns from Armenia to Iran, Tehrani IA may be viewed as a daughter of the 16th century dialects of Nakhichevan and Atropatene (Iranian Azerbaijan, Atrpatakan), having differentiated further within Iran over the centuries, and more recently having been subjected to prescriptive influences from SEA and modern Yerevan Armenian through education and literary and broadcast media. Moreover, we believe that the koineization of multiple

Iranian Armenian dialects in Tehran during the 20th century was compounded by improved schooling in SEA and increased cultural output from Yerevan. This led to leveling the more salient features of the lect and has in turn brought Tehrani Iranian Armenian (the Tehran koine) closer to SEA than to other local Iranian Armenian dialects like New Julfa Armenian. This is reflected in the tendency for some older speakers to employ more Persianisms and retain dialectical forms from their hometowns throughout Iran. Because of the close contact between Iranian Armenian and SEA, IA speakers likewise report perceiving that IA is a dialect of SEA. Adjarian himself discusses some difficulties in classifying IA, while using the name of Perso-Armenian (Աճառյան 1940: §1), where he says that Perso-Armenian is related to Tabriz and Astrakhan Armenian.

1.3 Sociolinguistics of the Iranian Armenian community

The Tehran community is diglossic or triglossic (Nercissians 1988, 2012). Armenians learn and speak Persian with non-Armenians, and code switching is common (Ghiasian & Rezayi 2014, Ghiasian & Rezaei 2014). Within the Armenian community, children acquire Iranian Armenian at home. This variety is spoken as an informal register. In Armenian schools, children learn Standard Eastern Armenian. The community uses Standard Eastern Armenian as a formal register in literature, newspapers, written communications, and formal speech. We discuss each code in §1.3.1, and then discuss the social stigmatization of the spoken vernacular with respect to Standard Eastern Armenian (§1.3.2).

Whereas the Iranian Armenian community in Tehran is diglossic or triglossic, the Iranian Armenian diaspora is much less so. For the diaspora in California, families may speak Iranian Armenian at home, but not necessarily Standard Eastern or Persian. The relative rarity of transmitting Persian to the youth makes sense because it is not a lingua franca among Armenians in the US. As for the Armenian registers, Standard Eastern Armenian is the formal register, while Iranian Armenian is the informal register. Thus the children of such communities acquire Iranian Armenian at home. Some but not all diaspora children attend Armenian schools where they acquire Standard Eastern.

1.3.1 Characteristics of the three codes

For Persian, Zamir (1982: §6.7) reports that Tehrani Armenians spoke a distinctive dialect of Persian. Their dialect involved various phonological changes. For example, standard Persian /æ/ was pronounced as /ɒ/ by speakers of this dialect

(Zamir 1982: 370); the history of /æ/ is discussed more in §2.1.4. Afsheen Sharifzadeh (AS) and others report that this Persian dialect died out over the last few decades (Barry 2017a: 154). This dialect is now more characteristic of the current generation's grandparents or great-grandparents, i.e., people who were adults around the time of Zamir (1982)'s study.

The modern community still has some level of awareness of this old dialect however; for example, the phonological accent of this old dialect is satirized in the work of Iranian Armenian comedian Gilbert Sinanian (Gibo Hopar).[6] For the modern community, speakers seem to use the same dialect of Persian as non-Armenians but with some noticeable phonological features. For example, Barry (2018: 220) reports:

> Furthermore, the Armenian accent is not simply something of which Iranian Armenians are self conscious; Muslim Iranians recognise it also. Two Iranian students in Melbourne stated that the Armenian accent in Persian is easily recognisable in its intonation.

There are similar reports on Armenian-accented Persian among Isfahan Armenians (Rezaei & Farnia 2023). Though the exact linguistic features of this accent are unclear to us. In AS's experience, some members of the Iranian Armenian speech community utilize the IA approximant /ɹ/ when speaking Persian, to an extent that is easily recognizable and stereotypical of their speech among Iranians (Barry 2018: 220).

As for the informal register of Iranian Armenian, this variety is natively acquired at home by speakers in the Tehran community. Outside of Tehran, various people have told us that the Tehrani variety is known in other Armenian-populated towns and villages in Iran. For example, Nercissians (2001: 64) explicitly states that "there is a clearly prestigious Tehrani dialect for Armenian." Specifically, spoken Tehrani Iranian Armenian is more prestigious than the spoken vernacular of other towns and villages, such as Isfahan, Tabriz, and so on.

It seems that other Armenian varieties in Iran are dying out and being replaced by Tehrani Iranian Armenian. For example, in AS's travels through Iran, he's found that many young people in New Julfa (Isfahan) no longer speak the New Julfa variety of their ancestors. Instead, the current generation speaks the Tehrani variety. The parents of this generation speak Tehrani and the local New Julfa vernacular; while the grandparents of this generation speak only the New Julfa vernacular.

---

[6]https://www.facebook.com/gibohopar/

Because of the prestige and language shifts, AS suggests that Tehrani Iranian Armenian has become a spoken koine or lingua franca among Armenians in Iran. The social prominence of Tehrani has likewise spread throughout the Iranian Armenian community in Los Angeles. Here, Varand Nikolaian (2016, p.c.) reports that the Tehrani variety is quite prominent among Iranian Armenians. In Los Angeles, Iranian Armenians from Isfahan, Tabriz, and other areas often shift to speaking Tehrani Iranian Armenian when talking to Iranian Armenians from other villages or towns. Some people likewise feel ashamed of their own local vernacular and have shifted to using Tehrani Iranian Armenian even in their own homes.

As for the formal register, it's more accurate to say that the formal register is Standard Eastern Armenian with an *Iranian Armenian accent*. That is, the community would say a Standard Eastern Armenian sentence but use Iranian Armenian phonology, such as using the rounded Iranian Armenian /ɒ/ instead of unrounded Standard Eastern /ɑ/.

1.3.2 Social stigmatization of the spoken vernacular

As a last note on sociolinguistics, we must mention the social status of Iranian Armenian with respect to Standard Eastern Armenian. Because of the diglossic situation in Tehran, the spoken vernacular of Tehrani Iranian Armenians is often stigmatized as "wrong", "broken", or "vulgar" speech, especially by the older generation of speakers. For example, in the early 2000s, one of the present authors (Bert Vaux, BV) gave a conference presentation at UCLA (University of California, Los Angeles) on Iranian Armenian. Before the conference, he received an aggressive email from a member of the Iranian Armenian community in California. We repeat parts of that email below, anonymized. We re-transcribe Armenian words in IPA. Bolding is our own; Persian words are romanized in italics.

> I am writing to you to express my deep concern about your thesis of the third literary dialect (the Persian-Armenian). The examples you cite to prove your findings, [gənɒts͡ʰim], [imɒts͡ʰɒm] (instead of [gənɒts͡ʰi, imɒts͡ʰɒ]), [me] (instead of [mek]) **are all dialectal forms**, they are used in spoken language but never, never, never in print. You mention the printed material before the revolution. I have not seen one example with such **vulgar errors**. As to [lev] or [lɒf] instead of [lɒv], this is truly **unheard of**. These are all spoken forms by **not-very-educated people** in Iran and those who are here, and there are many. As to the words *havich, xiar, jafari, xiarshur*, these are purely Persian words (not even borrowings) and **nonex-**

istent in the spoken language let alone in the Persian Armenian literary dialect which I think, such an animal does not exist at all...

Please **check your sources** before coming to these conclusions. I consider myself an educated Iranian Armenian, who writes in Eastern Armenian literary language (and there is **non** [*sic*] **other variations**) and also speaks with some dialectal forms but never mixes Persian words.

Your question of what form of literary language is/was taught in schools in Iran. I am very much familiar with the textbooks used in Iran before the revolution and after. The text, the syntax, the lexicon, and the grammar is that of Standard Eastern Armenian literary language. The same standards are used also in the media. I beg you again, revisit your findings and conclusions. Your presentation may **irritate** many Iranian Armenians. I was hoping you would speak about a **distinct** dialect of Iranian Armenians, like the Maragha dialect (the *er* branch: [etɑs eɾ] meaning I am going) or the Gharadagh dialect that is close to the Gharabagh dialect.

[Correction by BV: No one uses /etɑs eɾ/. Khoy/Urmia/Salmast have /eɾtʰɑs em/ 'I am going' and /eɾtʰɑs em eɾ/ 'I was going'. Maragha uses /etʰæli im/ 'I am going' and /etʰæli im eɾ/ 'I was going'.]

As is clear, the email shows that the spoken vernacular is extremely stigmatized by at least some members of higher social classes. The dialect is considered "vulgar", "un-educated", or even "non-existent". Paradoxically, the Iranian Armenian community legitimizes Armenian varieties that are spoken in the more peripheral areas of Iran. These varieties are deemed "exotic" and un-intelligible enough for Tehranis to consider them as legitimate languages. In contrast, the spoken language of the average Tehrani child or adult is erased. People pretend they don't speak this spoken vernacular, even though they do.

1.4 Fieldwork and language consultants

This grammar is based on fieldwork that was done by each of the authors, at different times, and with different people. We go through each phase of fieldwork below.

The first phase of fieldwork was undertaken in the 1990s and early 2000s by Bert Vaux (BV). BV is a trained generative phonologist and is a native speaker of English. He undertook fieldwork by collecting data from Armenian expatriates from Iran, especially in Boston and Los Angeles.

BV's main consultant was Karine Megerdoomian (KM, female), who was born and raised in Tehran until the age of 13. There, she acquired Iranian Armenian, Standard Eastern Armenian, and Persian. After that, she moved across Europe and North America until finally settling in the United States. KM is a trained generative syntactician and thus often gave meta-linguistic judgments as a linguist-speaker. At the time of BV's fieldwork, KM was in her early 30s.

BV also elicited data from other Iranian Armenian expatriates living in the US and Europe. One such consultant is AP. AP is a male from Peria, which is in the province of Isfahan, Iran. His judgments were relayed to BV through AP's wife.

The second phase was undertaken by Afsheen Sharifzadeh (AS). AS is a self-trained linguist and is a native speaker of Persian and English. His fieldwork was somewhat atypical. He initially was interested in merely learning the Armenian culture and language. He often visited the Armenian community in Iran and would befriend Iranian Armenian speakers. His exposure was some time in the late 2000s and early 2010s. Over time, he developed an advanced proficiency in Standard Eastern Armenian and Iranian Armenian. His data comes from his interactions with a wide community of Iranian Armenian speakers, both in Tehran and in expatriate communities in the US. His main consultants were people in their early to late 20s.

The third phase was undertaken by Hossep Dolatian (HD). HD is a trained generative morphophonologist and is a native speaker of Standard Western Armenian. He did fieldwork after discovering the data collected by BV and AS. He then undertook the task of synthesizing their data and replicating it with speakers of Iranian Armenian in California. He did fieldwork in 2021 and his main consultant was Nicole Khachikian (NK, female). Her parents and grandparents are from Tehran. She was born and raised in the US outside of Los Angeles, but was often within the Iranian Armenian community of LA. Her home languages were Iranian Armenian and English. She does not know Persian. She learned aspects of Standard Eastern Armenian both by a) learning the spoken formal register of Standard Eastern Armenian with the larger Armenian community in Los Angeles, and b) taking Armenian classes at university. She was in her early 20s during HD's fieldwork. HD at times elicited data from KM, who was in her early 50s in 2021. Recordings were made remotely, either with Praat (Boersma 2001) over Zoom or with Audacity. HD's recording methodology is documented on the associated archive of this grammar.

For some data points, HD elicited material on Standard Eastern Armenian in order to show a contrast between Standard Eastern and Iranian Armenian. Some other IA-speaking linguists were also consulted at times. Elicitations were done with the following speakers:

- Eastern Armenian

  - Mariam Asatryan (MA): female; born and raised in Tsovasar, Armenia, age was around late 20s.

  - Victoria Khurshudyan (VK): female; born and raised in Goris, Armenia, age was around early 40s.

  - Vahagn Petrosyan (VP): male; born and raised in Yerevan, Armenia; age was around mid 30s.

  - Arevik Torosyan (AT): female; born and raised in Yerevan, Armenia up until her late teens; age was around early 20s.

- Iranian Armenian

  - Anooshik Melikian (AM): female; born and raised in Tehran, Iran up until 2016; age was around early 50s.

  - Garoun Engström (GE): female; born and raised in Uppsala, Sweden; age was around early 30s.

As is clear, the three linguists did their fieldwork at different times and locations. However, we have found little to no discrepancies across these different pools of data. The main differences come from generational changes in the pronunciation of certain lexical items and morphemes, which we take note of.

Furthermore, neither BV, AS, nor HD are native speakers of Standard Eastern Armenian or Iranian Armenian. BV's and AS's data come from speakers who can be considered bi-dialectal, which means the speakers are proficient in both Iranian Armenian and Standard Eastern Armenian. This is because their speakers were born and raised in Iran and thus were exposed to Standard Eastern Armenian within the education system of the Armenian community. In contrast, HD's main consultants are mono-lectal and mainly speak Iranian Armenian. Because HD's consultants grew up in the US, his speakers did not acquire Standard Eastern Armenian within an educational system. We have found only minor differences between the grammars of bi-dialectal vs. mono-lectal speakers when it comes to Iranian Armenian judgments or pronunciations.

1.5 Orthography, transcription, and glossing

The Armenian language is normally written in the Armenian script (Sanjian 1996). There are two orthographic conventions or spelling systems for Armenian: Classical and Reformed. The Classical system is the original system of writing the Armenian script. It is used for Standard Western. It was originally used for Standard Eastern Armenian as well, but then a series of Soviet-era spelling reforms created the Reformed system. The Reformed system is used for Standard Eastern Armenian as spoken in Armenia and large parts of the Diaspora. But in Iran, Standard Eastern Armenian is still written with the Classical system. For an overview of these orthographic changes, see Dum-Tragut (2009: 5–6, 12).

For this grammar, we use the Reformed spelling to write Standard Eastern Armenian examples. We use Classical spelling to write Iranian Armenian examples out of respect to the community's orthographic customs. This is somewhat atypical because Iranian Armenian is an unwritten vernacular. We have decided to provide orthographic forms to make future cross-dialectal work easier. Note that the orthographic script does not indicate all phonetic aspects of Iranian Armenian pronunciation. All data is likewise transcribed in IPA.

For our glossed sentences, we first provide an IPA transcription, then gloss, then translation, and then the orthographic representation.

For glossing, we follow the Leipzig Glossing Rules, and we've added our own conventions for those morphosyntactic features that are absent from the Leipzig Glossing Rules.

In this grammar, we adopt a simple item-and-arrangement model of morphology (Hockett 1942). We try to segment as many affixes as possible. We adopt the word "morph" as a theory-neutral term to denote the surface form of morphemes, i.e., to simply denote morphological items (Haspelmath 2020). We at times provide realization rules to more clearly show how certain inflectional features are marked in Iranian Armenian; these rules should not be treated as explicit formal theoretical rules.

Full morpheme segmentation and glosses are given for sentences and for morphological paradigms. In the morphology section, we likewise segment zero morphemes. We generally avoid segmentation for the data in the phonology chapter in order to reduce clutter. Outside of the morphology chapter, we often segment the 3SG auxiliary (positive *ɒ* and negative *t͡ʃ-i*) as just '(NEG)-AUX' instead of '(NEG)-AUX.PRS.3SG' to reduce clutter.

For our bibliography, we do not romanize or transliterate Armenian entries. All Armenian entries are given in the Armenian alphabet, so that searching for those entries in the future (via library catalogs) is easier. Translations are provided to help preview the content of the entry.

2 Phonology

In this chapter we present the basic segmental inventory (§2.1) and suprasegmental phonology (§2.2) of Iranian Armenian.

2.1 Segmental phonology

Table 2.1 lists the consonant inventory of Iranian Armenian, including both phonemes and non-contrastive sounds in parentheses.

Table 2.1: Consonant inventory of Iranian Armenian

	Labial		Coronal				Dorsal/Back		
Stop	p b		t d				k g		
	pʰ		tʰ				kʰ		
Affricate			t͡s d͡z	t͡ʃ	d͡ʒ				
			t͡sʰ	t͡ʃʰ					
Nasal		m	n				(ŋ)		
Fricative	f	v	s z	ʃ	ʒ	χ	ʁ	h	
Liquid			ɹ	l					
			r						
Glide			j				(w)		

Iranian Armenian has largely the same phonemic inventory as Eastern Armenian. For example, both utilize a three-way laryngeal contrast for stops and affricates: D, T, Tʰ (§2.1.1). General overviews of Standard Eastern Armenian segmental phonology are found in Vaux (1998b: §1) and Johnson (1954: §1–3).

The lects do differ in a few aspects. In terms of rhotics (§2.1.2), Eastern has a phonemic trill /r/ and phonemic flap /ɾ/, while Iranian Armenian has a phonemic trill /r/ and phonemic approximant /ɹ/.

Both dialects have [ŋ] as a non-phonemic allophone of /n/ before velar stops. Iranian Armenian utilizes a glide [w] as a non-contrastive epenthetic segment, while this segment is absent for Standard Eastern (§2.1.3). We show these two sounds with parentheses in Table 2.1.

In terms of vowels (§2.1.4) in Figure 2.1, the low back vowel is unrounded /ɑ/ in Standard Eastern but rounded /ɒ/ in Iranian Armenian. Iranian Armenian also has a low front vowel /æ/ as a marginal phoneme.

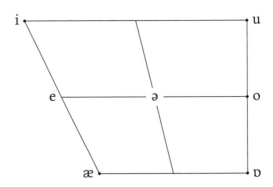

Figure 2.1: Vowel inventory of Iranian Armenian

2.1.1 Laryngeal qualities of consonants

Both Standard Eastern and Iranian Armenian utilize a three-way laryngeal contrast for stops and affricates based on voice onset time (VOT). There is a phonemic contrast between prevoiced or voiced (-VOT), voiceless unaspirated (0VOT), and voiceless aspirated (+VOT) consonants. We provide near-minimal pairs in Table 2.2 from Iranian Armenian. In general, there is a separate grapheme (orthographic letter) for each type of phonemic stop/affricate. We list the graphemes in the first column, and the phonemes in the second column.

Acoustic data on the three-way contrast can be found for both Iranian Armenian (Hacopian 2003, Amirian 2017, Toparlak 2017) and Standard Eastern (Seyfarth & Garellek 2018, Seyfarth et al. forthcoming). The contrast is maintained even word-finally. However, there are very few words that are pronounced with word-final voiced obstruents. The coronals have been reported to be dental in Standard Eastern (Խաչատրյան 1988: 110), but we are unsure if they are also dental in Iranian Armenian.[1]

For word-final voiceless unaspirated stops (p, t, k), it is reported that some Iranian Armenian speakers pronounce these sounds as ejectives (Fleming 2000, Toparlak 2017, Toparlak & Dolatian 2023), while some do not (Amirian 2017). For NK, we rarely heard any ejectivized tokens. Figure 2.2 shows an example of a

---

[1]NK self-reported a dental articulation for some tokens with initial coronal stops, but also reported alveolar articulation for other tokens.

Table 2.2: three-way laryngeal contrast for stops and affricates

		Initial		Medial		Final	
բ	/b/	'bɒɾ	'word' բառ	ɒ.ɾɒbe'.ɹen	'Arabic' արաբերէն	æ'.ɹæb	'Arab' արաբ
պ	/p/	pɒ'niɾ	'cheese' պանիր	ɒpɒ'ki	'glass' ապակի	kɒp	'connection' կապ
փ	/pʰ/	'pʰiʁ	'elephant' փիղ	tʃʰɒ'pʰel	'to measure' չափել	tupʰ	'box' տուփ
դ	/d/	'dɒɾ	'century' դար	bɒ'dik	'duckling' բադիկ	bɒd	'duck' բադ
տ	/t/	'tun	'house' տուն	pʰe'tuɾ	'feather' փետուր	'sut	'lie' սուտ
թ	/tʰ/	'tʰuɾkʰ	'Turk' թուրք	dʒu'tʰɒk	'violin' ջութակ	kɒtʰ	'milk' կաթ
գ	/g/	'giɾkʰ	'book' գիրք	ɒ'.ɹɒg-ə	'fast-DEF' արագը	'tʰɒg	'crown' թագ
կ	/k/	kɒɾ'tʰɒl	'to read' կարդալ	tʃɒ'kɒt	'forehead' ճակատ	bɒk	'yard' բակ
ք	/kʰ/	'kʰɒɾ	'rock' քար	mɒ'kʰuɾ	'clean' մաքուր	kʰɒ'ʁɒkʰ	'city' քաղաք
ձ	/dz/	'dzun	'snow' ձուն	hɒmɒ'dzɒjn	'agreeing' համաձայն	'indz	'me.DAT' ինձ
ծ	/ts/	'tsɒr	'tree' ծառ	kə'tsu	'spicy' կծու	'mets	'big' մեծ
ց	/tsʰ/	'tsʰɒv	'pain' ցավ	hɒ'tsʰ-i	'bread-GEN' հացի	'bɒtsʰ	'open' բաց
ջ	/dʒ/	'dʒuɾ	'water' ջուր	dʒən'dʒik	'eraser' ջնջիկ	kʰɒdʒ	'brave' քաջ
ճ	/tʃ/	tʃɒ'.ɹel	'to look for' ճարել	ɒ'tʃel	'to grow' աճել	'litʃ	'lake' լիճ
չ	/tʃʰ/	'tʃʰɒɾ	'evil' չար	ɒ'tʃʰ-itsʰ	'right-ABL' աջից	'votʃʰ	'no' ոչ

final ejectivized unaspirated /k/, along with an un-ejectivized one. The recordings for these two words can be found in our online archive.[2] There is a larger debate about whether any varieties of modern or ancient Armenian possess(ed) a glottalized or ejective series of voiceless stops; for discussion and references see Vaux (2022a).

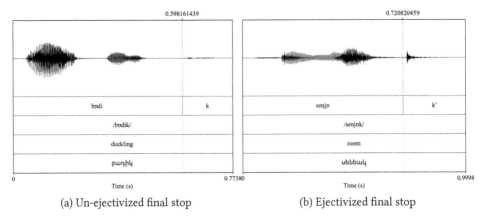

(a) Un-ejectivized final stop   (b) Ejectivized final stop

Figure 2.2: Variable ejectivization of final unaspirated stops from NK

In general, for a given morpheme that is shared between Iranian Armenian and Standard Eastern Armenian, the obstruents in that morpheme maintain the same laryngeal features in the two lects. That is, if a word begins with a prevoiced stop in Standard Eastern, then it also begins with a prevoiced stop in Iranian Armenian. This correspondence is the general case. But we have encountered some morphemes where the Iranian Armenian pronunciation utilizes a different laryngeal quality (Table 2.3). For example, the resultative participle suffix -ած is pronounced /-ɑts/ in Standard Eastern, but is often pronounced as /-ɒtsʰ/ in Iranian Armenian with aspiration in some speakers. NK always uses aspiration for this morpheme, while KM reports that she rarely does so.

Table 2.3: Unexpected aspiration in Iranian Armenian from NK

	SEA	IA		
երգած	jerˈkʰ-ats	jeɹˈkʰ-ɒtsʰ	sing-RPTCP	'sung'
կարդացած	kartʰ-ɑ-tsʰ-ats	kɒɹtʰ-ɒˈ-tsʰ-ɒtsʰ	read-TH-AOR-RPTCP	'read'

---

[2]https://github.com/jhdeov/iranian_armenian

From AS's personal experience, the unexpected use of aspiration for the affricate ծ /t͡s/ varies by speaker (Table 2.4). We speculate that this variable aspiration may be connected to variable ejectivization or glottalization of voiceless unaspirates. Variable ejectivization is reported for Standard Eastern (Schirru 2012, Seyfarth & Garellek 2018, Toparlak & Dolatian 2023). AS likewise finds variable ejectivization for /t͡s/. We speculate that what we report as aspiration might instead be a reflex of ejectivization. More data is of course needed.

Table 2.4: Unexpected but variable aspiration of affricate /t͡s/ in Iranian Armenian from NK

	SEA	IA	
ծնուել	t͡sən'vel	t͡sən'vel~t͡sʰənvel	'to be born'
գործածել	gort͡sa'tsel	goɹt͡sɒ'tsel~goɹt͡sʰɒt͡sʰel	'to use'

In NK's speech (and in her family's), there were some words where the voiced stops were (variably) devoiced in her speech, and some where voiceless stops were (variably) voiced (Table 2.4). KM felt that such variable voicing was more characteristic of heritage speakers in the diaspora than of speakers in Tehran. Note that these are all high-frequency words.

Table 2.5: High-frequency words with variable (de)voicing from NK and her family

	SEA	IA	
'(If) I come'	gɑm	gɒm, kɒm	գամ
'door'	dur	dur, tur	դուռ
'to put'	dənel	dənel, tənel	դնել
'dance'	pɑɹ	pɒɹ, bɒɹ	պար
'mouth'	beɾɑn	beɹɒn, peɹɒn	բերան
'to bring'	beɾel	beɹel, peɹel	բերել
'knife'	dɑnɑk	dɒnɒk, dɒnɒg	դանակ
'yesterday'	jeɾek	eɹek, eɹeg	երեկ, էրեկ
'drawer'	dɑɾɑk	dæɹæk, dæɹæg	դարակ

For such voicing differences, BV reports that using devoiced tokens like [tənel] instead of [dənel] 'to put' is the expected outcome in non-standard dialects of Iran, such as Urmia, Khoy, and Salmast (Ասատրյան 1962: 34–40), Maragha (Աճառ-յան 1926: 83–89) and Keyvan (Քեյվան) (Բաղրամյան 1985: 187). For Tehrani Iranian Armenian, such variation in devoicing may indicate the residue of dialect shift-ing, or possibly a diglossic continuum between Iranian Armenian and Standard Eastern Armenian.

2.1.2 Rhotics

A stark difference between the two lects concerns their rhotics. Standard Eastern Armenian has a phonemic contrast between a flap /ɾ/ and a trill /r/. The flap is more frequent than the trill. Orthographically, the flap is represented by the grapheme ռ, and the trill by ր. Although Iranian Armenian also has a two-way rhotic distinction, the Standard Eastern flap corresponds to an Iranian Armenian retroflex approximant /ɻ/. We contrast the two lects in Table 2.6.[3]

In general, if a word has a rhotic trill in Standard Eastern Armenian, then it has a trill in Iranian Armenian as well. However, there were some high-frequency words where NK and other speakers preferred using a trill /r/ where Standard Eastern would use a flap /ɾ/ (Table 2.7).

Some high-frequency words have a rhotic in Standard Eastern Armenian, but the rhotic is optionally deleted in Iranian Armenian (Table 2.8). The loss of the rhotic here may be related to the loss of rhotics in the perfective converb (§3.3).

The Standard Eastern flap /ɾ/ is typically spirantized in some positions, such as word-finally (Toparlak 2019: §5, Seyfarth et al. forthcoming). The Iranian Ar-menian retroflex approximant sounds similar to the American English alveolar approximant [ɹ] to our ears, but more retroflex like [ɻ]. A future acoustic or ar-ticulatory study can help in determining the exact place of articulation of this rhotic.

Cross-linguistically, it is common to find that dialects differ in the phonetic re-alization of rhotics (Ladefoged & Maddieson 1996, Chabot 2019). It is rather rare to find languages with a phonemic retroflex approximant [ɻ] (Arsenault 2018: 28). For example, the UCLA Phonological Segment Inventory Database (UPSID) lists only 17 out of 451 languages (3.77%) that have the phoneme /ɻ/ (Maddieson & Hanson 1990).[4] Most of these languages are in Australia. Similar results are ob-tained from the PHOIBLE 2.0 database at 306 out of 3020 languages (10%) (Moran

---

[3]The /f/ in 'Raffi' is variably geminated. The /b/ in Iranian Armenian 'thin' is variably devoiced for NK.

[4]http://menzerath.phonetik.uni-frankfurt.de/S/S0763.html

Table 2.6: Rhotic contrasts in Standard Eastern and Iranian Armenian

	SEA /ɾ/	IA /ɹ/	ɲ	SEA /r/	IA /r/	ɲ
Initial	ɾɑ'fi	ɹɒ'fi	'Raffi (a name)' Ռաֆֆի	re'zin	re'zin	'eraser' ռեզին
				raz'mik	rɒz'mik	'Razmik (a name)' Ռազմիկ
Medial	bɑ'ɾɑk	bɒ'ɹɒk	'thin' բարակ	'sarə	'sɒrə	'cold' սառը
	pɑ'ɾɑp	pɒ'ɹɒp	'available, empty' պարապ	he'ru	he'ru	'far' հեռու
Final	'sɑɾ	'sɒɹ	'mountain' սար	'bɑr	'bɒr	'word' բառ
	'kɑɾ	'kɒɹ	'string' կար	'tɑr	'tɒr	'letter' տառ

Table 2.7: High-frequency words that use a trill instead of an approximant

	SEA	IA	
'minute'	ɾope	rope	ռոպէ
'war'	pɑteɾɑzm	pɒterɒzm	պատերազմ

Table 2.8: High-frequency words that lose a rhotic in Iranian Armenian

	SEA	IA	
'to go'	jerthɑl, erthɑl,	eɹthɒl, ethɒl	երթալ, էրթալ, էթալ
'when'	jerpʰ	jeɹpʰ, jepʰ	երբ

& McCloy 2019). For the alveolar approximant [ɹ], this segment is acoustically quite similar to [ɻ]. This sound is cross-linguistically rare as well at 60 languages (2%) in the PHOIBLE database. This segment is found particularly in Southeast Asia and in English.

The origins of the Iranian Armenian approximant could be due to language contact with Persian. Persian has a rhotic /r/ whose realization varies between a trill, tap, fricative, and approximant (Majidi & Ternes 1991, Rafat 2010). In a study on Persian rhotics, Rafat (2010: 675) found that when they were realized as approximants, the approximants sounded retroflex.[5]

There is evidence that an approximant rhotic is attested in other Armenian dialects of Iran. In Vaux's translation of Աճառյան (1940)'s grammar of New Julfa (Isfahan) Armenian, Vaux uses the IPA symbol [ɹ] to transcribe the letter ռ (§6). Allen (1950: 195) likewise reports a speaker of New Julfa who has a retroflex fricative that he transcribes as [ɻ]. It is an open question if the Tehrani [ɻ] and New Julfa [ɹ] are articulatorily different or the same.[6]

Although the trill is phonemic in both lects, KM reports that the Iranian Armenian trill feels "not as trilled as in Eastern." This suggests that the trill uses a smaller number of tongue contacts in Iranian Armenian than in Standard Eastern. Coincidentally, some dialects like Standard Western Armenian have lost a phonemic trill for certain communities like in Lebanon (Vaux 1998b: 16).[7] Some communities in Canada still maintain weak phonemic and weak articulatory distinctions between trills and flaps (Tahtadjian 2020). KM's intuitions thus might indicate a slow language change toward losing the trill.[8]

---

[5]However, the role of contact is likely limited. It is a stereotype that when IA speakers speak Persian, they use the approximant /ɻ/ more often than Persian speakers. Classical Armenian may have had an approximant [ɹ] (Macak 2017: 1040), so it's possible that IA keeps [ɻ] as an archaism. But we suspect that it's more likely that the IA /ɻ/ is an innovation.

[6]The sound /ɹ/ is sometimes reported elsewhere in the Turkey-Caucasus-Iran region: queer Turkish speakers from Istanbul (Kontovas 2012: 11), and the Muslim variety of the Hamshen dialect spoken in the village of Köprücü (Hopa province, northeastern Turkey) (Vaux 2007: 258). The sound [ɻ] is also reported in the Iranian language of Kumzari in Oman (van der Wal Anonby 2015: 25). For Turkish, it seems that approximants are generally attested (Nichols 2016), possibly characteristic of "white" Turkish women and also found in the northeastern parts of Turkey (Nicholas Kontovas, p.c.). But it is unclear what is the exact place of articulation, with some sources reporting an alveolar place while others report a retroflex place (Tıraş 2021: 12).

[7]In Armenian dialectology, Jahukyan (Ջահուկյան 1972) reports feature 23 as about "confusion between /r/ and /ɾ/ in non-preconsonantal position" in the dialects of Kuty, Hadjin, Tabriz, Tbilisi, Burdur, and Maragha.

[8]Don Stilo (p.c.) suggests that such a trajectory makes sense. Given that the modern IA rhotic pair /ɻ, r/ likely descends from a /ɾ, r/ pair (wih a flap), it is possible that the trill is slowly simplifying to become a flap.

2.1.3 Other consonants

For completeness, we provide the rest of the consonantal inventory of Iranian Armenian in Table 2.9. To our knowledge, the phonological properties of these remaining consonants do not differ between Standard Eastern and Iranian Armenian.[9]

The nasal /n/ becomes [ŋ] before velar stops /k, kʰ, g/ (Table 2.10).

In addition to the above consonantal phonemes, Iranian Armenian has a surface glide [w] that is used to repair vowel hiatus (1). This glide is discussed in §3.1.2. It is not a contrastive or phonemic segment.

(1) /kɒˈtu =e-m/   → [kɒ.ˈtu.wem]
     cat   =AUX-1SG
     'I am a cat.'
     Կատու եմ:

2.1.4 Vowel inventory

The vowel inventory is largely the same in both lects. We provide the basic vowel inventory in the two lects in Table 2.11. Most occurrences of the schwa are unwritten in the orthography for Standard Eastern Armenian.

Between the two lects, the main difference is that the low back vowel is unrounded /ɑ/ in Standard Eastern but rounded /ɒ/ in Iranian Armenian. The rounding of the low vowel is likely due to contact between Iranian Armenian and Persian. Persian has a phonemic low back rounded vowel /ɒ/ (Majidi & Ternes 1991).[10]

---

[9]Don Stilo (p.c.) reports that the fricative /h/ of SEA and IA sounds like a voiced form [ɦ]. We are not sure if this impression is accurate. Instrumental work on SEA reports that the fricative is generally a voiceless [h], but it has a voiced variant [ɦ] when intervocalic (Խաչատրյան 1988: 182–184). In Armenian dialectology, early work by Adjarian (Աճառեան 1911, translated in Dolatian submitted) reports a (possibly phonemic) [ɦ] in some dialects in Turkey (Erzurum/Karin, Mush, Van, Şebinkarahisar, Sebastia), but not in modern-day Armenia or Iran. Adjarian does however report in later work that the dialect of New Julfa in Iran possesses the phoneme /ɦ/ (Աճառյան 1940: §5), to which Jahukyan (Ջահուկյան 1972: 60) adds Livasian (Chaharmahal). More recent sources also report /ɦ/ in many modern Armenian varieties spoken in the Republic of Armenia: Vardenis, Ashtarak, Koghb, Ghalacha/Berdavan, and Kamo/Gaver/New Bayazet (Ջահուկյան 1972: 58–59), and many more in the provinces of Gegharkunik (Կատվալյան 2018a) and Kotayk (Կատվալյան 2020).

[10]Anecdotally, BV has sometimes heard a rounded /ɒ/ in spoken Eastern Armenian in Yerevan. In modern Persian, the low back rounded vowel /ɒ/ is acoustically unstable and can approach /ɔ/ (Esfandiari et al. 2015, Mokari et al. 2017, Aronow et al. 2017, Jones 2019). In our impressions, the Iranian Armenian low vowel is much lower than the Armenian /o/. Although more acoustic data is needed, we speculate that the Iranian Armenian /ɒ/ is truly [ɒ] and not [ɔ].

Table 2.9: Other consonants in Iranian Armenian

		Initial		Medial		Final	
մ	/m/	ˈmɒˌtʰ մարդ	'man'	mɒˈm-it͡sʰ մամից	'mom-ABL'	dəˈɹɒm դրամ	'Arm. dram'
ն	/n/	ˈnɒv նավ	'ship'	kʰəˈnel քնել	'to sleep'	mɒˈt͡sun մածուն	'yogurt'
ֆ	/f/	fɒtʰiˈmɒ Ֆաթիմա	'Fatima'	ɹɒˈfi Ռաֆֆի	'Raffi (name)'	ˈkʰef քեֆ	'party, mood'
ւ, վ	/v/	vorˈteʁ որտեղ	'where'	təˈvoʁ տուող	'giver'	veˈɹev վերեւ	'up'
ս	/s/	siˈɹel սիրել	'to love'	ɒˈsel ասել	'to say'	pɒˈkɒs պակաս	'missing'
զ	/z/	ˈzɒŋg զանգ	'bell'	ɒzɒˈtel ազատել	'to free'	ˈkʰez քեզ	'you.DAT.SG'
շ	/ʃ/	ˈʃeŋkʰ շենք	'building'	pʰoˈʃi փոշի	'dust'	t͡ʃɒʃ ճաշ	'food'
ժ	/ʒ/	ʒəpˈtɒl ժպտալ	'to smile'	uˈʒeʁ ուժեղ	'strong'	ˈuʒ ուժ	'strength'
խ	/χ/	ˈχɒt͡ʃʰ խաչ	'cross'	t͡sɒˈχel ծախել	'to sell'	ˈmeχ մեխ	'nail'
ղ	/ʁ/	ʁɒzɒˈɹos Ղազարոս	'Lazarus'	uʁɒˌˈkel ուղարկել	'to send'	ˈpʰoʁ փող	'money'
յ, հ	/h/	ˈhɒt͡sʰ հաց	'bread'	mɒhɒˈnɒl մահանալ	'to die'	ˈʃɒh շահ	'gain'
լ	/l/	ˈlɒv լավ	'good'	moloˌˈvel մոլորվել	'to go astray'	ˈgɒl գալ	'to come'
յ	/j/	ˈjeˌkʰ երգ	'song'	tɒˈjim տայիմ	'I give (SBJV.PST)'	ˈtʰej թեյ	'tea'

Table 2.10: Examples of nasal place assimilation

/zɒng/	→	ˈzɒŋg	'bell'	զանգ
/menkʰ/	→	ˈmeŋkʰ	'we'	մենք
/tsʰɒnkɒnɒl/	→	tsʰɒŋkɒˈnɒl	'to wish'	ցանկանալ

Table 2.11: Vowel inventory across the lects

Grapheme	Phoneme		Example			
	SEA	IA	SEA	IA		
ա	/ɑ/	/ɒ/	tɑˈɾi	tɒˈɹi	'year'	տարի
է, ե	/e/	/e/	t͡sʰoˈɾen	t͡sʰoˈɹen	'wheat'	գորեն
ի	/i/	/i/	ˈkʰitʰ	ˈkʰitʰ	'nose'	քիթ
օ, ո	/o/	/o/	ˈvoɾ	ˈvoɹ	'that'	որ
ու	/u/	/u/	ˈdur	ˈdur	'door'	դուռ
ը	/ə/	/ə/	ˈmɑɾtʰə	ˈmɒɹtʰə	'the man'	մարդը
			gəˈɾel	gəˈɹel	'to write'	գրել

When the low vowel /ɒ/ is next to a glide /j/, the low vowel is still rounded (Table 2.12), but we suspect that it is not as rounded as in other contexts. More data is needed with finer acoustic measurements and across multiple speakers.[11]

Table 2.12: The low back vowel stays rounded next to glide /j/

[ˈhɒj]	'Armenian person'	հայ
[mɒɹˈjɒm]	'Mariam'	Մարիամ

Iranian Armenian likewise utilizes a low front vowel /æ/ as a marginal phoneme (Table 2.13). This vowel appears in Persian loanwords. Some of these loanwords likewise exist in Standard Eastern (sometimes via a different route, such as from Turkish). But in Standard Eastern, the loanwords are nativized with the low back vowel /ɑ/. In general, the front vowel does not appear in native Armenian words, but we did find a few native constructions that contain it.[12]

In the Armenian script, the front vowel /æ/ is represented as the symbol ա with umlaut in dialectological work. Because of variation across Iranian Armenian speakers, we do not adopt this symbol in our orthographic forms, but instead use a simple ա.

---

[11]For the word 'voice', the Iranian Armenian word is [d͡zen] ձեն while the Standard Eastern word is the cognate [d͡zɑjn] ձայն. NK reports that Iranian Armenians sometimes say the word [d͡zɑjn] as a type of Standard Eastern borrowing, sometimes nativized as [d͡zɒjn].

[12]The word 'drawer' is [dɑɾɑk] in Standard Eastern. In Iranian Armenian, bi-dialectal KM pronounces the final stop as [k], while mono-lectal NK uses [g]. We suspect this is just individual-level variation within the diaspora.

Table 2.13: Low front vowel /æ/ in Iranian Armenian

IA				cf. SEA
æˈɹæb	'Arab'	արաբ	from Persian	aˈɾab
mænˈʁæl	'grill'	մանղալ	from Persian	manˈʁal
læmæˈd͡ʒun	'lahmacun'	լահմաջուն	from Turkish/Persian	lahmaˈd͡ʒun
dæˈɹæg	'drawer'	դարակ	native	daˈɾak
mæˈhæt ~ ˈmæt	'a one'	մի հատ	native	mi ˈhat

The use of /æ/ is due to contact with Persian which has a phonemic /æ/ vowel (Mahootian 2002: 286). Although contemporary Iranian Armenian has /æ/ as a marginal phoneme, it is possible that earlier stages of Iranian Armenian did not. Zamir (1982: 368) reports that his sample of Iranian Armenians did not have the phoneme /æ/ when they spoke Persian. Their accent of Persian was characterized by replacing the Persian /æ/ with a back variant. Similarly for New Julfa Armenian in Isfahan, Adjarian (Աճառյան 1940: §7) reports that in the 1910s/1920s, /æ/ was slowly getting introduced in the speech of young Armenians. See the translation by Vaux (in preparation). This suggests that the introduction of /æ/ as a marginal phoneme is both recent and widespread in the Armenian dialects of Iran.[13]

As an interesting diachronic fact, there are some words that are pronounced with either [uj] or [ju] in Standard Eastern Armenian, but which are pronounced with [u] in Iranian Armenian (Table 2.14). But this is not a general rule because there are some words that are pronounced with [uj] or [ju] in both varieties.[14]

2.2 Suprasegmental phonology

In general, we did not find significant differences between Standard Eastern and Iranian Armenian in terms of syllable structure (§2.2.1). There are some differences in word stress (§2.2.2). Intonational differences are salient because Iranian Armenian has borrowed aspects of Persian intonation (§2.2.3).

---

[13] Allen (1950: 183) reports a speaker from New Julfa who only has a low vowel without any indication of rounding or fronting. This speaker does however self-report as being heavily influenced by Yerevan Standard Eastern Armenian.

[14] For SWA, the SEA [ju] sequence corresponds to [ɣ]: [t͡sɣn] 'snow'. Don Stilo reports that he may have heard some IA speakers use a front vowel as well [d͡zʏn]. Unfortunately, we have not been able to replicate this form with our speaker pool.

Table 2.14: Dialectal variation in [uj] and [ju] sequences

	Changing /uj/, /ju/ or [u]		Keeping /uj, ju/	
	'sister'	'snow'	'color'	'other'
SEA	[kʰujɾ]	[d͡zjun]	[gujn]	[mjus]
IA	[kʰuɹ]	[d͡zun]	[gujn]	[mjus]
	քույր	ձիւն	գույն	միւս

2.2.1 Syllable structure

The syllable structure of Iranian Armenian is not substantially different from that of Standard Eastern (Table 2.15). In Iranian Armenian, the typical syllable is at most CVCC. Complex onsets are limited to /Cj/ clusters, and intervocalic /Cj/ clusters are usually syllabified together into the same syllable. Complex codas generally have falling sonority. The segment /kʰ/ can follow any type of cluster. Phonologically, this segment is an extrasyllabic appendix.

Table 2.15: Syllable shapes in Iranian Armenian

V	'u	'and'	ու
CV	'du	'you (NOM.SG)'	դու
VC	'ɒpʰ	'shore'	ափ
CVC	'pʰiʁ	'elephant'	փիղ
CVCC	'mɒɹtʰ	'man'	մարդ
CjVCC	'kjɒŋkʰ	'life'	կեանք
CV.CjVC	se'njɒk	'room'	սենեակ
CVCkʰ	'petkʰ	'need'	պէտք
CVCCkʰ	'kuɹt͡skʰ	'breast'	կուրծք

All the above generalizations are likewise found in Standard Eastern Armenian. For general overviews of syllable structure in Standard Eastern Armenian, see Vaux (1998b: §1, 3). For a discussion of the final appendix *-kʰ* in Standard Eastern, see Vaux (1998b: 83), Vaux & Wolfe (2009), and Dolatian (2021a: §5).

An exception to the above generalizations concerns word-initial sibilant-stop sequences. Such clusters variably undergo schwa prothesis in both Standard Eastern and Iranian Armenian (Table 2.16). In modern Eastern, the norm is for schwa prothesis to not apply. In our elicitations from Iranian Armenian speakers, most cases of sibilant-stop clusters did not undergo prothesis. When a schwa is absent, the sibilant is analyzed as an extrasyllabic appendix (Vaux 1998b: 83ff, Vaux & Wolfe 2009, Dolatian 2023c).

Table 2.16: Schwa prothesis in sibilant-stop clusters

zgujʃ	'caution'	զգույշ
stɒnɒl	'to receive'	ստանալ
(ə)skəsel	'to start'	սկսել
əzgɒl	'to feel'	զգալ
skizb	'beginning'	սկիզբ

2.2.2 Lexical stress

Iranian Armenian seems to utilize the same lexical stress system as Standard Eastern Armenian. For an overview of lexical stress in Standard Eastern Armenian, see Vaux (1998b: §4) and Dolatian (2021a). But there are differences in irregular stress.

2.2.2.1 Regular stress

Within the morphological word, stress is generally final on the rightmost non-schwa vowel (2). This means that regular stress is on the final syllable if that syllable has a non-schwa nucleus. Suffixation of non-schwa suffixes triggers stress shift.[15]

(2)   a.   t͡ʃɒˈkɒt   'forehead'   ճակատ
            t͡ʃɒkɒt-ɒ-ˈgiɹ   'destiny'   ճակատագիր
      b.   uˈɹɒχ   'happy'   ուրախ
            uɹɒχ-uˈt͡ʃʰun   'happiness'   ուրախություն

Note that [ɒ-giɹ] is the compound linking vowel LV and the root [giɹ] 'writing'. The suffix [-ut͡ʃʰun] is a nominalizer suffix.

If the final syllable has a schwa, then stress is on the penultimate syllable (3).

---

[15]Prescriptively, the suffix -ություն (-ություն in Standard Eastern) is pronounced as [-utʰjun]. But in casual speech, the stop-glide sequence usually undergoes affrication.

(3)   a. t͡ʃɒˈkɒt-ə   'forehead-DEF'   ճակատը
          'the forehead'

      t͡ʃɒˈkɒt-əs   'forehead-POSS.1SG'   ճակատս
          'my forehead'

      t͡ʃɒˈkɒt-ət   'forehead-POSS.2SG'   ճակատդ
          'your forehead'

Besides final schwas, stress is avoided on clitics (4).

(4)   a. t͡ʃɒˈkɒt=el   'forehead=also'   ճակատ էլ
          'also forehead'

      t͡ʃɒˈkɒt=ɒ   'forehead=AUX'   ճակատ ա
          'is forehead'

      b. uˈɾɒχ=el   'happy=also'   ուրախ էլ
          'also happy'

      uˈɾɒχ=ɒ   'happy=AUX'   ուրախ ա
          'is happy'

If the word takes a cluster of clitics, stress stays inside the word (5).

(5)   a. t͡ʃɒˈkɒt=el=ɒ   'forehead=also=AUX'   ճակատ էլ ա
          'is also a forehead'

      b. uˈɾɒχ=el=ɒ   'happy=also=AUX'   ուրախ էլ ա
          'is also happy'

2.2.2.2 Irregular stress

We catalog some morphological contexts which trigger exceptional non-final stress.

A systematic exception to final stress involves the negation prefix /t͡ʃʰ-/ (pronounced [t͡ʃʰə-] before consonants), as in Table 2.17. In both periphrastic and synthetic tenses, the negation prefix attracts primary stress. For periphrastic tenses, the prefix is added to the auxiliary, and the auxiliary takes stress. In synthetic tenses, the prefix is added directly to the verb. The first syllable of the verb takes stress, even if the first syllable has a schwa.

Negation stress is reported in Iranian Armenian dialogues from Shakibi & Bonyadi (1995). In HD's experience, negation stress is likewise attested in Standard Western Armenian in both synthetic and periphrastic tenses. However in Standard Eastern Armenian, negation attracts stress in only periphrastic tenses,

Table 2.17: Irregular stress in negation

	Positive	Negative
'I am singing'	je.ɾ'kʰ-**um** e-m	**t͡ʃʰ-e-m** je.ɾkʰ-um
	sing-IMPF.CVB AUX-1SG	NEG-AUX-1SG sing-IMPF.CVB
	երգում եմ	չեմ երգում
'he took'	ve.ɾ-t͡s'ɾ-ᴅ-v	t͡ʃʰə-ve.ɾ-ts.ɾ-ᴅ-v
	take-CAUS-PST-3SG	NEG-take-CAUS-PST-3SG
	վերցրաւ	չվերցրաւ
'he did'	ᴅ'ɾ-ᴅ-v	t͡ʃʰ-ᴅ.ɾ-ᴅ-v
	do-PST-3SG	NEG-do-PST-3SG
	արաւ	չարաւ
'he fell'	əŋ'g-ᴅ-v	t͡ʃʰ-əŋg-ᴅ-v
	fall-PST-3SG	NEG-fall-PST-3SG
	ընկաւ	չընկաւ

not synthetic (Մարգարյան 1997: 77). The fact that Iranian Armenian has negation-sensitive stress may be due to language contact with Persian, where negation is a stressed prefix (Kahnemuyipour 2009).

Another morphological exception for final stress comes from ordinals (Table 2.18). The ordinal suffixes /-ɾo.ɾtʰ, -e.ɾo.ɾtʰ/ assign stress to the previous syllable (cf. Vaux 1998b: 132ff). For more examples, see §5.4.2. When an inflectional suffix or clitic is added after the ordinal suffix, irregular stress is lost and we get regular stress on the rightmost non-schwa and non-clitic vowel.

Beyond this section, we generally avoid marking stress in order to reduce clutter. Unless otherwise stated, stress is on the rightmost non-schwa and non-clitic vowel.

2.2.3 Prosodic phonology and intonation

Above the word, there is relatively little known about the prosodic structure of phrases and clauses in any Armenian lect (Fairbanks 1948: 27ff, Johnson 1954: 14ff, Ղուկասյան 1990, Toparlak & Dolatian 2022, Dolatian 2022b). There is however one aspect of Iranian Armenian prosodic phonology which stands out from Standard Eastern Armenian. This concerns the intonational structure of questions. We briefly overview the main properties of Iranian Armenian interroga-

Table 2.18: Irregular stress in ordinals in Iranian Armenian

a. Cardinal	'two'	eɾˈku	2	երկու
	'five'	ˈhiŋg	5	հինգ
b. Ordinal	'second'	ˈjek-ɾoɾtʰ	2-ORD	երկրորդ
	'fifth'	ˈhiŋg-eɾoɾtʰ	5-ORD	հինգերորդ
c. Adding /-i/	'to the second one'	jek-ɾoɾˈtʰ-i-n	2-ORD-DAT-DEF	երկրորդին
	'to the fifth one'	hiŋg-eɾoɾˈtʰ-i-n	2-ORD-DAT-DEF	հինգերորդին
d. Adding /-ə/	'the second one'	jek-ˈɾoɾtʰ-ə	2-ORD-DEF	երկրորդը
	'the fifth one'	hiŋg-eˈɾoɾtʰ-ə	5-ORD-DEF	հինգերորդը
e. Adding clitic	'he is second'	jek-ˈɾoɾtʰ =ɒ	2-ORD=AUX	երկրորդ ա
	'he is fifth'	hiŋg-eˈɾoɾtʰ=ɒ	5-ORD=AUX	հինգերորդ ա

tives, using common notation from the autosegmental-metrical tradition on intonational phonology (Pierrehumbert 1980, Ladd 1986, Jun 2005). The recordings from this subsection can be found in the online archive.[16]

In a basic SOV sentence in the present tense (6a), verbal inflection is periphrastic. The verb is in the form of the imperfective converb, and tense-agreement marking is on an auxiliary. If the object is morphologically bare, then it carries sentential stress (nuclear stress, underlined). The auxiliary is cliticized to the bare object.[17] Declarative sentences end in falling intonation.

(6) a. *Declarative SOV sentence with an auxiliary*
        i.   mɑɾjɑ-n   giɾkʰ   =e   kɑɾtʰ-um↘   (SEA)
             Մարիան գիրք է կարդում:
        ii. mɒɾjɒ-n   giɾkʰ   =ɒ   kɒɾtʰ-um↘   (IA)
             Maria-DEF   book   =AUX   read-IMPF.CVB
             'Maria is reading books.'
             Մարիան գիրք ա կարդում:
     b. *Polar question*
        i.   mɑɾjɑ-n   giɾkʰ↗   =e   kɑɾtʰ-um↘   (SEA)
             Մարիան գի՞րք է կարդում:
        ii. mɒɾjɒ-n   giɾkʰ↗   =ɒ   kɒɾtʰ-um↗   (IA)
             Maria-DEF   book   =AUX   read-IMPF.CVB
             'Is Maria reading books?'
             Մարիան գի՞րք ա կարդում:

---

[16] https://github.com/jhdeov/iranian_armenian
[17] The distribution of this auxiliary is complex in Standard Eastern and Iranian Armenian (§3.3.1). For further data and discussion, see Tamrazian (1994), Megerdoomian (2009), Kahnemuyipour & Megerdoomian (2011, 2017).

To form polar questions, the only strategy in Standard Eastern and Iranian Armenian is intonational. In Standard Eastern Armenian, there is a significant rise in pitch on the bare object in (6b-i). The sentence ends in falling intonation (cf. Ունկասյան 1990, 1999). In contrast in Iranian Armenian, there is both a rise on the object and a sentence-final rise (6b-ii).

For illustration, Figure 2.3 shows the pitch track of the declarative sentence (6a) and its corresponding polar question (6b) in both Standard Eastern and Iranian Armenian. The Iranian Armenian recordings are from NK. The Standard Eastern Armenian recordings are from AT. We annotate the perceived nucleus with the H* symbol, sentence-final fall with L%, and sentence-final rise with H%.

As is clear, both declarative sentences end in L%. The Iranian Armenian polar question has H%. For Standard Eastern, both the declarative and polar question end in a L%. The main difference is the level of pitch on the nuclear stressed word [girkʰ] 'book'.

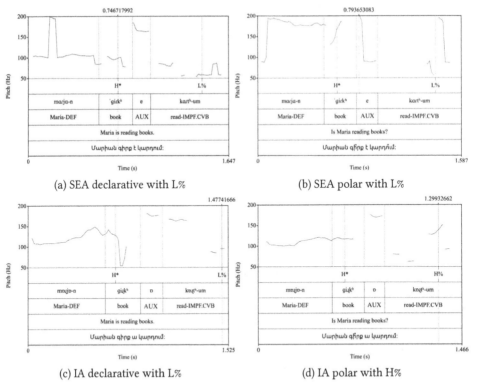

    (a) SEA declarative with L%   (b) SEA polar with L%

    (c) IA declarative with L%   (d) IA polar with H%

Figure 2.3: Pitch track of declarative (6a) and polar question (6b) in SEA an IA

The use of a sentence-final rise is likely due to two factors: one language-internal, and the other is language contact with Persian.

In Persian, polar questions end in a sentence-final rise as a type of Intonational Phrase boundary H% (Sadat-Tehrani 2007, 2011: 111, Mahjani 2003: 55). Furthermore, AS reports that some Iranian Armenian speakers draw out the last syllable, i.e., they apply sentence-final lengthening. This is also reported in Persian polar questions (Sadat-Tehrani 2011: 113).

As for language-internal factors, prescriptively, Standard Eastern Armenian uses L% for polar questions when nuclear stress is on a non-final word. However, AT informs us that Colloquial Eastern Armenian (as spoken in Yerevan) does allow a final H%. She said that the use of this H% is socially judged as "improper" for her Eastern Armenian community. We provide a pitch track in Figure 2.4. Another parallelism is that Colloquial Eastern Armenian can also use the colloquial auxiliary [ɑ] (like IA) instead of the standard [e].

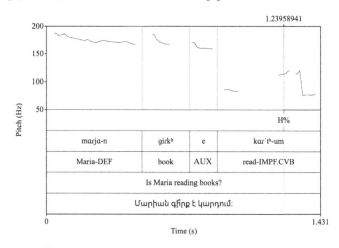

Figure 2.4: Polar question in Standard Eastern (6a-i) with optional H%

For Iranian Armenian, the final syllable in a polar question can be considerably lengthened in order to indicate politeness. AS reports that final lengthening in Iranian Armenian is common in order to indicate a non-aggressive and polite inquiry.

Phonologically, the sentence-final H% is on the final syllable of the polar question, regardless of whether that syllable carries lexical stress. For example, consider the following declarative sentence and its polar question form (7a). Morphologically, the sentence consists of a verb in a non-finite form, plus a cliticized auxiliary. In the declarative, lexical stress and nuclear stress H* are on the last syllable of the verb, while the clitic is unstressed and carries L%.

(7) a. *Declarative V-Aux with lexical stress on the V*
     i. t͡səχ-um   =e-s↘   (SEA)
     ii. t͡səχ-um   =e-s↘   (IA)
         smoke-IMPF.CVB   AUX-2SG
         'You smoke.'
         Ծխում ես:

     b. *Polar question*
     i. t͡səχ-um↗   =e-s↘   (SEA)
     ii. t͡səχ-um   =e-s↗   (IA)
         smoke-IMPF.CVB   AUX-2SG
         'Do you smoke?'
         Ծխո՞ւմ ես:

In the polar form, the Standard Eastern version simply makes the nuclear stress more prominent, while the clitic keeps its L% tone. But in Iranian Armenian, sentence-final H% is placed on the clitic. The proximity of H% and the verb causes the verb to lose its nuclear stress. We show a pitch track for these sentences in Figure 2.5 from NK and AT.

Such lengthening and rising are also found in wh-questions (8). In a subject wh-question in the present tense, the subject is replaced by the wh-word, takes nuclear stress, and is cliticized with the inflected auxiliary. There is a significant rise on the wh-word. The sentence ends with a falling intonation in Standard Eastern (Johnson 1954: 15). For Iranian Armenian, the sentence can end in a falling intonation in casual speech. However, speakers can also apply a sentence-final rise in order to indicate a degree of politeness.

(8) *Subject wh-question*
     a. ov↗   =e   girkʰ   kartʰ-um↘   (SEA)
         Ո՞վ է գիրք կարդում:
     b. ov↗   =ɒ   giɾkʰ   kɒɾtʰ-um↘   (IA - Casual)
     c. ov↗   =ɒ   giɾkʰ   kɒɾtʰ-um↗   (IA - Polite)
         who   =AUX book   read-IMPF.CVB
         'Who is reading books?'
         Ո՞վ ա գիրք կարդում:

Figure 2.6 (page 38) shows the recordings for the above wh-question, one with a final fall L%, and one with a final rise H%. Data is from NK. She at first produced the falling sentence, but in subsequent elicitations preferred the rising sentence.

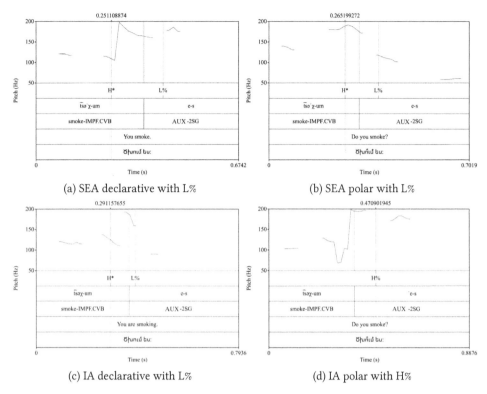

Figure 2.5: Pitch track of declarative (7a) and polar question (7b) in SEA and IA

In Persian, wh-questions likewise end in falling intonation (Sadat-Tehrani 2011: 118). Such questions can undergo a final rise and lengthening in order to indicate politeness, curiosity, or a sense of not asserting the question (Sadat-Tehrani, p.c.). The use of a final rise in wh-questions seems to have become somewhat conventionalized in Iranian Armenian. For example, NK produced some wh-questions with final rises, and some wh-questions with final falls. But she more often used final rises than final falls. More data is however needed to establish the frequency of using sentence-final rises vs. falls in wh-questions across multiple speakers.

Finally, recall that Standard Eastern Armenian is used by the Armenian community in Iran as a formal register. It is possible that a contributing factor to the intonational difference between Standard Eastern and Iranian Armenian is the fact that Persian utilizes lower pitch in formal contexts (Falahati 2020). Thus, Iranian Armenian might have conventionalized the use of sentence-final rises in order to further reinforce the sociolinguistic distinction between formal Standard Eastern and informal Iranian Armenian.

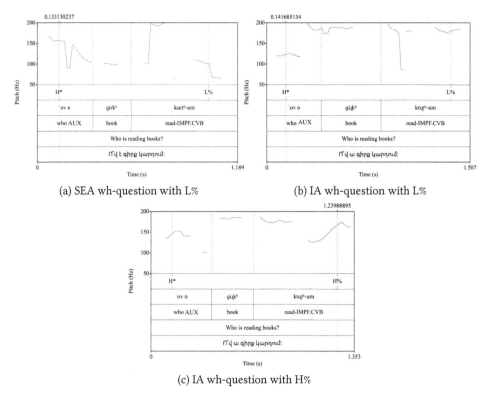

(a) SEA wh-question with L% (b) IA wh-question with L%

(c) IA wh-question with H%

Figure 2.6: Pitch track of wh-question from (8) with a final fall (8a,b) or with a final rise (8c) in Standard Eastern and Iranian Armenian

In sum, Iranian Armenian has adopted aspects of Persian intonation. Such aspects are not due to code switching. It seems that in general, Iranian Armenian speakers born in the diaspora (like NK) do not acquire Persian at the home.

3 Morphophonology

In terms of the interaction between morphology and phonology, we discuss morphologically-induced phonological processes (§3.1), phonologically-conditioned allomorphy (§3.2), and a phonosyntactic process that references both phonology and syntax (§3.3).

3.1 Morphophonological alternations

Besides general phonology, Armenian dialects show various morphophonological rules which operate at morpheme boundaries. This includes root-initial glide insertion (§3.1.1), vowel hiatus repair under suffixation/cliticization (§3.1.2), and high vowel reduction under suffixation (§3.1.3).

In general, morphophonological processes that are attested in Standard Eastern Armenian are also attested in Iranian Armenian. But in the judgments of KM, "phonological changes at morpheme boundaries are becoming simpler in Iranian Armenian." This "simplicity" suggests that such processes apply less often in Iranian Armenian than in Standard Eastern Armenian. For an overview of such morphophonological processes in Standard Eastern and Western Armenian, see Vaux (1998b: §1) and Dolatian (2020: §2).

3.1.1 Root-initial glide insertion

Armenian is primarily suffixing, and there are few morphophonological rules that are sensitive to prefix boundaries. The most noticeable process is root-initial "diphthongization" or glide insertion.

The Classical Armenian grapheme ե was a mid vowel *e* (Macak 2017). In the diachronic development from Classical Armenian to modern Armenian, this grapheme later underwent root-initial glide insertion (Weitenberg 2008). For example in Standard Eastern Armenian, the word-initial pronunciation of this grapheme is [je] (Table 3.1). In Standard Eastern, the glide is prescriptively supposed to delete after inflectional prefixes like the synthetic future *k-* and negative $\widehat{tf^h}$-, but the retention of the glide has become more common in Colloquial Eastern Armenian (Dum-Tragut 2009: 15). For Iranian Armenian, the retention seems obligatory based on our elicitations, at least for NK and her family. These prefixes trigger schwa epenthesis before a consonant.

However, there are some lexemes which have the initial <#ե> [#je] in Standard Eastern Armenian, but where the glide is lost in Iranian Armenian (Table 3.2). For some of these lexemes, Colloquial Eastern Armenian also has dialectal forms without the glide. The loss of the glide in Iranian Armenian is likely a sporadic and idiosyncratic diachronic process because the relevant lexemes are high-frequency words, and oftentimes function words.[1]

The words that show this glide-to-zero change are all polysyllabic. We have found monosyllabic words that have an invariant glide, such as [je.ɹpʰ] 'when' երբ and [je.ɹkʰ] 'song' երգ. But we have not been able find monosyllabic roots where the glide is deleted. It is possible that glide deletion is only allowed in polysyllabic roots.

When glide insertion applies word-initially, the orthographic convention is to write the word with an initial letter <ե>. When the glide is absent, the convention is to use the letter <է>. For example, the word 'to cook' with a glide [jepʰel] is spelled եփել, while the glide-less form [epʰel] is spelled էփել.

A related process is how the letters <ո, o> are pronounced [vo, o] root-initially, but both as [o] root-medially (Table 3.3). For the letter ո, it seems that this letter is always pronounced as [vo] word-initially in both monosyllables and polysyllables. In Standard Eastern Armenian, a root-initial and word-medial [vo] changes to [o] in prefixation, but Colloquial Eastern Armenian and Iranian Armenian prefer keeping this root-initial [vo] as [vo] (Dum-Tragut 2009: 16). More data is needed to verify these tendencies.

3.1.2 Vowel hiatus repair

Within the word, vowel-vowel sequences (vowel hiatus) are typically repaired, such as via [j] epenthesis or by changing [u] to [v]. Iranian Armenian seems to utilize all the vowel hiatus repair rules that are used by Standard Eastern. Iranian Armenian is however innovative in that it can also epenthesize a [w] glide.

Across the stem-inflection boundary in Standard Eastern Armenian, pre-vocalic /i/ tends to delete (1a) while pre-vocalic /u/ tends to de-vocalize or change to [v] (1b). Less common strategies are to epenthesize a glide [j] in these contexts. The following data uses the instrumental suffix /-ov/.

---

[1]For the word 'yesterday' in Iranian Armenian, NK and her family tend to say this word as [e.ɹeg], while KM and AS report [e.ɹek].

Table 3.1: Root-initial glide insertion from NK

	SEA	IA		
երգել	jeɾkʰ-e-l	je.ɽkʰ-e-l	√-TH-INF	'to sing'
երգեմ	jeɾkʰ-e-m	je.ɽkʰ-e-m	√-TH-1SG	'I sing (SBJV)'
կերգեմ	k-eɾkʰ-e-m		FUT-√-TH-1SG	'I will sing'
	kə-jeɾkʰ-e-m	kə-je.ɽkʰ-e-m		
չերգեմ	t͡ʃʰ-eɾkʰ-e-m		NEG-√-TH-1SG	'I don't sing (SBJV)'
	t͡ʃʰə-jeɾkʰ-e-m	t͡ʃʰə-je.ɽkʰ-e-m		

Table 3.2: Loss of initial glides in Iranian Armenian

	SEA	IA	
երեկ	jeɾek ~ eɾek	e.ɽek	'yesterday'
երթալ	jeɾtʰal ~ eɾtʰal ~ etʰal	e.ɽtʰɒl ~ etʰɒl	'to go'
երկու	jeɾku ~ eɾku	e.ɽku	'two'
եփել	jepʰel ~ epʰel	epʰel	'to cook'
ելնել	jelnel ~ elnel	elnel	'to rise' (SEA); 'to be' (IA)
եկել	jekel ~ ekel	ekel ~ eke.ɽ	'to come (RPTCP)'

Table 3.3: Maintaining initial [v] in Iranian Armenian

	SEA	CEA	IA	
ոսպ	vosp	vosp	vosp	'lentil'
որոշել	voɾoʃel	voɾoʃel	vo.ɽoʃel	'to decide'
կորոշեմ	k-oɾoʃem	kə-voɾoʃem	kə-vo.ɽoʃem	'I will decide'

41

(1) */u/ devocalization and /i/ deletion in vowel hiatus*

	SEA	IA		
a.	ɑjgi	ɒjgi	'garden'	այգի
	ɑjg-ov	ɒjg-ov	'garden-INS'	այգով
	ɑjgi-jov	ɒjgi-jov		այգիյով
b.	lezu	lezu	'tongue'	լեզու
	lezv-ov	lezv-ov	'tongue-INS'	լեզվով (Reformed)
				լեզուով (Classical)
	lezu-jov	lezu-jov		լեզույով

In KM's judgments for pre-vocalic /u/, Iranian Armenian utilizes /u/-devocalization and /i/-deletion less often than Standard Eastern, while Iranian Armenian utilizes /j/-insertion more often than Standard Eastern.

Unlike Standard Eastern, Iranian Armenian utilizes /w/-insertion to repair vowel hiatus in a cliticized /u=V/ sequence (2). Inserting a glide /w/ is obligatory if the /u/ is part of the future converb. The second vowel is part of the inflected auxiliary, and the vowel can be /e, ɒ, i/. We provide stress markings to reinforce the fact that the final vowel is a clitic. We do not provide a finer segmentation for the auxiliary.

(2) */w/-insertion for cliticized future converbs*

/jeɹkʰ-e-l-u=em/	jeɹ.kʰe.ˈlu.wem	'I will sing'
		երգելու եմ
/jeɹkʰ-e-l-u=iɹ/	jeɹ.kʰe.ˈlu.wiɹ	'you were going to sing'
		երգելու իր
/jeɹkʰ-e-l-u=ɒ/	jeɹ.kʰe.ˈlu.wɒ	'he will sing'
√-TH-INF-FUT.CVB=AUX		երգելու ա

Rule 1 is a rule for vowel hiatus repair in the future converb.

Rule 1: Morpheme-specific rule of w-*epenthesis*

$$\emptyset \rightarrow [w] \ / \ u_1 \_ V_2$$
where /u_1/ is the future converb suffix,
and /V_2/ is the auxiliary

Insertion of /w/ is also attested outside of the future converb (3). When an enclitic is attached to a /u/-final noun, the typical vowel hiatus repair rule is to insert [j]. But NK and AS report that /w/-insertion is also possible.

(3) */w/-insertion outside of the future converb*
   a.   /kɒtu=e-m/
       kɒ.ˈtu.jem *or* kɒ.ˈtu.wem
       cat=AUX-1SG
       'I am a cat.'
       Կատու եմ:
   b.   /kɒtu=el=e-m/
       kɒ.ˈtu.je.lem *or* kɒ.ˈtu.we.lem
       cat=also=AUX-1SG
       'I am also a cat.'
       Կատու էլ եմ:

It is possible that Iranian Armenian innovated a rule of /w/-insertion because of contact with Persian. Persian allows various types of vowel hiatus repair rules (Ariyaee & Jurgec 2021: 3). One such rule inserts the glide [w] after a back vowel /u/ (Dehghan & Kambuziya 2012: 20).

3.1.3 Destressed high vowel reduction

Armenian utilizes a process of destressed high vowel reduction (Vaux 1998b, Khanjian 2009, Dolatian 2020, 2021a). When a root undergoes suffixation, regular final stress typically shifts to the suffix (Table 3.4). In Standard Eastern and Iranian Armenian, destressed high vowels from the root reduce before derivational suffixes, but generally not before consonant-initial inflectional suffixes. Some words exceptionally reduce before the consonant-initial *-neɾ*.[2]

Table 3.4: Destressed high vowel reduction

SEA	IA		
amuˈsin	ɒmuˈsin	'husband'	ամուսին
amusn-uˈtʰjun	ɒmusn-uˈt͡ʃʰun	'marriage'	ամուսնություն
amusin-ˈneɾ	ɒmusin-ˈneɾ	'husbands'	ամուսիններ
ˈskizb	ˈskizb	'beginning'	սկիզբ
skizb-ˈneɾ	skizb-ˈneɾ	'beginnings'	սկիզբներ
skəzb-ˈneɾ	skəzb-ˈneɾ	'beginnings'	սկզբներ

---

[2] See footnote 15 in Chapter 2 on the difference in the pronunciation of the suffix /-utʰjun/.

Before vowel-initial inflectional suffixes, the tendency in Standard Eastern Armenian is for reduction to apply (4). For Iranian Armenian, KM feels that reduction applies less often in this context than in Standard Eastern.

(4) *Variation in vowel reduction before V-initial inflection*

    a.   kɒmˈuɹd͡ʒ   'bridge'   կամուրջ
         kɒmuɹˈd͡ʒ-itsʰ 'bridge-ABL'   կամուրջից
         kɒməɹˈd͡ʒ-itsʰ   կամրջից
    b.   jeɹˈkiɹ   'world'   երկիր
         jeɹkiˈɹ-um   'world-LOC'   երկիրում
         jeɹkˈɹ-um   երկրում
    c.   ˈtun   'house'   տուն
         tuˈn-um   'house-LOC'   տունում
         təˈn-um   տնում

Before vowel-initial inflectional suffixes, there is widespread cross-dialectal and lexical variation in the application of high vowel reduction (Ղարագյուլյան 1974, Մարգարյան 1997). For an overview, see Dum-Tragut (2009: 41ff) and Dolatian (2021a: §2.7).

3.2 Phonologically-conditioned allomorphy

This section presents some examples of phonologically-conditioned allomorphy in Iranian Armenian. These include syllable-counting allomorphy of the plural suffix (§3.2.1), schwa-zero and schwa-nasal alternations for the possessive and definite suffixes (§3.2.2), and variable voicing assimilation in the synthetic future prefix (§3.2.3).

3.2.1 Syllable-counting allomorphy of the plural suffix

For the plural, the regular suffix is *-eɹ* for monosyllabic bases, and *-neɹ* for polysyllabic bases (Vaux 2003, Dolatian 2021b). This is a relatively straightforward case of syllable-counting allomorphy, as a form of phonologically-conditioned allomorphy (Table 3.5).

Words that have only one syllable and the appendix *-kʰ* count as monosyllabic for plural-counting (Table 3.6).[3] Words with an initial appendix /s/ + a syllable are treated as polysyllabic.

---

[3]Compounds have complicated rules for plural allomorphy in Armenian (Vaux 1998b: 21). For discussion, see Dolatian (2021b, 2022c).

Table 3.5: Distribution of regular plural suffixes

Monosyllabic			Polysyllabic		
bɒr	'word'	բառ	senjɒk	'room'	սենեակ
bɒr-eɹ	'words'	բառեր	senjɒk-neɹ	'rooms'	սենեակներ

Table 3.6: Pluralization of exceptional syllable structures

syllable + /-kʰ/			/s/ + syllable		
pɒɹtkʰ	'debt'	պարտք	skizb	'beginning'	սկիզբ
pɒɹtkʰ-eɹ	'debts'	պարտքեր	skizb-neɹ	'beginnings'	սկիզբներ
			skəzb-neɹ		սկզբներ
kuɹt͡skʰ	'breast'	կուրծք			
kuɹt͡skʰ-eɹ	'breasts'	կուրծքեր			
Syllable + [CəC]					
vɒgəɹ	'tiger'	վագր	pʰokʰəɹ	'small'	փոքր
vɒgɹ-eɹ	'tigers'	վագրեր	pʰokʰɹ-eɹ	'small ones'	փոքրեր
vɒgəɹ-neɹ		վագրներ	pʰokʰəɹ-neɹ		փոքրներ

Bisyllabic words that end in a [CəC] sequence have an epenthetic schwa, such as [vɒgəɹ] 'tiger' from /vɒgɹ/ (Vaux 2003, Dolatian 2023c). For modern Standard Eastern Armenian, the plural ignores this schwa and the word is treated as monosyllabic with [-eɾ], such 'tigers' [vɑgr-eɾ] (Dum-Tragut 2009: 65). But in older or colloquial registers, the form [-neɾ] is attested like [vɑgər-neɾ] (Մարգսյան 1987: 217). For Iranian Armenian, Anooshik Melikian (AM) reports that the modern community likewise almost always uses [-eɹ], while older members (such as her grandfather) would use [-neɹ].

3.2.2 Schwa alternations in the determiner slot

In nominal inflection, the determiner slot is occupied by either a possessive suffix or a definite suffix. Both types of suffixes display allomorphy conditioned by consonant- vs. vowel-final stems. The definite suffix likewise displays outwardly-conditioned allomorphy to subsequent vowels.

The possessive suffixes are *-s, -t* for vowel-final bases. A schwa is epenthesized after consonant-final bases (Table 3.7). The epenthetic schwa is maintained between a C-final base and a V-initial clitic.

Table 3.7: Allomorphy in possessive marking

No epenthesis after V-final base			
kɒtu		'cat'	կատու
kɒtu-s	cat-POSS.1SG	'my cat'	կատուս
kɒtu-s=el	cat-POSS.1SG=also	'also my cat'	կատուս էլ
kɒtu-t	cat-POSS.2SG	'your cat'	կատուդ
kɒtu-t=el	cat-POSS.2SG=also	'also your cat'	կատուդ էլ
Schwa epenthesis after C-final base			
gumɒɹ		'amount'	գումար
gumɒɹ-əs	amount-POSS.1SG	'my amount'	գումարս
gumɒɹ-əs=el	amount-POSS.1SG=also	'also my amount'	գումարս էլ
gumɒɹ-ət	amount-POSS.2SG	'your amount'	գումարդ
gumɒɹ-ət=el	amount-POSS.2SG=also	'also your amount'	գումարդ էլ

The definite suffix has three allomorphs: *-ə, -n, -ən* (Table 3.8). The choice of suffix is conditioned by the preceding segment and the following segment. When there is no following segment, the suffix is *-n* after vowel-final bases, but *-ə* after consonant-final stems.

Table 3.8: Forms of the definite suffix in Standard Eastern and Iranian Armenian

	SEA	IA			
	kaˈtu	kɒˈtu		'cat'	կատու
V_	kaˈtu-n	kɒˈtu-n	cat-DEF	'the cat'	կատուն
V_V	kaˈtu-n=el	kɒˈtu-n=el	cat-DEF=also	'also the cat'	կատուն էլ
	kaˈtu-n=e	kɒˈtu-n=ɒ	cat-DEF=AUX	'is the cat'	կատուն է/ա
	guˈmar	guˈmɒɹ		'amount'	գումար
C_	guˈmar-ə	guˈmɒɹ-ə	amount-DEF	'the amount'	գումարը
C_V	guˈmar-n=el	guˈmɒɹ-ən=el	amount-DEF=also	'also the amount'	գումարն էլ
	guˈmar-n=e	guˈmɒɹ-ən=ɒ	amount-DEF=AUX	'is the amount'	գումարն է/ա

The lects differ when the definite suffix is between a C-final base and V-initial clitic (5). In this context, Standard Eastern Armenian uses the *-n* form of the definite. In Iranian Armenian, the form is *-ən*. More examples are shown below.

(5) *Other examples of the /-ən/ form before clitics in Iranian Armenian*

'mɒɹtʰ-**ən**=ɒ   man-DEF=AUX   '(he) is the man'   մարդն ա

'iŋkʰ-**ən**=ɒ   he-DEF=AUX   'it is he'   ինքն ա

dɒ'nɒk-**ən**=ɒ   knife-DEF=AUX   '(it) is the knife'   դանակն ա

Iranian Armenian also uses the *-ən* form between a C-final word and a V-initial word (6).

(6) *Use of -ən before a V-initial word*

a. 'iŋkʰ-**ən** iɹ
    him-DEF he.GEN
    'himself'   (KM)
    ինքն իր

b. mɒɹtʰ-**ən** ɒɹtʰn-ɒ-t͡sʰ-ɒ-v
    man-DEF wake.up-LV-AOR-PST-3SG
    'The man woke up.'   (KM)
    Մարդն արթնացավ:

The form [ən] is attested in colloquial Western Armenian speech (Dolatian 2022a), so it is likely that Iranian Armenian developed its [ən] via language-internal grammaticalization. BV also reports that he has come across [ən] forms in published texts from some Iran-adjacent areas such as Astrakhan (Ախվերդեան 1852: 121)[4] which has had close trade connections with Armenians in New Julfa, Isfahan. It is an open question how widespread this [ən] form is for Iranian communities outside of Tehran.[5]

Prosodic phrasing and pauses can block the use of the *-ən* form between a C-final word and V-initial word (7). For example, in the sentence below, it is common to have a pause between the subject and the object. The presence of a pause blocks the *-ən* form.

(7) d͡ʒɒn-**ə** indz mɒkʰɹ-ɒ-v
    John-DEF me.DAT clean-PST-3SG
    'John cleaned me.'   (NK)
    Ջոնը ինձ մաքրաւ:

---

[4]See the accessible page at Google Books (https://www.google.co.uk/books/edition/Sajeath_N%C3%B4waj/-bg-AAAAcAAJ).

[5]Stevick (1955) documents a speaker from Tabriz/Tehran who seems to largely speak in Standard Eastern Armenian, such as by not using the suffix /-m/ for the aorist 1SG (p. 19). But this speaker does show minor traces of Iranian Armenian morphophonology, such as using the definite suffix /-ən/ (p. 3, 27).

In sum, the shape of the definite suffix is sensitive to the type of the preceding and following segments and to prosodic pauses. This amounts to a case of phrasal allomorphy that is outwardly-sensitive. Such phenomena are cross-linguistically rare (Paster 2006). For an analysis of the definite suffix in Iranian Armenian and other Armenian lects, see Dolatian (2022a).

3.2.3 Voicing assimilation in the synthetic future prefix

There are reports of limited phonologically-conditioned allomorphy for the synthetic future prefix. See §6.5.3 for a morphological description of this prefix.

Some speakers seem to have this process, some do not. The process resembles a mildly long-distance assimilation process whereby velar stops in a /CV-C/ context can assimilate in voice. For some speakers this process is limited to a few or no lexical items, while for others it is more widespread.

The synthetic future prefix is underlyingly /k-/ (8a). Before a consonant, schwa epenthesis resolves the consonant cluster. Before a voiced velar stop [g], AS reports that the prefix assimilates to [gə-] for some speakers (8b). However, one consultant (NK) does not produce any alternation (8c). Though for the word *gɒm* 'I come', NK's family reports variable voicing changes (8d).

(8)   *Voicing assimilation for synthetic future prefix /k-/*

    a.   k-uɾɒχɒnɒm   'I will be happy'   կուրախանամ
          kə-tesnem   'I will see'   կը տեսնեմ

    b.   From AS's contacts
          gə-gəɾem   'I will write'   կը գրեմ
          gə-gɒm   'I will come'   կը գամ

    c.   From NK
          kə-kɒɾtʰɒm   'I will read'   կը կարդամ
          kə-gəɾem   'I will write'   կը գրեմ
          kə-kʰənem   'I will sleep'   կը քնեմ

    d.   From NK's family
          kə-gɒm   'I will come'   կը գամ
          gə-gɒm
          gə-kɒm

The cognate of this prefix assimilates in voicing and aspiration to a root-initial consonant in many varieties of modern Armenian, including Ararat (the set of varieties to which the Yerevan dialect belongs; Մարկոսյան 1989: 150), Goris (Մարգարյան 1975), Karabakh (Աճառեան 1911: 68), New Nakhichevan (Աճառեան

1925, Ачарян 1961: 85), and in Iran in Maragha (Ачарян 1926: 273–274) and New Julfa (Vaux 1997, 1998a, 1998b: 39, 215ff, Ачарян 1940: §287, translated in Vaux in preparation: 287). It is possible that the traces of this process in (Tehrani) Iranian Armenian ultimately come from one of these Iranian varieties.

3.3 Phonosyntax: Auxiliary-induced segment deletion

We examine the behavior of the final segment of the perfective converb suffix: *-el* or *-eɭ*. This phenomenon is the most complex morphophonological process that we describe in this grammar, because it involves syntax-phonology interactions. Phonologically, this segment can delete in different morphosyntactic contexts. To make this segment surface, we find that the ultimate conditioning factor is syntactic and long-distance. This factor is that the suffix has to precede the auxiliary 'to be' within the same clause or verb phrase. The suffix and auxiliary can be adjacent or non-adjacent.

This section focuses on describing as much as we can about the behavior of this suffix. This process counts as a phonosyntactic or syntax-sensitive phonological process (perhaps syntax-sensitive allomorphy) because of the deep interaction between phonology and syntax. We postpone a complete theoretical analysis to future work.

We present some basics of Armenian syntax, with regards to the mobile auxiliary (§3.3.1). We then discuss the basic data on liquid deletion in §3.3.2. Long-distance factors are examined in §3.3.3. An identical deletion process is attested in irregular imperfectives (§3.3.4). We discuss the diachronic origin of liquid deletion from Standard Eastern Armenian (§3.3.5).

There are other Armenian lects in Iran which alternate in the form of the perfective converb suffix based on whether the auxiliary is to the right vs. the left of the verb.[6] For Tehrani Iranian Armenian, this difference manifests in the presence/absence of the final liquid: V-*el/eɭ* vs. V-*e*. But in Iran, there are other Armenian lects where the difference is manifested in using a completely different allomorph for the alternating suffix. For example in Salmast (Vaux 2022b: 53), the pre-auxiliary form of the imperfective converb is V-*s*, while the post-auxiliary form is V-*li*. Other such dialects include Urmia (Դարբիյան 1941: 275). It is an open question whether all the generalizations for Tehrani Armenian likewise extend to these other Armenian varieties.

---

[6]The alternation is also attested in Armenian lects that developed outside of Iran, such as the Karin or Erzurum dialect which developed in modern-day Turkey (Bezrukov 2022: 120).

3.3.1 Background on the mobile auxiliary

Before we discuss the main morphophonological process, we survey the basic features of Iranian Armenian syntax. We focus on the use of converbs and the mobile auxiliary. The syntactic data has been discussed in previous works on Standard Eastern Armenian, but previous analyses extend to Iranian Armenian (Comrie 1984, Kahnemuyipour & Megerdoomian 2011, 2017).

As in Standard Eastern Armenian, many verbal tenses are marked by periphrasis. For example, the present indicative is marked by using the form of the verb that we call the "imperfective converb" (9). Tense and agreement are marked on the auxiliary 'to be'. See §6.3.1 for full morphological paradigms.

(9) a. jes giɹkʰ-ə **gəɹ-um** =e-m
        I   book-DEF write-IMPF.CVB AUX-1SG

        'I am writing the book.'   (NK)

        ես գիրքը գրում եմ:

    b. du giɹkʰ-ə **kɒɹtʰ-um** =e-s
        you book-DEF read-IMPF.CVB AUX-2SG

        'You are reading the book.'   (NK)

        Դու գիրքը կարդում ես:

Throughout this section we underline the relevant converb form. We highlight the auxiliary. We mark the nuclear stress of the sentence via boldface, because this information is quite relevant to the syntax of the auxiliary. In the above sentences, nuclear stress is on the verb.

The auxiliary is phonologically cliticized to the word to its left, i.e., the converb. The auxiliary is a clitic that unambiguously syllabified with the converb: [gə.ɹu.mem] 'I am writing'. In terms of stress, the auxiliary is an unstressed clitic in general (§2.2.2).[7]

In the simple sentences above, the auxiliary appears by default after the verb. However, in more complex types of sentences, we find that this auxiliary can shift or move leftwards. Hosts for the mobile clitic include the negation marker (10).

(10) jes giɹkʰ-ə **t͡ʃʰ-e-m** gəɹ-um
     I   book-DEF NEG=AUX-1SG write-IMPF.CVB

     'I am not writing the book.'   (NK)

     ես գիրքը չեմ գրում:

---

[7]The auxiliary takes stress when it is negated, as seen in (10).

Negation is marked by using the prefix $\widehat{tʃ^h}$-. When the verb is periphrastic, the negation prefix is placed directly before the verb, and then the auxiliary moves leftwards and attaches to the prefix. The prefix-auxiliary combination acts as its own phonological word, and carries the nuclear stress of the sentence.

Another context for leftward movement involves bare objects. In the above sentences, the object of the verb is definite and resists taking nuclear stress. But if the object lacks any morphological markers of definiteness or indefiniteness, then the object is considered bare, takes nuclear stress, and acts as a host for the auxiliary (11).

(11) jes **giɹkʰ** =e-m   gəɹ-um
      I   book =AUX-1SG write-IMPF.CVB
      'I am writing books.'   (NK)
      Ես գիրք եմ գրում:

For descriptions and analyses of bare objects in other Armenian lects, see Standard Eastern (Comrie 1984, Megerdoomian 2009, Yeghiazaryan 2010, Crum 2020) and Standard Western (Sigler 1997, Sağ 2019, Kalomoiros 2022).

Another context is narrow focus. If a word has narrow focus and precedes the verb, then the auxiliary moves and attaches to the focused word (12).

(12) a. jes **giɹkʰ-ən** =e-m   gəɹ-um
          I   book-DEF =AUX-1SG write-IMPF.CVB
          'I am writing **THE BOOK**.'   (NK)
          Ես գիրքն եմ գրում:

      b. **jes** =e-m   giɹkʰ-ə gəɹ-um
          I   =AUX-1SG book-DEF write-IMPF.CVB
          '**I** am writing the book.'   (NK)
          Ես եմ գիրքը գրում:

      c. **esoɹ** =e-m   giɹkʰ-ə gəɹ-um
          today =AUX-1SG book-DEF write-IMPF.CVB
          'I am writing the book **TODAY**.'   (NK)
          Էսօր եմ գիրքը գրում:

It is obvious that there are strong correlations between auxiliary movement and nuclear stress. Essentially, the auxiliary moves to the pre-verbal phrase that carries nuclear stress. Such correlations have been modeled in the past with various frameworks and analyses (Tamrazian 1994, Megerdoomian 2009, Kahnemuyipour 2009, Kahnemuyipour & Megerdoomian 2011, 2017, Giorgi & Haroutyunian 2016, Hodgson 2019a). We do not analyze or provide a larger catalog of contexts for auxiliary movement. For our purposes, we focus on the effects of auxiliary movement on converbs.

3.3.2 Non-constant form of the perfective converb

Having surveyed the syntax of auxiliaries, this section shows how auxiliary movement interacts with the morphophonology of the perfective converb suffix.

The imperfective converb suffix *-um* is phonologically constant. Its segments never delete or change, regardless of whether the suffix precedes the auxiliary or not. In contrast, the perfective converb is formed with the suffix *-el* or *-eɹ*. The liquid deletes when the auxiliary has moved.

When the perfective converb suffix precedes the auxiliary, some speakers produce this suffix as *-el*, some as *-eɹ*, and some as either (13). The choice of liquid varies by speaker and perhaps by generation or geographic origin. For consistency, we mostly use the *-eɹ* form in this chapter because HD's main consultant NK preferred it.

(13) jes giɹkʰ-ə   **gəɹ-el/eɹ**   =e-m
    I   book-DEF write-PERF.CVB =AUX-1SG
    'I have written the book.'   (NK)
    ես գիրքը գրել եմ:
    ես գիրքը գրեր եմ:

When the auxiliary is attached to the suffix, the auxiliary is syllabified with the suffix: [gə.ɹe.lem] or [gə.ɹe.ɹem].

When the auxiliary shifts leftwards, the perfective converb suffix loses its liquid (14). We find deletion in configurations involving negation (14a), bare objects (14b), or narrow focus (14c-14d), among others.

(14) a. jes giɹkʰ-ə   t͡ʃʰ **-e-m**   gəɹ-e
        I   book-DEF NEG=AUX-1SG write-PERF.CVB
        'I have not written the book.'   (NK)
        ես գիրքը չեմ գրե:

    b. jes **giɹkʰ** =e-m   gəɹ-e
        I   book =AUX-1SG write-PERF.CVB
        'I have written books.'   (NK)
        ես գիրք եմ գրե:

c. **jes** =e-m giɹkʰ-ə   gəɹ-e
   I   AUX-1SG book-DEF write-PERF.CVB

   '**I** have written the book.'   (NK)
   Ես եմ գիրքը գրե:

d. **esoɹ** =e-m   giɹkʰ-ə   gəɹ-e
   today AUX-1SG book-DEF write-PERF.CVB

   I have written the book **TODAY**.'   (NK)
   Էսօր եմ գիրքը գրե:

Note that in the above sentences, the final liquid of the suffix has deleted. NK sometimes would produce sentences where the deleted liquid was replaced with what HD and NK heard as an [h]. However, this [h] was so weak that it may be an extragrammatical sentence-final voiceless interval rather than an allomorph of the underlying final liquid.

As we discuss in §6.3.2, the perfective converb is analyzable as a suffix /e<ɹ>/ or /-e<l>/ with a floating segment. This segment surfaces based on the location of the auxiliary.

Auxiliary movement and liquid deletion are quite common in answers to wh-questions which naturally create narrow focus, as the following set of questions and answers illustrate (15). Focus is on the wh-word *intʃʰ* in the question (15a), and on the focused word 'song' in the answer (15a). Because the auxiliary is to the left of the verb, the final liquid of the verb is either dropped or pronounced as [h]. It seems that the choice of deletion vs. [h] is unpredictable and due to random chance.

(15)   a. **intʃʰ** =e-s   jeɹkʰ-e(h)
           what =AUX-2SG sing-PERF.CVB

           'What have you sung?'   (NK)
           Ինչ ես երգե՞:

    b. jes es jeɹkʰ-ən =e-m   jeɹkʰ-e(h)
        I   this song-DEF =AUX-1SG sing-PERF.CVB

        'I have sung this song.'   (NK)
        Ես էս երգն եմ երգե՞:

The deletion of the liquid is not a prosodic process. It is not conditioned by the sentence-final pause. For example, in the following ditransitive constructions (16), the verb appears between two noun phrases in a focus-neutral declarative sentence (16a). In the corresponding interrogative sentence, the auxiliary moves leftward and is placed on the wh-word. The verb can be sentence-final (16b) or sentence-medial (16c). In both cases, the verb lacks a final liquid.

(16) a. es gi̯kʰ-ə **təv-e̯** =e-m d͡ʒon-i-n
     this book-DEF give-PERF.CVB =AUX-1SG John-DAT-DEF
     'I have given this book to John.' (NK)
     Ես գիրքը տուեր եմ Ջոնին:

   b. es gi̯kʰ-ə **um-i-n** =e-s təv-e
     this book-DEF who-DAT-DEF AUX-2SG give-PERF.CVB
     'Who have you given this book to?' (NK)
     Ես գիրքը ումին ես տուե:

   c. **um-i-n** =e-s təv-e es gi̯kʰ-ə
     who-DAT-DEF =AUX-2SG give-PERF.CVB this book-DEF
     'Who have you given this book to?' (NK)
     Ումին ես տուե էս գիրքը:

In (16c) the post-verbal word starts with a vowel /e/, but this vowel does not block liquid deletion. Vowel hiatus between the suffix [-e] and the subsequent word [es] 'this' is not repaired by glide epenthesis. In our recordings, we notice a very slight transitional glide: [... təv-e ʲes..].

When a word is focused, the most typical situation is to place the focused word before the verb (17a). In this case, the auxiliary shifts onto the focused word. The direct object is optional and can be added at the end of the sentence. If the sentence is negated (17b), we again find auxiliary shift and liquid deletion. Thus, the uncliticized verb surfaces without the final liquid, regardless of whether it is sentence-medial or sentence-final (17a).

(17) a. jes d͡ʒon-i-n =e-m təv-e (es gi̯kʰ-ə)
     I John-DAT-DEF =AUX-1SG give-PERF.CVB this book-DEF
     'I have given this book to **JOHN**.' (NK, KM)
     Ես Ջոնին եմ տուե (էս գիրքը):

   b. jes d͡ʒon-i-n **t͡ʃʰ =e-m** təv-e (es gi̯kʰ-ə)
     I John-DAT-DEF NEG=AUX-1SG give-PERF.CVB this book-DEF
     'I have not given this book to John.' (NK, KM)
     Ես Ջոնին եմ տուե (էս գիրքը):

An alternative construction places the focused answer after the verb (18). In this case, the auxiliary does not shift leftwards and it remains cliticized to the verb. Thus, the verb surfaces with a liquid.[8]

---

[8]Focus can never move the auxiliary rightward from the verb. That is, we cannot have a construction like V+X+Aux.

(18) es gi.ɨkʰ-ə təv-eɹ =e-m d͡ʒon-i-n
      this book-DEF give-PERF.CVB =AUX-1SG John-DAT-DEF
      'I have given this book to **JOHN**.'   (NK)
      Ես գիրքը տուեր եմ Ջոնին:

Similarly, the following question-answer set again shows that the uncliticized converb loses its liquid in sentence-medial position (19).

(19) a. **jeɹpʰ** =e-s gi.ɨkʰ-ə təv-e d͡ʒon-i-n
            when =AUX-2SG book-DEF give-PERF.CVB John-DAT-DEF
            'When did you give John the book?'   (NK)
            Երբ ես գիրքը տուէ Ջոնին:

    b. jes **esoɹ** =e-m təv-e d͡ʒon-i-n
            I   today =AUX-1SG give-PERF.CVB John-DAT-DEF
            'I have given it to John **TODAY**.'   (NK)
            Ես էսօր եմ տուէ Ջոնին:

AS's fieldwork likewise reports the deletion of the liquid in uncliticized converbs, and the retention of the liquid in cliticized forms (20),

(20) a. **voɹteʁ** =e-s tsən-v-e
            where =AUX-2SG birth-PASS-PERF.CVB
            'Where were you born?'   (AS)
            Որտեղ ես ծնուէ:

    b. ek-eɹ   =e-Ø-ɹ ,   ek-eɹ   =Ø-i-m
            come-PERF.CVB =AUX-PST-3SG, come-PERF.CVB =AUX-PST-1SG
            'He had come. I had come.'   (AS)
            Եկեր էր, եկեր իմ:

    c. gəʒ-v-eɹ   =e-n
            insane-PASS-PERF.CVB =AUX-3PL
            'They have gone insane.'   (AS)
            Գժուեր են:

3.3.3 Long-distance conditions

So far, we have seen cases where the liquid is dropped when the auxiliary shifts leftward. Based on the data so far, one could hypothesize that the liquid surfaces when the auxiliary is *immediately* to the right. We find evidence against this hypothesis. In order for the liquid to surface, the liquid does not need to be adjacent to the auxiliary, just (non-immediately) before it. Data comes from intervening coordination and clitics. The data constitutes a type of suspended affixation (Kabak 2007, Kornfilt 2012, Erschler 2018, Fenger 2020, Dolatian 2023d).

In simple cases of coordination, two verbs can be coordinated each with their own auxiliary. In a sentence such as (21a), the liquids of both verbs surface because each appears before an auxiliary. But this sentence can be paraphrased with a simpler type of coordination which we call reduced coordination (21b).

(21) Coordination and liquid deletion

	Verb1	Aux	Conj	Verb2	Aux
a.	χəm-eɹ	=e-m	kɒm	**keɹ-eɹ**	=e-m
	drink-PERF.CVB	=AUX-1SG	or	eat-PERF.CVB	=AUX-1SG
	'I have drunk or have eaten.'			(NK)	
	Խմեր եմ կամ կերեր եմ:				
b.	χəm-eɹ		kɒm	**keɹ-eɹ**	=e-m
	drink-PERF.CVB		or	eat-PERF.CVB	=AUX-1SG
	'I have drunk or eaten.'			(NK)	
	Խմեր կամ կերեր եմ:				

In reduced coordination, only one auxiliary is used. The auxiliary follows the second verb, and it licenses the liquids of both verbs. This auxiliary licenses the liquid of the first verb (Verb1) even though they are not adjacent.

In the positive form, some speakers prefer to repeat the conjunction on both verbs (22a). The single auxiliary licenses the liquids on both verbs. Also when negating reduced coordination, an alternative construction is to delete the conjunction entirely (22b). However, the only crucial point for now is the positioning of the auxiliary leftward of the verb forms, which gives rise to liquid deletion here as expected.

(22) a. kɒm χəm-el   kɒm keɹ-el   =e-m

      or   drink-PERF.CVB or   eat-PERF.CVB be-1SG

      'I have drunk or eaten.'   (KM)

      Կամ խմել կամ կերել եմ:

  b. t͡ʃʰ -e-m   keɹ-e   χəm-e

      NEG=AUX-1SG eat-PERF.CVB drink-PERF.CVB

      'I have not eaten or drunk.'   (KM)

      Չեմ կերէ խմէ:

The generalization so far is that, in reduced coordination, the single auxiliary can license the appearance of the liquid of both verbs without being adjacent to both of them. Similar behavior is found in clitics.

The clitic [=el] is polysemous and can have a host of meanings based on its position and presence of negation. We gloss it as 'also' because that is its basic meaning. For verbs without negation, the clitic can appear between the verb and the auxiliary (23a), or after the auxiliary (23b). In neither case does the clitic prevent the liquid from surfacing. This is because the auxiliary is to the right of the liquid.

(23) Liquid deletion and clitics without negation

    a. <u>keɹ-eɹ</u>   =el   =e-m

       eat-PERF.CVB =also =AUX-1SG

       'I have also eaten.'   (NK)

       Կերեր էլ եմ:

    b. <u>keɹ-eɹ</u>   =e-m   =el

       eat-PERF.CVB =AUX-1SG =also

       'I have eaten already!'[9]   (NK)

       Կերեր եմ էլ:

In contrast, in the context of verbal negation, the clitic can be placed either after the auxiliary (24a) or after the verb (24b). In both cases, the liquid is deleted for NK and KM because the auxiliary has shifted leftward. The clitic is vowel-initial and in the same prosodic word as the suffix, but the clitic cannot license the liquid.

(24) Liquid deletion and clitics with negation

    a. **t͡ʃʰ -e-m**   =el keɹ-e

       NEG=AUX-1SG =also eat-PERF.CVB

       'Also, I have not eaten.'   (NK, KM)

       Չեմ էլ կերէ:

    b. **t͡ʃʰ -e-m**   <u>keɹ-e</u>   =el

       NEG=AUX-1SG eat-PERF.CVB =also

       'I have not eaten anymore.'   (NK, KM)

       Չեմ կերէ էլ:

We have found some speaker variation in cases where the suffix appears after the auxiliary but before a clitic. Whereas NK and KM drop the liquid (24b), Garoun Engström (GE) reports that she can maintain the liquid: [t͡ʃʰ-e-m keɹ-el =el]. GE likewise reports that in cases of reduced coordination like

---

[9]NK found the Aux-Clitic sequence rather odd but acceptable, while KM felt it too odd.

V+*kɒm*+V+Aux (22), she also maintains the liquid. Thus for some speakers, the rule is that the liquid is licensed either long-distance by the auxiliary, or locally by an adjacent clitic. At this point, we do not have enough data and resources to construct a large-scale variationist study on the phonosyntax of this process across multiple speakers, but it is a worthwhile future endeavor.

Setting aside microvariation between speakers, the data can be categorized in theoretical terms in terms of a post-lexical rule that is syntactically conditioned. Such cases are relatively rarer than purely prosodic rules, but still attested (Selkirk 1986, Kaisse 1985). However, to our knowledge, most attested cases of syntax-sensitive phonology involve adjacency between the target and trigger/blocker. For example, such locality or adjacency constraints are common for phonosyntactic processes in Romance and Germanic (Ackema & Neeleman 2003, 2004, Sampson 2016, Weisser 2019).

The Iranian Armenian data is thus cross-linguistically rare in allowing long-distance conditioning. To our knowledge, the closest attested case of long-distance syntax-sensitive phonology is long-distance and discontinuous vowel harmony in Wolof (Sy 2005) and Guébie (Dąbkowski & Sande 2021).[10] For Wolof (25), vowel harmony applies across words, specifically between a head and its complement. This makes vowel harmony a type of syntax-sensitive phonology. Harmony can ignore certain intervening words between the source and target vowels. This invisibility of intervening words is what makes Wolof a case of long-distance syntax-sensitive phonology.

(25)   Long-distance ATR agreement in Wolof, taken from Sy (2005: 95, (1))

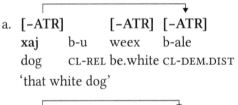

a. **[–ATR]**   **[–ATR] [–ATR]**
   xaj   b-u   weex   b-ale
   dog   CL-REL be.white CL-DEM.DIST
   'that white dog'

b. **[+ATR]**   **[+ATR] [+ATR]**
   béy   w-u   réy   w-ëlé
   goat   CL-REL be.big CL-DEM.DIST
   'that big goat'

---

[10]We thank Kie Zuraw for bringing the Wolof case to our attention. Another potential case is iterative or pervasive propagination in the Verbicaro dialect of Italian (Silvestri 2022: 7).

3.3.4 Irregular imperfective converb

All the preceding data focused on the perfective converb suffix. This suffix shows an inconstant or variable form, with or without a final liquid: [-el/ɹ] or [-e]. Whether a liquid surfaces or not is based on the presence and location of the auxiliary. We find exactly the same behavior in another suffix: the irregular imperfective [-i(s)].

For regular verbs and most irregular verbs, the imperfective converb is formed by adding the suffix -um onto the verb root or stem. In contrast, there are two irregular verbs 'to give' and 'to come' which form their imperfective converb by adding the suffix -is to the infinitive (Table 3.9). Paradigms for these irregular verbs are given in §6.7.2.[11]

Table 3.9: Formation of regular and irregular imperfective converbs

	Regular		Irregular		
	'to sing'		'to give'	'to come'	
INF	jeɹkʰ-e-l	√-TH-INF	t-ɒ-l	g-ɒ-l	√-TH-INF
	երգել		տալ	գալ	
IMPF.CVB	jeɹkʰ-um	√-IMPF.CVB	t-ɒ-l-is	g-ɒ-l-is	√-TH-INF-IMPF.CVB
	երգում		տալիս	գալիս	

In §3.3.1, we saw that the regular suffix -um has a constant form and never alternates. In contrast, the irregular suffix surfaces as -is before the auxiliary, and as -i when the auxiliary has shifted leftwards (26).

(26) a. jes giɹkʰ-ə **t-ɒ-l-is**   =e-m
         I   book-DEF give-TH-INF-IMPF.CVB =AUX-1SG
         'I am giving the book.'   (NK)
         ես գիրքը տալիս եմ:

      b. jes giɹkʰ-ə   t͡ʃʰ -e-m   t-ɒ-l-i
         I   book-DEF NEG=AUX-1SG give-TH-INF-IMPF.CVB
         'I am not giving the book.'   (NK)
         ես գիրքը չեմ տալի:

---

[11]Standard Eastern Armenian utilizes the same irregular imperfective forms for the verbs 'to come' [g-a-l], 'to give' [t-a-l], and 'to cry' [l-a-l]. But in Iranian Armenian, the verb [l-a-l] 'to cry' is replaced by regular [lɒts͡ʰ-e-l] 'to cry' which forms its imperfective converb with -um: [lɒts͡ʰ-um]. See §6.7.4 for discussion of this verb.

c. jes **giɹkʰ** =e-m   t-ɒ-l-i
   I   book =AUX-1SG give-TH-INF-IMPF.CVB
   'I am giving books.'   (NK)
   Ես գիրք եմ տալի:

d. **jes** =e-m   giɹkʰ-ə   t-ɒ-l-i
   I   AUX-1SG book-DEF give-TH-INF-IMPF.CVB
   '<u>I</u> am giving the book.'   (NK)
   Ես եմ գիրքը տալի:

The imperfective [-is]~[-i] alternation happens in the same contexts as the perfective [-el/ɹ]~[-e] alternation. We report additional data from AS's work (27). The same generalization stands: if the auxiliary has shifted leftwards, then the suffix [-is] alternates with [-i].

(27) a. **uʃ** =e-n   g-ɒ-l-i
        late =AUX-3PL come-TH-INF-IMPF.CVB
        'They are coming late.'   (AS)
        Ուշ են գալի:

   b. **mez** =e-n   t-ɒ-l-i
      us.DAT =AUX-3PL give-TH-INF-IMPF.CVB
      'They are giving it to us.'   (AS)
      Մեզ են տալի:

   c. jes d͡zez-i   **χoskʰ** =e-m   t-ɒ-l-i   voɹ
      I   you.PL-DAT promise =AUX-3PL give-TH-INF-IMPF.CVB that
      ɒχt͡ʃʰik-əs   el   jeɹpʰekʰ sent͡sʰ bɒn-er   t͡ʃʰ-i-∅
      daughter-POSS.1SG ever never   these thing-PL NEG-AUX-3SG
      ɒn-e-l-u
      doTH-INF-FUT.CVB
      'I promise you that my daughter will never do these things.' (AS)
      Ես ձեզի խոսք եմ տալի որ աղջիկս էլ երբեք սենց բաներ չի անելու:

We likewise see the same long-distance conditions in reduced coordination (28). The suffix surfaces as [-is] when the auxiliary is to the right within the phrase, even if not adjacent to the suffix. The suffix surfaces as [-i] when the auxiliary shifts leftwards.

(28) a. t-ɒ-l-is   =e-m   kɒm t͡sɒχ-um   =e-m
        give-TH-INF-IMPF.CVB =AUX-1SG or sell-IMPF.CVB =AUX-1SG
        'I am giving or I am selling.'   (NK)
        Տալիս եմ կամ ծախում եմ:

b. t-ɒ-l-is   kɒm t͡sɒχ-um   =e-m
    give-TH-INF-IMPF.CVB or   sell-IMPF.CVB =AUX-1SG
    'I am giving or selling.'   (NK)
    Տալիս կամ ծախում եմ:

c. t͡ʃʰ -e-m   t-ɒ-l-i   kɒm t͡sɒχ-um
    NEG=AUX-1SG give-TH-INF-IMPF.CVB or   sell-IMPF.CVB
    'I am not giving or selling.'   (NK)
    Չեմ տալի կամ ծախում :

3.3.5 Diachronic origins and effects of adjacency

The previous section examined the synchronic behavior of the perfective converb suffix -el/e.ɭ and how this suffix loses its liquid when the auxiliary has shifted. This section describes the diachronic origins of this behavior in Standard and Colloquial Eastern Armenian.

In Standard Eastern Armenian, the perfective converb suffix is -el, and the irregular imperfective converb suffix is -is. Whereas these suffixes alternate in Iranian Armenian, they do not in Standard Eastern (29). The forms of the suffixes remain constant regardless of whether the auxiliary has shifted leftwards.

(29)   Constant forms in Standard Eastern Armenian

a. **gər-el**   =e-m ,   t-a-l-is   =e-m
    write-PERF.CVB =AUX-1SG, give-TH-INF-IMPF.CVB =AUX-1SG
    'I have written, I am giving.'
    Գրել եմ, տալիս եմ:

b. **t͡ʃʰ -e-m**   **gər-el,**   **t͡ʃʰ -e-m**   t-a-l-is
    NEG=AUX-1SG write-PERF.CVB, NEG=AUX-1SG give-TH-INF-IMPF.CVB
    'I have not written, I am not giving.'
    Չեմ գրել, չեմ տալիս:

The Iranian Armenian suffix [-el/-e.ɭ] developed from the same historical source as the Standard Eastern suffix. It is reported that across Armenian lects, the liquid of the perfective suffix can sometimes change from /l/ to a rhotic (Գրիգորյան 2018; dialectological feature #85 in Ջահուկյան 1972: 101).

However, in Colloquial Eastern Armenian (CEA) as spoken in Yerevan, it is reported that speakers can optionally drop the liquid /l/ and the fricative /s/ when the auxiliary has shifted (30) (Պառագյունյան 1981: 101, Dum-Tragut 2009: 213, 223, Դամդյան et al. 2014: 37).

(30)   Optional deletion in Colloquial Eastern Armenian

    a.   <u>gər-el</u>   =e-m ,   t-a-l-is   =e-m

        write-PERF.CVB =AUX-1SG, give-TH-INF-IMPF.CVB =AUX-1SG

        'I have written, I am giving.'

        Գրել եմ, տալիս եմ:

    b.   t͡ʃʰ -e-m   gər-e(l),   t͡ʃʰ -e-m   t-a-l-i(s)

        NEG=AUX-1SG write-PERF.CVB, NEG=AUX-1SG give-TH-INF-IMPF.CVB

        'I have not written, I am not giving.'

        Չեմ գրել, չեմ տալիս:

The deletion of the final liquid is reported to be unique to the perfective converb suffix [-el] in Colloquial Eastern Armenian. This colloquial process is likewise attested in the Colloquial Eastern Armenian spoken by immigrant communities in Los Angeles (Karapetian 2014: 72).

There is some experimental evidence that this optional deletion process in Colloquial Eastern Armenian is related to the prosodic weakening of liquids (Գրիգորյան 2018).

One speaker of CEA (VP) informed us that the clitic [=el] 'also, even' can also optionally delete its liquid in CEA (31).

(31)   Colloquial Eastern Armenian

    jes e(l) kʰez   =e-m   spas-um

    I   also you.SG.DAT =AUX-1SG wait-IMPF.CVB

    'I am also waiting for you.'   (VP)

    Ես էլ քեզ եմ սպասում:

For Colloquial Eastern Armenian, we asked young speakers from Armenia (around 20–40 years old) for their sociolinguistic intuitions about the optional deletion in the suffixes [-el] and [-is] (Table 3.10). Some speakers told us that they themselves have this optional process in their speech, some told us they do not do it at all. Some told us that this process is common, while others told us that it is judged as "vulgar" and uncommon. Some told us that they can apply the deletion in some verbs, but not others.

Table 3.10: Consultants on Colloquial Eastern Armenian and their meta-linguistic judgments

Speaker	Age	Sex	What verbs?	Social judgment?
MA	late-20s	F	'open', 'close', 'eat', 'drink'	"it's colloquial"
VP	mid-30s	M	any verb	"any social class/region"
HH	early-20s	M	N/A	"it's colloquial and vulgar"

The above reports suggest that this colloquial process is attested but stigmatized. The use of this process varies by speaker, and sometimes by verb. There is little to no work on the variationist sociolinguistics of Armenian,[12] so we do not know if any demographic factors are correlated with this deletion process.

Diachronically, there is an obvious path of historical development for the perfective suffix in Iranian Armenian. 1) In some stage of the dialect, there was no deletion at all [-el] (like modern Standard Eastern Armenian). 2) Later on, the dialect developed optional deletion [-e(l)] (like modern Colloquial Eastern Armenian). 3) Finally, the deletion became obligatory [-e] (as in modern Iranian Armenian). As we discuss below, stages 2 (for CEA) and 3 (for IA) also seem to differ in terms of adjacency requirements between the suffix and the auxiliary.

Data on this colloquial process is sparse, but we suspect that Colloquial Eastern and Iranian Armenian differ in the role of adjacency between the verb and auxiliary. Briefly, in Iranian Armenian, non-adjacent auxiliaries cause the liquid to surface, while non-adjacent auxiliaries can cause the liquid to delete. We illustrate below.

Consider the sentences in (32), in both Colloquial Eastern and Iranian Armenian. In (32a), the sentence has un-reduced coordination with two verbs and two auxiliaries. The verb's liquid surfaces in both dialects. But in reduced coordination (32b) with just one auxiliary, Verb1 keeps its liquid in Iranian Armenian but can optionally delete it in Colloquial Eastern Armenian. No deletion is found in Standard Eastern. We use -P, =AUX instead of -PERF.CVB, =AUX-1SG.

(32)   Effect of verb-auxiliary adjacency in Colloquial Eastern and Iranian Armenian

    a. Un-reduced coordination with two auxiliaries

	Verb1	Aux	Conj	Verb2	Aux		
i.	χəm-el	=e-m	kɑm	keɾ-el	=e-m	(SEA)	(MA, VP)
ii.	χəm-el	=e-m	kɑm	keɾ-el	=e-m	(CEA)	(MA, VP)

       Խմել եմ կամ կերել եմ:

iii.	χəm-eɭ	=e-m	kɒm	keɭ-eɭ	=e-m	(IA)	(NK)
	drink-P	=AUX	or	eat-P	=AUX		

       'I have drunk or have eaten.'

       Խմեր եմ կամ կերեր եմ:

---

[12]To our knowledge, the closest work is Zakaryan (Զաքարյան 1981), a study of social factors in different Armenian morphophonological choices.

b. Reduced coordination with one auxiliary

	Verb1	Conj	Verb2	Aux		
i.	χəm-el	kɑm	keɾ-el	=e-m	(SEA)	(MA, VP)
ii.	χəm-e(l)	kɑm	keɾ-el	=e-m	(CEA)	(MA, VP)

Խմել կամ կերել եմ:

iii.	χəm-eɾ	kɒm	keɾ-eɾ	=e-m	(IA)	(NK)
	drink-P	or	eat-P	=AUX		

'I have drunk or eaten.'

Խմեր կամ կերեր եմ:

When reduced coordination is negated, Standard Eastern keeps the liquid in Verb1, while Iranian Armenian deletes the liquids in both Verb1 and Verb2 (33). For Colloquial Eastern Armenian, either both liquids surface or both delete. Other permutations are not possible for our informants (liquid + no liquid, no liquid + liquid).

(33) Reduced coordination with negation and consonant-initial conjunction

	Neg-Aux	Verb1	Conj	Verb2		
i.	t͡ʃʰ -e-m	χəm-el	kɑm	keɾ-el	(SEA)	(MA, VP)
ii.	t͡ʃʰ -e-m	χəm-el	kɑm	keɾ-el	(CEA)	(MA, VP)
	t͡ʃʰ -e-m	χəm-e	kɑm	keɾ-e		(MA, VP)
	*t͡ʃʰ -e-m	χəm-e	kɑm	keɾ-el		(*MA, *VP)
	*t͡ʃʰ -e-m	χəm-el	kɑm	keɾ-e		(*MA, *VP)

Չեմ խմել կամ կերել:

iii.	t͡ʃʰ -e-m	χəm-e	kɒm	keɾ-e	(IA)	(NK)
	NEG=AUX	drink-P	or	eat-P		

'I have not drunk or eaten.'

Չեմ խմէ կամ կերէ:

The generalization so far is the following. In both Iranian Armenian and Colloquial Eastern Armenian, the auxiliary licenses the floating liquid of the perfective converb. In Iranian Armenian, the suffix and auxiliary do not need to be adjacent, but they do need to be adjacent in Colloquial Eastern Armenian.

The above generalization is however too simplified for Colloquial Eastern Armenian, because we have found some variation across speakers. In reduced coordination with a vowel-initial conjunction, one Standard Eastern speaker told us that they can delete the liquid on Verb1 (VP), while another said that they could not (MA). This data suggests that some speakers can allow other adjacent vowel-initial words to license the perfective liquid (34).

(34) Effect of other vowel-initial words in Colloquial Eastern Armenian and in
      Iranian Armenian

a. Un-reduced coordination with two auxiliaries

	Verb1	Aux	Conj	Verb2	Aux		
i.	χəm-el	=e-m	u	keɾ-el	=e-m	(SEA)	
ii.	χəm-el	=e-m	u	keɾ-el	=e-m	(CEA)	

Խմել եմ ու կերել եմ:

	Verb1	Aux	Conj	Verb2	Aux		
iii.	χəm-eɹ	=e-m	u	keɹ-eɹ	=e-m	(IA)	(NK)
	drink-P	=AUX	and	eat-P	=AUX		

'I have drunk and have eaten.'

Խմեր եմ ու կերեր եմ:

b. Reduced coordination with one auxiliary

	Verb1	Conj	Verb2	Aux		
i.	χəm-el	u	keɾ-el	=e-m	(SEA)	(MA, VP)
ii.	χəm-el	u	keɾ-el	=e-m	(CEA)	(VP, MA)
	χəm-e	u	keɾ-el	=e-m	(CEA)	(VP, *MA)

Խմել կամ կերել եմ:

	Verb1	Conj	Verb2	Aux		
iii.	χəm-eɹ	u	keɹ-eɹ	=e-m	(IA)	(NK)
	drink-P	and	eat-P	=AUX		

'I have drunk and eaten.'

Խմեր ու կերեր եմ:

The variation can cause ineffability when reduced coordination involves negation and a vowel-initial conjunction (35). In the sentences below, the auxiliary
has to shift because of negation, and Verb1 precedes a vowel. Our consultants
VP and MA are fine with deleting neither liquid. VP is fine with deleting both
liquids, but MA is not. Neither speaker is fine with deleting only one liquid. For
Iranian Armenian, our main consultant required deletion in both verbs. However,
another speaker (GE) reports that deletion of the first liquid is optional.

(35) Reduced coordination with negation and vowel-initial conjunction

	Neg-Aux	Verb1	Conj	Verb2		
i.	t͡ʃʰ -e-m	χəm-el	u	keɾ-el	(SEA)	(VP, MA)
ii.	t͡ʃʰ -e-m	χəm-el	u	keɾ-el	(CEA)	(VP, MA)
	t͡ʃʰ -e-m	χəm-e	u	keɾ-e		(VP, *MA)
	*t͡ʃʰ -e-m	χəm-e	u	keɾ-el		(*VP, *MA)
	*t͡ʃʰ -e-m	χəm-el	u	keɾ-e		(*VP, *MA)

Չեմ խմել ու կերել:

iii. $\widehat{\text{tʃ}}^h$ **-e-m**   χəm-e   u   keɹ-e   (IA)   (NK)
      $\widehat{\text{tʃ}}^h$ **-e-m**   χəm-e(l)   u   keɹ-e   (IA)   (GE)
      NEG=AUX   drink-P   and   eat-P
      'I have not drunk and eaten.'
      Չեմ խմէ ու կերէ:

The data from Colloquial Eastern Armenian and Iranian Armenian is quite complicated and our analysis is incomplete. More variation-oriented data is required from larger pools of people from different areas and generations. But crucially, the overarching generalization is that whereas IA allows non-local conditioning between the suffix and the auxiliary, CEA seems to require local conditioning. Some IA speakers also allow both generalizations simultaneously (non-local or local conditioning).

4 Nominal morphology

This chapter covers the basics of nominal inflection in Iranian Armenian. In general, we have not found any significant differences between Standard Eastern and Iranian Armenian in this domain. We thus keep this chapter brief, with an overview of the basic paradigms. For larger paradigms and for work on the noun phrase of Armenian, we refer readers to other sources for Standard Eastern Armenian (Kozintseva 1995, Yeghiazaryan 2010, Tamrazian 1994: §4, Megerdoomian 2009: §5, Dum-Tragut 2009: §2.1, Hodgson 2019b: §2.1.1) and Standard Western Armenian (Sigler 1997, Khanjian 2013: §2.3, Bale & Khanjian 2014).

4.1 Basic template for nominal inflection

Nominal inflection is agglutinative for number, case, possession, and definite marking. The basic template for nominal inflection is given in Table 4.1. The rightmost column is dedicated to possessive and definiteness marking, which we refer to collectively as a Determiner slot. We list productive suffixes within each cell, including suffixal allomorphs.

Table 4.1: Template for nominal inflection and the set of productive suffixes

N	Number		Case (ĸ)			Determiner (DET)		
SG	-Ø		NOM/ACC	-Ø		unmarked	-Ø	
PL	-eɹ	-եր	DAT/GEN	-i	-ի	POSS.1SG	-(ə)s	-ս
	-neɹ	-ներ	ABL	-itsʰ	-ից	POSS.2SG	-(ə)t	-դ
			INS	-ov	-ոմ	DEF	-ə	-ը
			LOC	-um	-ում		-n	-ն
							-ən	-ն

Some of the above morphemes have multiple realizations due to phonological-ly-conditioned allomorphy. Such allomorphy is discussed in §3.2.

To illustrate nominal inflection, we show the paradigms of a singular case-marked noun, a plural case-marked noun, and a plural case-marked possessed noun (Table 4.2). Note that possessive marking follows case marking.

Table 4.2: Paradigm for singular noun, plural noun, and plural possessed noun

	N-K	N-PL-K	N-PL-K-POSS.1SG
NOM/ACC	senjɒk սենեակ	senjɒk-neɾ սենեակներ	senjɒk-neɾ-əs սենեակներս
DAT/GEN	senjɒk-i սենեակի	senjɒk-neɾ-i սենեակների	senjɒk-neɾ-i-s սենեակներիս
ABL	senjɒk-itsʰ սենեակից	senjɒk-neɾ-itsʰ սենեակներից	senjɒk-neɾ-itsʰ-əs սենեակներիցս
INS	senjɒk-ov սենեակով	senjɒk-neɾ-ov սենեակներով	senjɒk-neɾ-ov-əs սենեակներովս
LOC	senjɒk-um սենեակում	senjɒk-neɾ-um սենեակներում	senjɒk-neɾ-um-əs սենեակներումս
	'room'	'rooms'	'my rooms'

In Standard Eastern Armenian, the word for 'case' is /holov/ հոլով. The names of the different cases are in Table 4.3.

Table 4.3: Names of cases in Standard Eastern Armenian

Nominative	uʁʁakan	ուղղական
Accusative	hajtsʰakan	հայցական
Genitive	serakan	սեռական
Dative	tərakan	տրական
Ablative	batsʰarakan	բացառական
Instrumental	gortsijakan	գործիական
Locative	nergojakan	ներգոյական

In terms of syncretism and exponence, nominative and accusative are zero-marked, singular number is unmarked, and dative and genitive are syncretic for common nouns. However, this syncretism does not apply to personal pronouns, which we discuss in §5.1.

Standard Eastern Armenian can use the instrumental case marker *-ov* to denote either the meaning of 'to use X as an instrument' or 'to go along with X'.
The latter meaning is considered a comitative meaning (Dum-Tragut 2009: 93).
Standard Western Armenian can likewise use the instrumental as a comitative.
However in Iranian Armenian, the comitative meaning of the instrumental suffix
is considered atypical and odd. Speakers prefer to express the comitative meaning through an alternative postpositional construction.[1]

For example, sentence (1a) places an instrumental suffix on the noun. The intended interpretation is comitative: to go along with the sister. Such a meaning is
possible for some speakers in Standard Eastern Armenian, but not in Iranian Armenian. The typical Iranian Armenian reading would be purely instrumental: to
go to the cinema by using the sister. To express the comitative meaning, speakers
strongly prefer using the postposition *het* (1b).[2]

(1) a. kʰəɹ-otʃʰ-ov-əs   gən-ɒ-tsʰ-i-ŋkʰ   sinemɒ
         sister-DAT-INS-POSS.1SG go-TH-AOR-PST-1PL cinema

         Intended meaning: 'We went to the cinema along with my sister.'
         Actual meaning: 'We went to the cinema by using my sister.'
         Քրոջովս գնացինք սինեմա: (KM)

     b. kʰəɹ-otʃʰ-əs   het gən-ɒ-tsʰ-i-ŋkʰ   sinemɒ
         sister-GEN-POSS.1SG with go-TH-AOR-PST-1PL cinema

         'We went to the cinema along with my sister.'
         Քրոջս հետ գնացինք սինեմա: (KM)

The suffixes in Table 4.1 are the regular or default suffixes for the corresponding morphosyntactic features. Iranian Armenian has limited morphologically-
conditioned allomorphy with irregular suffixes. We have not found any significant differences for irregular inflection in Iranian Armenian vs. Standard Eastern
Armenian. At most, it seems that Iranian Armenian is slowly leveling out irregular inflection.

---

[1]However, a reviewer states that a possibly more accurate description of SEA is that the instrumental can be used for activities that are carried out as a group (for example as a family), and
not alongside a person. If we take this description of SEA as accurate, then both SEA and IA
lack comitative instrumentals, while SWA has them. However, KM did report that she encountered such comitative readings in SEA before, so it is possible that there is variation among
SEA speakers. Our SEA consultant AT said that such a comitative reading is "not okay" but
that it is possible that someone might use it in a disparaging way, e.g., a misogynist might use
the comitative instrumental of the word 'sister'.

[2]For the word 'sister', the nominative form is [kʰuɹ] քույր. In the dative/genitive, the word uses
an irregular allomorph for both the root and the suffix: [kʰəɹ-otʃʰ]. The dative/genitive stem is
then further inflected to form the instrumental. Note that the prescriptive form of the irregular
dative/genitive suffix is [-odʒ], but in Iranian Armenian it is more often pronounced as [-otʃʰ].

To illustrate, the regular dative/genitive suffix is *-i.* In both Standard Eastern and Iranian Armenian, the dative/genitive suffix has a wide set of irregular allomorphs or realizations. For example, the suffix -ությին /-ut^{h}jun/ is a productive nominalizer (2). This suffix forms an irregular dative/genitive by using a different allomorph for the entire nominalizer suffix: -ություն /-ut^{h}jɒn/. The use of this allomorph is the prescriptive rule in Standard Eastern and Iranian Armenian, but KM reports that Iranian Armenian speakers much more frequently apply a regularized form /-ut^{h}jun-i/.

(2)   *Leveling out of irregular dative/genitive of /-ut^{h}jun/*
   a. այոχ   'happy'   ուրախ
      այոχ-ut^{h}jun   happy-NMLZ   'happiness'   ուրախություն
   b. այոχ-utjɒn   happy-NMLZ.DAT/GEN   'to/of happiness' ուրախության
   c. այոχ-ut^{h}jun-i happy-NMLZ-DAT/GEN   'to/of happiness' ուրախությինի

For complete paradigms of these irregular declensions in Standard Eastern Armenian, see Dum-Tragut (2009: §2.1.2). These paradigms apply to the formal prescriptive speech of Iranian Armenians. But in casual speech, KM and AS report the loss of various irregular case suffixes.

4.2 Constraints on definite marking and case marking

The determiner slot can be realized by either nothing, the 1SG possessive, 2SG possessive, or the definite suffix. The 1SG possessive and 2SG possessive can follow any type of case marker. This was illustrated in section §4.1 in Table 4.2 for the 1SG possessive. However, the definite suffix cannot follow the genitive, ablative, or instrumental (Dum-Tragut 2009: 104, Yeghiazaryan 2010: 7, Hodgson 2019b: 48, 2022).[3]

To illustrate, Table 4.4 shows definite marking on singular and plural nouns. For the genitive, ablative, and instrumental, the noun is semantically ambiguous in terms of being definite or not. The gloss K is a placeholder for case marking.[4]

---

[3]We treat the definite and possessive morphemes as suffixes and not clitics. Morphosyntactically, there is no obvious evidence for treating them as separate words (clitics) instead of suffixes. Phonologically, these morphemes are unstressed (like clitics). But because these morphemes lack a non-schwa vowel, a suffix account already correctly predicts that they are unstressable (§2.2.2.1).

[4]The morpheme sequence of instrumental-definite is judged as ungrammatical by NK. In Standard Eastern Armenian it is also judged as odd. However, BV found around 29 instances of this morpheme sequence as [senjɑk-um-ə] սենյակումը 'in the room' on the EANC. Victoria Khurshudyan reported that such a sequene can be uttered, "but it will be clearly perceived as a non-standard form."

Table 4.4: Paradigm of definite singular noun and definite plural noun

	N-K-DEF		N-PL-K-DEF	
NOM/ACC	senjɒk-ə	սենեակը	senjɒk-neɹ-ə	սենեակները
DAT	senjɒk-i-n	սենեակին	senjɒk-neɹ-i-n	սենեակներին
GEN	senjɒk-i	սենեակի	senjɒk-neɹ-i	սենեակների
	*senjɒk-i-n		*senjɒk-neɹ-i-n	
ABL	senjɒk-itsʰ	սենեակից	senjɒk-neɹ-itsʰ	սենեակներից
	*senjɒk-itsʰ-ə		*senjɒk-neɹ-itsʰ-ə	
INS	senjɒk-ov	սենեակով	senjɒk-neɹ-ov	սենեակներով
	*senjɒk-ov-ə		*senjɒk-neɹ-ov-ə	
LOC	senjɒk-um	սենեակում	senjɒk-neɹ-um	սենեակներում
	*senjɒk-um-ə		*senjɒk-neɹ-um-ə	
	'the room'		'the rooms'	

It is interesting that the dative and genitive are syncretic with the suffix -*i*. However, the definite suffix can be used after the dative form, but not the genitive form. This is illustrated in the following sentences.

In sentence (3a), the suffix -*i* marks dative case. It can take the definite suffix -*n*. But in (3b), the suffix -*i* marks genitive case. It cannot be followed by the definite suffix.

(3) a. senjɒk-i-n   giɹkʰ təv-ɒ-m
        room-DAT-DEF book give-PST-1SG
        'I gave books to the room.'   (NK)
        Սենեակին գիրք տուամ:

    b. senjɒk-i(*-n)   gujn-ə
        room-GEN-*DEF color-DEF
        'the color of the room'   (*NK)
        սենեակի գոյնը

This co-occurrence restriction applies equally to both non-human nouns and to human nouns, such as the given name Aram (4).

(4) a. ɒɹɒm-i-n   giɹkʰ təv-ɒ-m
        Aram-DAT-DEF book give-PST-1SG
        'I gave books to Aram.'   (NK)
        Արամին գիրք տուամ:

71

    b. ɒɾɒm-i(*-n)   giɾkʰ-ə
         Aram-GEN-*DEF book-DEF
         'the book of Aram'   (NK)
         Արամի գիրքը

The co-occurrence restriction between the genitive and the definite suffix is limited to just the definite suffix (5). Other determiner suffixes like the 1SG possessive can freely co-occur with either the dative *-i* or the genitive *-i*.

(5)   a. senjɒk-i-s   giɾkʰ təv-ɒ-m
           room-DAT-POSS.1SG book give-PST-1SG
           'I gave books to my room.'   (NK)
           Սենեակիս գիրք տուամ:

       b. senjɒk-i-s   gujn-ə
           room-GEN-POSS.1SG color-DEF
           'the color of my room'   (NK)
           սենեակիս գոյնը

The definite suffix has an additional function of helping to mark third person possessives. This is discussed in the following section.

4.3 Constraints on possessive marking

The determiner slot can be occupied by either the possessive suffixes or the definite suffix. There are likewise co-dependencies between this slot and the possessive pronouns.

Iranian Armenian has a set of 8 genitive/possessive pronouns which mark possession. The 3SG and 3PL each have two members. One member is intensive or emphatic, while the other member is non-intensive or non-emphatic. This is discussed in §5.1.

If a noun is possessed by the first person singular, then the noun can surface in one of three forms (6a). It can surface without a possessive pronoun and with the 1SG possessive suffix. Or, it can surface with the possessive pronoun and the 1SG possessive suffix. Or, it can surface with the possessive pronoun but with the definite suffix. Similar options are found for 2SG possessives (6b).

(6) a. *Variation in 1SG possessive marking*

      a.   senjɒk-**əs**   սենեակս

                   room-POSS.1SG

      b. **im**   senjɒk-**əs**   իմ սենեակս

            my   room-POSS.1SG

      c. **im**   senjɒk-**ə**   իմ սենեակը

            my   room-DEF

           'my room'

   b. *Variation in 2SG possessive marking*

      a.   senjɒk-**ət**   սենեակդ

                   room-POSS.2SG

      b. **kʰo** senjɒk-**ət**   քո սենեակս

            my   room-POSS.2SG

      c. **kʰo** senjɒk-**ə**   քո սենեակը

            my   room-DEF

           'your room'

Sociolinguistically, the simultaneous use of the possessive pronoun and the possessive suffix is deemed prescriptively incorrect for Standard Eastern Armenian (Dum-Tragut 2009: 113). The use of both the pronoun and the possessive suffix is instead restricted to colloquial speech and often stigmatized. But it is the preferred strategy for casual speech in Iranian Armenian.

For the other combinations of person and number, there is no dedicated possessive suffix (Table 4.5). Instead, the possessed noun takes the genitive/possessive pronoun and the definite suffix.

Table 4.5: Possessive marking for person-number combinations beyond 1SG-2SG

3SG	iɹɒ	senjɒk-ə	'his room'	իրա սենեակը
	nəɹɒ	senjɒk-ə	'his room'	նրա սենեակը
1PL	meɹ	senjɒk-ə	'our room'	մեր սենեակը
2PL	d͡zeɹ	senjɒk-ə	'your.PL room'	ձեր սենեակը
3PL	iɹɒnt͡sʰ	senjɒk-ə	'their room'	իրանց սենեակը
	nəɹɒnt͡sʰ	senjɒk-ə	'their room'	նրանց սենեակը
	PRO.GEN	room-DEF		

4.4 Synthetic constructions for plural possessors

When the noun has a plural possessor, the most typical construction is to use a genitive pronoun and the definite suffix (7a). Both Standard Eastern and Iranian Armenian allow a synthetic alternative that is very restricted in usage (Dum-Tragut 2009: 113–114). In Standard Eastern Armenian, one can use the plural suffix *-ner* to encode a plural possessor (7b).

(7) Standard Eastern Armenian (adapted from Khurshudian 2020: 339,340)

    a. mer   at͡ʃʰkʰ-er-ə, mer   het-ə
       us.GEN eye-PL-DEF, us.GEN with-DEF
       'our eyes, with us'
       մեր աչքերը, մեր հետը

    b. at͡ʃʰkʰ-ner-əs,   het-ner-əs
       eye-PL-POSS.1SG, with-PL-POSS.1SG
       'our eyes, with us'
       աչքներս, հետներս

For SEA, note how the plural *-ner* suffix is supposed to attach only to polysyllabic stems, while the allomorph *-er* attaches to monosyllables. But the suffix *-ner* is exceptionally used to mark plural possession on monosyllables in the above examples (§3.2.1).

In Standard Western Armenian, such constructions are productive, using different morphological templates (Arregi et al. 2013, Bezrukov 2016). In contrast in Standard Eastern Armenian, the use of this synthetic construction for plural possessors is quite unproductive, and limited to a small set of concepts, such as talking about one's body parts 'our eyes' or using an adposition 'with us'. The SEA-style of plural possessives is also attested in Iranian Armenian (8).[5]

(8) Iranian Armenian

    a. meɹ   ʋt͡ʃʰkʰ-eɹ-ə, meɹ   het-ə
       us.GEN eye-PL-DEF, us.GEN with-DEF
       'our eyes, with us'   (NK)
       մեր աչքերը, մեր հետը

---

[5]In SEA, the prescriptive norm is that the postposition /het/ 'with' assigns dative case to its argument. In contrast, CEA uses genitive marking (Dum-Tragut 2009: 297–299). IA also uses genitive marking.

b. ɒtʃʰkʰ-neɾ-əs, het-neɾ-əs
eye-PL-POSS.1SG, with-PL-POSS.1SG
'our eyes, with us' (NK)
աչքներս, հետներս

This construction seems particularly common for body parts which come in pairs, like feet or eyes (9).[6]

(9) Iranian Armenian

a. meɾ votkʰ-eɾ-ə, meɾ dzer-eɾ-ə
us.GEN foot-PL-DEF, us.GEN hand-PL-DEF
'our feet, our hands' (NK)
մեր ոտքերը, մեր ձեռերը

b. votkʰ-neɾ-əs, dzer-neɾ-əs
foot-PL-POSS.1SG, hand-PL-POSS.1SG
'our feet, our hands' (NK)
ոտքներս, ձեռներս

As in Standard Eastern Armenian, this construction is restricted and unproductive in Iranian Armenian (10). NK found it odd to add it to nouns that were for animals.

(10) Iranian Armenian

a. meɾ muk-ə, meɾ kov-ə, meɾ kɒtu-n
us.GEN mouse-DEF, us.GEN cow-DEF, us.GEN cat-DEF
'our mouse, our cow, our cat' (NK)
մեր մուկը, մեր կովը, մեր կատուն

b. *muk-neɾ-əs, kov-neɾ-əs, kɒtu-neɾ-əs
mouse-PL-POSS.1SG, cow-PL-POSS.1SG, cat-PL-POSS.1SG
Intended: 'our mouse, our cow, our cat' (*NK)

4.5 Differential object marking

For nouns in the subject position, nominative case is covert or zero. But in the object position, we see a distinction between nouns with human referents and

---

[6]AS reports that for the word 'foot', the default form is /votkʰ/, as in [votkʰ-eɾ-əs]. However, the form /vot/ can be used as well: [vot-eɾ-əs]. However, he suspects that such a form is more permissible if the preceding genitive pronoun is singular and not plural. That is, this smaller form is used when there is no plural possessor: /im vot-eɾ-əs/ 'my feet'.

nouns with non-human referents. Non-human nouns are not overtly marked for morphological case, i.e., they take covert accusative case. In contrast, human nouns in object position take dative -*i* as a form of differential object marking. The same pattern occurs in Standard Eastern Armenian (Dum-Tragut 2009: 61, Scala 2011) and the Iranian dialect of Maragha (Աճառյան 1926: 160).

To illustrate, consider the sentences in (11). If the object is non-human (11a), then the noun is unmarked for case. If the object is human, such as the given name Aram (11b), then the object must take dative case. Our consultants felt that if the dative marker was absent (11c), then the sentence reads as if Aram was a non-human entity.

(11) a. senjɒk-ə mɒkʰɹ-ɒ-m
    room-DEF clean-PST-1SG
    'I cleaned the room.'   (NK)
    Սենեակը մաքրամ:

  b. ɒɹɒm-i-n mɒkʰɹ-ɒ-m
    Aram-DAT-DEF clean-PST-1SG
    'I cleaned Aram.'   (NK)
    Արամին մաքրամ:

  c. *ɒɹɒm-ə mɒkʰɹ-ɒ-m
    Aram-DEF clean-PST-1SG
    Intended: 'I cleaned Aram'.
    Actual: 'I cleaned some entity called an "Aram".'

The above discussion focused on humans vs. inanimates. Differential object marking on animals is more complicated (Dum-Tragut 2009: §2.1.1.1).

4.6 Indefinites and classifiers

Like Standard Eastern Armenian, Iranian Armenian has grammaticalized the numeral 'one' into an indefinite proclitic. Iranian Armenian likewise utilizes a classifier [hɒt] for counting. The combination of the indefinite and classifier has some semantic and phonological idiosyncrasies (Hodgson 2020a, Sargsyan 2022).

The numeral 'one' in Iranian Armenian is [mek]. The *k* segment is retained in the citation form (12a). But when the numeral is used as a modifier for a noun, the *k* can be dropped: *me rope* 'one minute' (12b).[7] The *me* morph is also grammaticalized as an indefinite proclitic (12c). It is spelled as մի <mi> because the Standard Eastern equivalent is [mi].

---

[7]For the word 'minute', the rhotic is a flap [ɾope] in Standard Eastern Armenian, but it is a trill in NK and KM's speech [rope] (§2.1.2).

(12) a. mek
          one
          'one'   (KM)
          մէկ

      b. mek/me rope
          one   minute
          'one minute'   (NK, KM)
          մէկ րոպէ

      c. me   bɒn
          INDF thing
          'A thing; something'   (NK)
          մի բան

The indefinite morph /me/ is also the indefinite article in some of the traditional dialects of Iran (Khoy/Urmia: Ասատրյան 1962: 84; Maragha: Աճառյան 1926:
1.78; and Salmast).[8] The *mek/me* alternation could be connected to how in colloquial Persian, the word [yek] is used to mean the cardinal 'one' while [ye] is used
as an indefinite article (Mahootian 2002: 328; Geoffrey Haig, p.c.).

The indefinite can be used alongside the classifier *hɒt* (13) (Sigler 2003, Bale
& Khanjian 2008, Sağ 2019). The classifier *hɒt* can also be used as a noun meaning 'piece' (13a). As in Standard Eastern and Western Armenian, the classifier is
used in number + noun constructions. Here, the *me* is on the surface ambiguous
between an indefinite proclitic and a numeral (13b). But when it precedes the
classifier *hɒt*, the morpheme *me* is unambiguously a numeral (13c).

(13) a. me   hɒt
          INDF/one piece
          'a piece; one'   (KM)
          մի հատ

      b. me   mɒɹt^h
          INDF/one man
          'a/one man'   (KM)
          մի մարդ

      c. me hɒt mɒɹt^h
          one CLF man
          'one man'   (KM)
          մի հատ մարդ

---

[8]For Salmast, BV found an example of an indefinite /me/ in a newspaper article called Խայու
Լաճ from the periodical Պսակ (date October 11, 1880, volume 30): https://tert.nla.am/archive/
NLA%20TERT/Psak/1880/1880(30).pdf

The construction *me hɒt* can undergo vowel lowering and fronting as *mæ hæt* (14). This phrase can be further reduced into a single morph *mæt*. Note the use of [æ], which is otherwise a marginal phoneme in Iranian Armenian.

(14) a. {mæt / mæ hæt} mɒɹtʰ
         INDF.CLF / INDF CLF man
         'a man'   (NK)
         մի հատ մարդ.

      b. {mæt / mæ hæt} χɒʁɒlikʰ
         INDF.CLF / INDF CLF toy
         'a toy'   (AS)
         մի հատ խաղալիք

      c. VDʁ-ə   k-eɹtʰ-ɒ-m   χɒnutʰ-itsʰ mæt   χɒʁɒlikʰ
         tomorrow-DEF FUT-go-TH-1SG store-ABL INDF.CLF toy
         veɹ-tsʰn-e-m   iɹɒ   zɒvɒk-neɹ-i hɒmɒɹ
         buy-CAUS-TH-1SG he.GEN child-PL-DAT for
         'Tomorrow I'm going to go pick up a toy for his children from the
         store'   (AS)
         Վաղը կեռթամ խանութից մի հատ խաղալիք վերցնեմ իրա զավակների
         համար:

The combination of indefinite + classifier is also used as an adverb to denote a sense of transience, roughly translatable to 'for a moment' or 'a little bit' (15).

(15) a. mæt   ɒɹi   ste
         INDF.CLF come.IMP.2SG here
         'Come here for a moment.'   (AS)
         Մի հատ արի ստէ:

      b. mæt   mətɒtsʰ-i   mjus-i   zgɒtsʰmuŋkʰ-neɹ-i mɒs-i-n
         INDF.CLF think-IMP.2SG other-GEN feeling-PL-GEN   about-GEN-DEF
         'Think a little bit about the other person's feelings.'   (AS)
         Մի հատ մտածէ մէւսի զգացմունքների մասին:

      c. mæt   hɒŋgəst-ɒ-tsʰɹ-u   senjɒk-um-ət
         INDF.CLF relax-LV-CAUS-IMP.2SG room-LOC-POSS.2SG
         'Rest for a while in your room.'   (AS)
         Մի հատ հանգստացրու սենեակումդ:

5 Function words

We go over basic function words in this chapter, including personal pronouns (§5.1), demonstratives (§5.2), interrogative pronouns or wh-words (§5.3), numerals (§5.4), and other function words (§5.5). We have not found many significant differences between Iranian Armenian and Standard Eastern Armenian when it comes to pronouns.

5.1 Personal pronouns

Iranian Armenian uses the personal pronouns in Table 5.1. Whereas common nouns are syncretic for dative and genitive, pronouns distinguish the two cases. The Iranian Armenian pronouns do not significantly differ from Standard Eastern (Dum-Tragut 2009: 123) except that the intensive 3SG dative is *iren* in Standard Eastern but *iɾɒn* in Iranian Armenian. The form [iɾan] is attested in Colloquial Eastern Armenian (Dum-Tragut 2009: 128).

For the 3SG and 3PL, there are two series of pronouns. One series is intensive (Dum-Tragut 2009: 126) or emphatic (Donabédian 2018) and starts with the segment *i*, while the other series is a generic third person pronoun and starts with *n*. For the syntactic distribution of Armenian pronouns, see Sigler (2001), Donabédian-Demopoulos (2007). For both NK and KM, the intensive pronoun is considered more "conversational", while the non-intensive pronoun feels more formal. For the 3PL non-intensive, the initial /nəɹɒ-/ sequence was often lenited in NK's speech, e.g., ACC/DAT/GEN plural [nəɹɒnts͡ʰ] or lenited [nɒnts͡ʰ] 'they'.[1]

For the accusative/dative series, outside of the third person, the pronoun has two forms: one bare and one suffixed with -*i*. For example, accusative/dative 1SG is *ind͡z* or *ind͡z-i*. The bare form is the more common form, but there is significant speaker variation on the preferred form. For example, NK almost always used the bare form in our elicitations, while AS reports that his consultants often used the suffixed form.

---

[1]Compare New Julfa ACC/DAT/GEN plural [nɰɒnts͡ʰ] նոնց, which in its Indian subdialect is [nan-ts͡ʰan] նանցան 'those over there.ACC/DAT/GEN', ablative [nantsʰane] նանցանէ 'from those' (Աճառյան 1940: §266).

Table 5.1: Paradigm of personal pronouns in Iranian Armenian

	Nominative PRO	Acc/Dative PRO-(DAT)	Genitive PRO	Ablative PRO-(NX)-ABL	Instrumental PRO-(NX)-INS	Locative PRO-(NX)-LOC
1SG	jes	ind͡z, ind͡z-i	im	ind͡z-ɒn-it͡sʰ	ind͡z-ɒn-ov	ind͡z-ɒn-um
	ինձ	ինձ, ինձի	իմ	ինձանից	ինձանով	ինձանում
2SG	du	kʰez, kʰez-i	kʰo	kʰez-ɒn-it͡sʰ	kʰez-ɒn-ov	kʰez-ɒn-um
	դու	քեզ, քեզի	քո	քեզանից	քեզանով	քեզանում
3SG	iŋkʰ-ə	iɾɒn	iɾɒ	iɾɒn-it͡sʰ	iɾɒn-ov	iɾɒn-um
	ինքը	իրան	իրա	իրանից	իրանով	իրանում
	nɒ	nəɾɒn	nəɾɒ	nəɾɒn-it͡sʰ	nəɾɒn-ov	nəɾɒn-um
	նա	նրան	նրա	նրանից	նրանով	նրանում
1PL	meŋkʰ	mez, mez-i	meɾ	mez-ɒn-it͡sʰ	mez-ɒn-ov	mez-ɒn-um
	մենք	մեզ, մեզի	մեր	մեզանից	մեզանով	մեզանում
2PL	dukʰ	d͡zez, d͡zez-i	d͡zeɾ	d͡zez-ɒn-it͡sʰ	d͡zez-ɒn-ov	d͡zez-ɒn-um
	դուք	ձեզ, ձեզի	ձեր	ձեզանից	ձեզանով	ձեզանում
3PL	iɾɒŋkʰ	iɾɒnt͡sʰ	iɾɒnt͡sʰ	iɾɒnt͡sʰ-it͡sʰ	iɾɒnt͡sʰ-ov	iɾɒnt͡sʰ-um
	հիրանք	հիրանց	հիրանց	հիրանցից	հիրանցնով	հիրանցնում
	nəɾɒŋkʰ	nəɾɒnt͡sʰ	nəɾɒnt͡sʰ	nəɾɒnt͡sʰ-it͡sʰ	nəɾɒnt͡sʰ-ov	nəɾɒnt͡sʰ-um
	նրանք	նրանց	նրանց	նրանցից	նրանցնով	նրանցնում

In pronouns, the accusative is syncretic with the dative (and with the genitive in the 3PL). This syncretism is shown in the following sentences (1).

(1) a. d͡ʒɒn-ə   ind͡z   mɒkʰɾ-ɒ-v
    John-DEF me.DAT clean-PST-3SG
    'John cleaned (or washed) me.'   (NK)
    Ջոնը ինձ մաքրաւ:

   b. d͡ʒɒn-ə   ind͡z   giɾkʰ təv-ɒ-v
    John-DEF me.DAT book give-PST-3SG
    'John gave a book to me.'   (NK)
    Ջոնը ինձ գիրք տուաւ:

Morphotactically, the ablative, instrumental, and locative are built on top of the dative form. For the non-third person series, the dative form and the added case suffix are separated by the meaningless morph -ɒn-. This morph sequence can be weakened to either -ən- or -n-: [ind͡z-ɒn-it͡sʰ, ind͡z-n-it͡sʰ] 'I-NX-ABL'.

We have received conflicting judgments on the frequency of such weakening. NK always lenited the 1SG obliques to -ən-, e.g. 1SG ablative ind͡z-ən-it͡sʰ. Yet she always lenited the other non-third person series to just -n-, e.g., dative 2SG *kʰez-n-itsʰ*. In contrast, AS reports that for speakers in Iran, the deletion of /ɒ/ is not frequent.

For the instrumental and locative series, they are quite difficult to elicit in natural speech. Alternative syntactic strategies are preferred. For example, for instrumentals, the comitative meaning of the instrumental ('to go alongside X') is expressed by using a postpositional construction with the genitive pronoun (Table 5.2). Similarly, the locative meaning is expressed by using a postposition [met͡ʃʰ] մէջ 'in'.

Table 5.2: Expressing comitative-instrumental with postpositions

1SG	im	het	'with me'	իմ հետ
2SG	kʰo	het	'with you.SG'	քո հետ
3SG	iɹɒ	het	'with him'	հրա հետ
	nəɹɒ	het	'with him'	նրա հետ
1PL	meɹ	het	'with us'	մեր հետ
2PL	dzeɹ	het	'with you.PL'	ձեր հետ
3PL	iɹɒntsʰ	het	'with them'	հրանց հետ
	nəɹɒntsʰ	het	'with them'	նրանց հետ
PRO.GEN		with		

5.2 Demonstratives

Iranian Armenian uses a small set of demonstrative pronouns. These show a three-way contrast for deixis: proximal, medial, and distal. There are different forms for when the pronoun is a modifier in a noun phrase vs. when the pronoun stands on its own as a substantive.

For illustration, we focus on the proximal series in (2). This series is characterized by starting with the segmental sequence /es-/ or /s/. When the proximal pronoun is a modifier in a noun phrase, it is realized as [es]. It can modify either a singular noun or plural noun.

(2) a. es giɹkʰ-ə
         this book-DEF
         'this book'
         էս գիրքը

  b. es giɹkʰ-eɹ-ə
      this book-PL-DEF
      'these books'
      էս գիրքերը

Table 5.3 shows the set of demonstrative pronouns when the pronoun is a modifier.

Table 5.3: Demonstrative pronouns when acting as a modifier

	Proximal	Medial	Distal
	es էu	et էın	en էu
	'this'	'that (close)'	'that (yonder)'
Usage	The item is by the speaker	The item is by the listener	The item is not by the speaker or listener

In Standard Eastern Armenian, these demonstratives have cognate forms that are phonologically larger. For example, the proximal-medial-distal series in Standard Eastern Armenian is {/ɑjs/, /ɑjd/ or /ɑjt/, /ɑjn/} (այu, այդ, այù). The Iranian Armenian forms /es, et, en/ are likely diachronically reduced versions of these larger Standard Eastern Armenian forms. A reviewer informs us that these reduced forms are also attested in Colloquial Eastern Armenian in Armenia. BV reports that this is just the regular change of Classical /ɑi̯/ <ay, այ > to /e/ in Eastern dialects.

When the pronoun is substantivized and stands for an entire noun phrase, it can be realized in one of three forms (3). For the proximal pronoun, the singular forms are *es*, *esi*, and *esikə*. The plural form of the substantivized pronoun is *səɹɒŋkʰ*.

(3) a. es/esi/esikə giɹkʰ   =ᴅ
      this   book-ᴅᴇꜰ =ᴀᴜx
      'This is a book.'   (NK)
      էu/էuh/էuhկ̣ə գhրp̣ ա:

    b. səɹɒŋkʰ giɹkʰ-eɹ =e-n
      these   book-ᴘʟ =ᴀᴜx-3ᴘʟ
      'These are books.'   (NK)
      Սrաùp̣ գhրp̣եr եù:

The final schwa of the long pronoun *esikə* is likely part of the definite suffix (4). Evidence for this is that the schwa becomes a schwa-nasal sequence when cliticized. See similar patterns for the definite suffix in §3.2.2.

(4) esik-ən e-m   uz-um
     this-DEF AUX-1SG want-IMPF.CVB
     'I want this one.'   (NK)
     Էսիկն եմ ուզում:

Etymologically, it is possible that forms like /esik-ə/ 'this' derive from adding the definite suffix onto a hypothetical earlier form like *esik (cf. Աճառյան 1954: 195ff). Alternatively, BV suggests that the modern complex form /esik-ə/ may have a more complicated origin. First, the form was *esikɒ. Second, the form underwent final vowel reduction to *esikə. Third, the form underwent morphological reanalysis as /esik-ə/ with a definite suffix. But Hrach Martirosyan (p.c.) suggests the first is more probable.

When these demonstratives are substantivized, they inflect for case (5).

(5) a. səɹɒn t͡ʃɒʃ təv-ɒ-m
         this.DAT food give-PST-1SG
         'I gave food to this one.'   (NK)
         Սրան ճաշ տուամ:

     b. səɹɒ   gujn-ə
         this.GEN color-DEF
         'the color of this one'   (NK)
         սրա գոյնը

Table 5.4 shows the paradigm of substantivized demonstratives. Note that the inflected forms of the substantivized distal are identical to the non-intensive third-person personal pronouns from Table 5.1. The Iranian Armenian paradigm does not significantly differ from that of Standard Eastern Armenian (Dum-Tragut 2009: 129). For the medial series, the plurals and the case-marked forms use [d] in Standard Eastern Armenian: [dəraŋkʰ, dəra]. Some Iranian Armenian speakers like KM use [d] too, while some Iranian Armenian speakers like NK use [t].

5.3 Interrogative pronouns

Iranian Armenian seems to use the same set of interrogative pronouns (wh-words) as Standard Eastern Armenian (Dum-Tragut 2009: 247). Full declension paradigms are found in the Dum-Tragut grammar for Standard Eastern Armenian. We have not found significant differences between Standard Eastern and

Table 5.4: Paradigm for substantivized demonstratives

	Nom/Acc PRO	Dative PRO	Genitive PRO	Ablative PRO-ABL	Instrumental PRO-INS	Locative PRO-LOC
Singular						
Prox.	es, esi, esikə	saɹɒn	saɹɒ	saɹɒn-itsʰ	saɹɒn-ov	saɹɒn-um
	էս, էսի, էսիկը	սրան	սրա	սրանից	սրանով	սրանում
Med.	et, eti, etikə	daɹɒn	daɹɒ	daɹɒn-itsʰ	daɹɒn-ov	daɹɒn-um
		taɹɒn	taɹɒ	taɹɒn-itsʰ	taɹɒn-ov	taɹɒn-um
	էտ, էտի, էտիկը	դրան	դրա	դրանից	դրանով	դրանում
Dist.	en, eni, enikə	naɹɒn	naɹɒ	naɹɒn-itsʰ	naɹɒn-ov	naɹɒn-um
	էն, էնի, էնիկը	նրան	նրա	նրանից	նրանով	նրանում
Plural						
Prox.	saɹɒŋkʰ	saɹɒntsʰ	saɹɒntsʰ	saɹɒntsʰ-itsʰ	saɹɒntsʰ-ov	saɹɒntsʰ-um
	սրանք	սրանց	սրանց	սրանցից	սրանցով	սրանցում
Med.	daɹɒŋkʰ	daɹɒntsʰ	daɹɒntsʰ	daɹɒntsʰ-itsʰ	daɹɒntsʰ-ov	daɹɒntsʰ-um
	taɹɒŋkʰ	taɹɒntsʰ	taɹɒntsʰ	taɹɒntsʰ-itsʰ	taɹɒntsʰ-ov	taɹɒntsʰ-um
	դրանք	դրանց	դրանց	դրանցից	դրանցով	դրանցում
Dist.	naɹɒŋkʰ	naɹɒntsʰ	naɹɒntsʰ	naɹɒntsʰ-itsʰ	naɹɒntsʰ-ov	naɹɒntsʰ-um
	նրանք	նրանց	նրանց	նրանցից	նրանցով	նրանցում

Iranian Armenian when it comes to the use or form of these interrogative pronouns, and therefore keep this section rather brief. In the following sentences, we provide examples of the different types of interrogative pronouns in bold.

The pronoun 'who' (6) is [ov] in the nominative (6a). But it uses a different root allomorph *um* when case suffixes are added.[2] Instrumentals and locative suffixes are generally avoided, and replaced with postpositional constructions.

(6) a. **ov** ɒ uɹɒχ
        who AUX happy
        'Who is happy?'   (NK)
        Ո՞վ ա ուրախ:

    b. **um**-i-n   e-s   mɒkʰɹ-um
        who-DAT-DEF AUX-2SG clean-IMPF.CVB
        'Who are you washing?'   (NK)
        Ումի՞ն ես մաքրում:

---

[2]This allomorph /um/ is actually the genitive-dative form of this morpheme in Standard Eastern Armenian (Dum-Tragut 2009: 148).

c. giˌkʰ-ə **um**-i-n   e-s   t-ᴅ-l-i
book-ᴅᴇꜰ who-ᴅᴀᴛ-ᴅᴇꜰ ᴀᴜx-2sɢ give-ᴛʜ-ɪɴꜰ-ɪᴍᴘꜰ.ᴄᴠʙ
'Who do you give the book to?'   (NK)
Գիրքը ումի՞ն ես տալի:

d. **um**-i   giˌkʰ-ə
who-ɢᴇɴ bookᴅᴇꜰ
'Whose book?'   (NK)
Ումի՞ գիրքը:

e. **um**-itsʰ
who-ᴀʙʟ
'From who?'   (NK)
Ումի՞ց:

f. **um**-i   het, **um**-i   metʃʰ
who-ɢᴇɴ with, who-ɢᴇɴ in
'With who? In who?'   (NK)
Ումի՞ հետ: Ումի՞ մէջ:

The pronoun 'what' is [intʃʰ], and there is no case-conditioned suppletion or stem allomorphy involved (7).

(7) a. **intʃʰ** ᴅ   kᴅput. **intʃʰ** e-s   uz-um
what ᴀᴜx blue.   what ᴀᴜx-2sɢ want-ɪᴍᴘꜰ.ᴄᴠʙ
'What is blue? What do you want?'   (NK)
Ի՞նչ ա կապուտ: Ի՞նչ ես ուզում:

b. **intʃʰ**-i(-n)   e-s   t-ᴅ-l-i   giˌkʰ-ə
what-ᴅᴀᴛ(-ᴅᴇꜰ) ᴀᴜx-2sɢ give-ᴛʜ-ɪɴꜰ-ɪᴍᴘꜰ.ᴄᴠʙ book-ᴅᴇꜰ
'To what do you give the book?'   (NK)
Ինչի՞ն/ինչի՞ ես տալի գիրքը:

c. **intʃʰ**-i   gujn-ə
what-ɢᴇɴ color-ᴅᴇꜰ
'The color of what?'   (NK)
Ինչի՞ գույնը:

d. **intʃʰ**-itsʰ, **intʃʰ**-ov, **intʃʰ**-um
what-ᴀʙʟ, what-ɪɴs, what-ʟᴏᴄ
'From what? With what? In what?'   (NK)
Ինչի՞ց: Ինչո՞վ: Ինչու՞մ:

The word for 'where' can vary between [vo.tes] and [u.]. NK reports that [u.]
feels more informal (8).

(8)   a.   ke.ɒku.-ə **vo.tes** ɒ
           food-DEF   where   AUX
           'Where is the food?'   (NK)
           Կերակուրը որտե՞ղ ա:

      b.   ke.ɒku.-ə **u.**   ɒ
           food-DEF   where   AUX
           'Where is the food?'   (NK)
           Կերակուրը ո՞ր ա:

      c.   **vo.tes**-its^h. **vo.tes**-um e-s   t͡sən-v-e
           where-ABL. where-LOC AUX-2SG born-PASS-IMPF.CVB
           'From where? Where were you born?'   (NK)
           Որտեղի՞ց: Որտեղու՞մ ես ծնուէ:

The pronoun 'when' is prescriptively [je.p^h], but the rhotic can be deleted in
colloquial speech [jep^h] (9a). The pronoun takes a special dative/genitive suffix
-vɒn or -vɒ (9b). This suffix is also used before oblique case suffixes like the ablative (9c), as a type of oblique stem.

(9)   a.   tɒ.edɒ.t͡s^h-ət   **je.p^h/jep^h** ɒ
           birthday-POSS.2SG when   AUX
           'When is your birthday?'   (NK)
           Տարեդարձդ ե՞րբ ա:

      b.   **je.p^h**-vɒ
           when-GEN
           'Of when?'   (NK)
           Երբուա՞յ:

      c.   **je.p^h**-vɒn-it͡s^h
           when-DAT-ABL
           'From when?'   (NK)
           Երբուանի՞ց:

For the pronoun 'why' (10), the Eastern Armenian version is [int͡ʃ^hu]. This word
is used by the Iranian Armenian community as well, but it has a formal connotation. A common colloquial version is [he.] հեր, which Sargsyan et al. (Սարգսյան
et al. 2001: vol. 4: p. 227) report for New Nakhichevan and several dialects around

Lake Van (Moks, Shatakh, Mush, Van). Adjarian (Աճառեան 1926) cites a form /heɾ/ հէր for Tabriz (p. 658) and Maragha (p. 119) and derives it from Classical Armenian /ēɾ/ էր, also meaning 'why'. Given the presence of [he.ɹ] հէր in so many of the neighboring southeastern dialects, particularly in Iran, we should not be surprised to come across it in Tehran.

(10) a. **intʃʰu**
why
'Why?'   (NK)
Ինչո՞ւ:

b. **he.ɹ** uʃ-ɒ-t͡sʰ-ɒ-n
why late-LV-AOR-PST-3PL
'Why are they late?"   (AS)
Հէ՞ր ուշացան:

NK reports that her family uses [he.ɹ] more often than [intʃʰu] (11). She further reports that [intʃʰu] is restricted to more formal speech.

(11) a. **he.ɹ** e-s   et hɒkʰ-e
why AUX-2SG that wear-PERF.CVB
'Why are you wearing that?'   (NK)
Հէ՞ր ես էդ հագէ:

b. **he.ɹ** e-s   et ut-um
why AUX-2SG that eat-IMPF.CVB
'Why are you eating that?'   (NK)
Հէ՞ր ես էդ ուտում:

c. **he.ɹ** t͡ʃʰ-e-s   zɒŋg-um
why NEG-AUX-2SG call-IMPF.CVB
'Why don't you call?'   (NK)
Հէ՞ր չես զանգում:

For the pronoun 'how', Standard Eastern Armenian uses [intʃʰpes] while Colloquial Eastern Armenian uses [vontsʰ] (Dum-Tragut 2009: 154). Iranian Armenian uses [intʃʰpes] (12). The modifier version is [intʃʰpesi].

(12) a. ke.ɹɒku.ɹ-ət **intʃʰpes** ɒ
food-POSS.2SG how   AUX
'How is your food?'   (NK)
Կերակուրդ ինչպէ՞ս ա:

b. **int͡ʃʰpesi** mɒɹtʰ ɒ
what.kind man AUX
'What kind of man is he?' (NK)
ինչպէսի մա̃րդ ա:

5.4 Numerals

Iranian Armenian uses essentially the same set of numerals and morphological operations to create complex numerals, as Standard Eastern Armenian. We focus on cardinals (§5.4.1) and ordinals (§5.4.2). For cardinals, there are only minor lexical differences between Standard Eastern Armenian and Iranian Armenian. For ordinals, Iranian Armenian displays a difference from Standard Eastern Armenian in the use of irregular morphology in complex numerals. All numeral data in this section was gathered from NK. She gave useful meta-linguistic judgements on variation within the Iranian Armenian community in Los Angeles. Standard Eastern Armenian forms were taken from Wiktionary and double-checked against grammars, the EANC's lexicon,[3] and speakers.

5.4.1 Cardinal numerals

Table 5.5 lists the basic numerals from 0 to 10. Numeral 9 includes the definite suffix /-ə/. We include stress markers because ordinals will later present exceptional stress patterns.

Some minor points of difference between Standard Eastern and Iranian Armenian: a) the numeral 0 has different vowels in SEA and IA, b) the numeral 2 has an initial glide in SEA [jeɾku] but not in IA [eɹku],[4] c) the numeral 9 has an extra nasal [inn-ə] in IA, and d) numeral 10 includes a definite suffix in SEA but not IA. Note however that an unsuffixed form [tɑs] is attested in Colloquial Eastern Armenian.

The final schwa in these cardinals is morphologically the definite suffix, but it is being used here meaninglessly without contributing definiteness. One cannot add another definite suffix onto these suffixed roots. And also, this schwa /-ə/ shows the same allomorphy patterns as the definite suffix (§3.2.2), such as a prevocalic /-n-/ (13).

---

[3]https://bitbucket.org/timarkh/uniparser-grammar-eastern-armenian/src/master/
[4]As discussed in §3.1.1, many polysyllabic words start with /je/ in SEA but an initial /e/ in IA. It is odd how the numerals 2 and 3 are both bisyllabic but behave differently.

Table 5.5: Cardinal numerals 0–10

Value	Iranian Armenian			cf. SEA		
0	ze'ɹo	zero	զէրօ	zə'ro	zero	զրօ
1	'mek	one	մէկ	'mek	one	մէկ
2	eɹ'ku	two	էրկու	jeɹ'ku	two	էրկու
3	je'ɹekʰ	three	էրէք	jeɹekʰ	three	էրէք
4	t͡ʃʰoɹs	four	չորս	t͡ʃʰors	four	չորս
5	'hiŋg	five	հինգ	'hiŋg	five	հինգ
6	'vets͡ʰ	six	վեց	'vets͡ʰ	six	վեց
7	'jotʰ	seven	եօթ	'jotʰ	seven	յօթ
8	'utʰ	eight	ութ	'utʰ	eight	ութ
9	'inn-ə	nine-DEF	իննը	'in-ə	nine-DEF	ինը
10	'tɒs	ten	տաս	'tɑs-ə	ten-DEF	տասը

(13) tɑs-n =e (SEA)
      tɒs-n =ɒ (IA)
      ten-DEF AUX
      '(The time) is ten.'
      Տասն է/ա:

For numerals 11–19, Iranian Armenian admits more variability than Standard
Eastern Armenian (Table 5.6). In Standard Eastern Armenian, a number like 11 is
expressed by concatenating the numerals for 10 [tɑs] and 1 [mek]; the two numerals are separated by the definite suffix /-n-/ and a meaningless connective suffix
/-ə-/: [tɑs-n-ə-mek]. Colloquial Eastern Armenian allows a simpler construction
whereby the intervening 'DEF-CON' morphs are omitted: [tɑs-mek]. NK reports
that in her Iranian Armenian community, both strategies are attested, and she
feels that neither is dominant over the other. She reports that she herself uses
the 'DEF-CON' template more often for 15 than for 16. She also had vowel hiatus
in words like 12.

A point of difference between Iranian Armenian and Standard Eastern Armenian concerns numerals 12, 13, and 18 where the ones digit starts with a glide
or vowel: SEA 2 [jeɹku], 3 [jeɹekʰ], 8 [utʰ]. For SEA, the connective schwa and
glide are absent: 12 [tɑs-n-eɹku], 13 [tɑs-n-eɹekʰ], 18 [tɑs-n-utʰ]. Colloquial Eastern Armenian allows the retention of the schwa and of the numeral's glide: 12

Table 5.6: Cardinal numerals 11–19 in Iranian Armenian

Value	Using SEA-style template			Using CEA-style template		
11	tɒs-n-ə-'mek	10-DEF-CON-1	տասնմէկ	tɒs-'mek	10-1	տասմէկ
12	tɒs-n-ə-eɹ'ku	10-DEF-CON-2	տասներկու	tɒs-eɹ'ku	10-2	տասերկու
13	tɒs-n-ə-je'ɹekʰ	10-DEF-CON-3	տասներեք	tɒs-je'ɹekʰ	10-3	տասերեք
14	tɒs-n-ə-ʧʰoɹs	10-DEF-CON-4	տասնչորս	tɒs-ʧʰoɹs	10-4	տասչորս
15	tɒs-n-ə-'hiŋg	10-DEF-CON-5	տասնհինգ	tɒs-'hiŋg	10-5	տասհինգ
16	tɒs-n-ə-'vetsʰ	10-DEF-CON-6	տասնվեց	tɒs-'vetsʰ	10-6	տասվեց
17	tɒs-n-ə-'jotʰ	10-DEF-CON-7	տասնեօթ	tɒs-'jotʰ	10-7	տասեօթ
18	tɒs-n-ə-'utʰ	10-DEF-CON-8	տասնութ	tɒs-'utʰ	10-8	տասութ
19	tɒs-n-ə-'inn-ə	10-DEF-CON-9-DEF	տասնիննը	tɒs-'inn-ə	10-9-DEF	տասիննը

[tɑs-n-ə-jeɾku], 13 [tɑs-n-ə-jeɾekʰ], 18 [tɑs-n-ə-utʰ]. Iranian Armenian patterns like CEA in keeping the connective and the glide, except for 12.[5]

Moving onto the higher numbers (Table 5.7), most multiples of ten like 30 consist of a root and suffix /-sun/. For illustration, we don't separately segment the root and suffix because their allomorphy is quite opaque.

Table 5.7: Higher cardinal numerals (decades, 100, 1000) in Iranian Armenian

20	'kʰsɒn	twenty	քսան
30	jeɹe'sun	thirty	երեսուն
40	kʰɒrɒ'sun	forty	քառասուն
50	hi'tsʰun	fifty	յիսուն
60	vɒ'tsʰun	sixty	վաթսուն
70	jotʰɒnɒ'sun	seventy	եօթանասուն
80	ut'tsʰun	eighty	ութսուն
90	innə'sun	ninety	իննսուն
100	hɒ'ɹuɹ	hundred	հարուր
1000	hɒ'zɒɹ	thousand	հազար

Numbers 20, 100, and 1000 have their own special forms. For the decade 20, the initial consonant cluster can contain a schwa in careful speech [kʰəsɒn], but it is usually omitted in natural speech (cf. SEA data from Hovakimyan 2016). NK never produced a schwa for this form.

---

[5]No such differences arise for numeral 17: SEA [tɑs-n-ə-jotʰ] and IA [tɒs-n-ə-jotʰ].

The lects differ for numerals 50, 60, 80, and 100. For Standard Eastern Armenian, these numerals end in /sun/: 50 [hi-sun], 60 [vɑtʰ-sun], 80 [utʰ-sun]. In Colloquial Eastern Armenian, it's possible to affricate the /s/ in these numerals, as in [hit͡sʰun, vɑt͡sʰun, ut͡sʰun]. Iranian Armenian speaker NK always affricates these numerals, sometimes also including a /t/ before the affricate: [hi-t͡sʰun, vɒt͡sʰun, utt͡sʰun].

For the number 100, Standard Eastern Armenian uses [hɑɾjuɾ] with a glide, while Iranian Armenian uses [hɒɹuɹ] without a glide.

To create complex cardinals, Iranian Armenian and Standard Eastern Armenian use the same strategy as English. Numerals are concatenated from the highest number to the lowest. For example, the number 35 is just a concatenation of the numerals 30 and 5: [jeɹesun jeɹekʰ] երեսուն երեք. Our archive includes more examples of complex cardinals that we elicited.

As a final note, these cardinals can act as nouns and take nominal inflection (14a). When the numeral 2 takes inflection, it uses a special allomorph [eɹkus] (14b).

(14)   a. jeɹekʰ-ən e-m   uz-um
           three-DEF AUX-1SG want-IMPF.CVB
           'I want the three of them.'   (NK)
           Երեքն եմ ուզում:

       b. eɹkus-ən e-m   uz-um
           two-DEF AUX-1SG want-IMPF.CVB
           'I want the two of them.'   (NK)
           Երկուսն եմ ուզում:

5.4.2 Ordinal numerals

Iranian Armenian uses essentially the same set of ordinal numerals and ordinal morphology as Standard Eastern Armenian. However, the two varieties differ in the use of irregular allomorphy in complex ordinals (Stump 2010, Dolatian 2023b). Briefly, the numeral one displays allomorphy for 'first' but not for higher numerals. Numerals 2–4 show allomorphy for their simple ordinals, but their allomorphy is variably percolated to higher numbers.

First, consider numerals 1–10 (Table 5.8). The ordinal of 1 [mek] is a special suppletive lexeme [ɒrɒt͡ʃʰin].[6] Numerals 2–4 utilize allomorphy with a special

---

[6]The ordinal [ɒrɒt͡ʃʰin] 'first' is morphologically related to the word [ɒrɒt͡ʃʰ] which means 'forward, before' in the modern language. In Classical Armenian, the word also had other meanings like 'previous', while the root had other meanings like 'front'. The etymological connection between these words is cross-linguistically common (Veselinova 1997: 441).

root allomorph and short suffix allomorph /-ɹoɹtʰ/. For example, 2 is [eɹku] but 2nd is [jek-ɹoɹtʰ].[7] The ordinals of 5–10 are formed by combining the cardinal root with the default ordinal suffix /-eɹoɹtʰ/: 5 [hiŋg] and 5th [hiŋg-eɹoɹtʰ]. The ordinal suffixes /-ɹoɹtʰ, -eɹoɹtʰ/ are morphologically exceptional because they are prosodically prestressing (§2.2.2.2).

Table 5.8: Ordinal numerals 1–10

Value	Iranian Armenian			cf. SEA	
1st	ɒrɒt͡ʃʰin	first	առաջին	arɑt͡ʃʰin	առաջին
2nd	ˈjek-ɹoɹtʰ	two-ORD	երկրորդ	ˈjeɾk-ɾoɾtʰ	երկրորդ
3rd	ˈje-ɹoɹtʰ	three-ORD	երրորդ	ˈjeɾ-ɾoɾtʰ	երրորդ
4th	t͡ʃʰo-ɹoɹtʰ	four-ORD	չորրորդ	ˈt͡ʃʰoɾ-ɾoɾtʰ	չորրորդ
5th	ˈhiŋg-eɹoɹtʰ	five-ORD	հինգերորդ	ˈhiŋg-eɾoɾtʰ	հինգերորդ
6th	ˈvetsʰ-eɹoɹtʰ	six-ORD	վեցերորդ	ˈvetsʰ-eɾoɾtʰ	վեցերորդ
7th	ˈjotʰ-eɹoɹtʰ	seven-ORD	եոթերորդ	ˈjotʰ-eɾoɾtʰ	յոթերորդ
8th	ˈutʰ-eɹoɹtʰ	six-ORD	ութերորդ	ˈutʰ-eɾoɾtʰ	ութերորդ
9th	ˈinn-eɹoɹtʰ	nine-ORD	իննֆերորդ	ˈin-n-eɾoɾtʰ	իննֆերորդ
10th	ˈtɒs-eɹoɹtʰ	ten-ORD	տասներորդ	ˈtɑs-n-eɾoɾtʰ	տասներորդ

Standard Eastern Armenian uses essentially the same morphemes, with some additional segments for ordinals 2–4, cf. SEA [jeɾk-ɾoɾtʰ] against IA [jek-ɾoɾtʰ] '2nd'. Ordinals 9 and 10 include the definite suffix /-n-/ in SEA.

The ordinal suffix /-eɹoɹtʰ/ is the default suffix for ordinal formation. Higher numbers like decades use this suffix as well (Table 5.9).

For complex numbers like 35, the default strategy is to add the ordinal suffix /-eɹoɹtʰ/ to the entire complex cardinal. For example, 35 is [jeɹesun hiŋg] երեսուն հինգ, thus the ordinal 'thirty-fifth' is [jeɹesun hiŋg-eɹoɹtʰ] երեսուն հինգերորդ.

Complications arise for complex numerals where the ones digit is 1–4. Recall that for the numeral 1, the cardinal is [mek] and the ordinal is [ɒrɒt͡ʃʰin]. For numerals 2–4, the cardinal is one root allomorph like 2 [eɹku], while the ordinal uses special root and suffix allomorphs [jek-ɹoɹtʰ]. These two groups of numerals differ in whether their allomorphy is inherited by higher complex cardinals.

First consider the numeral 1 and its higher forms (Table 5.10). For complex ordinals like 31st, we simply add the ordinal suffix without using the lexeme [ɒrɒt͡ʃʰin], such as [jeɹesun-mek-eɹoɹtʰ]. The lexeme [ɒrɒt͡ʃʰin] is not used for higher forms *jeɹesun-ɒrɒt͡ʃʰin.

---

[7]For 2, NK uses a glide in the ordinal but not the cardinal. AM reports more ordinal variation as [je(ɹ)g-ɹoɹtʰ, je(ɹ)k-ɹoɹtʰ].

Table 5.9: Higher ordinal numerals (decades, 100, 1000) in Iranian Armenian

20th	kʰsɒn-eɹoɹtʰ	twenty-ORD	քսաներորդ
30th	jeɹeˈsun-eɹoɹtʰ	thirty-ORD	երեսուներորդ
40th	kʰɒrɒˈsun-eɹoɹtʰ	forty-ORD	քառասուներորդ
50th	hi͡tsʰun-eɹoɹtʰ	fifty-ORD	յիսուներորդ
60th	vɒ͡tsʰun-eɹoɹtʰ	sixty-ORD	վաթսուներորդ
70th	jotʰɒnɒˈsun-eɹoɹtʰ	seventy-ORD	եօթանասուներորդ
80th	ut͡tsʰun-eɹoɹtʰ	eighty-ORD	ութսուներորդ
90th	innəˈsun-eɹoɹtʰ	ninety-ORD	իննսուներորդ
100th	hɒɹɹuɹ-eɹoɹtʰ	hundred-ORD	հարուրերորդ
1000th	hɒˈzɒɹ-eɹoɹtʰ	thousand-ORD	հազարերորդ

Table 5.10: Allomorphy of numeral 1 in complex ordinals in Iranian Armenian

1	mek	1	մեկ
1st	arɑ͡tʃʰin	first	առաջին
21	kʰsɒn-ˈmek	20-1	քսան մեկ
21st	kʰsɒn-ˈmek-eɹoɹtʰ	20-1-ORD	քսան մեկերորդ
31	jeɹesun-ˈmek	30-1	երեսուն մեկ
31st	jeɹesun-ˈmek-eɹoɹtʰ	30-1-ORD	երեսուն մեկերորդ
41	kʰɒrɒsun-ˈmek	40-1	քառասուն մեկ
41st	kʰɒrɒsun-ˈmek-eɹoɹtʰ	40-1-ORD	քառասուն մեկերորդ

Such patterns of limited allomorphy in higher numbers have been called external marking (Stump 2010). The idea is that the ordinal of a complex cardinal like 31 is treated as an exocentric construction, and that the component 1 numeral cannot use its special allomorph in complex cardinals.

Standard Eastern Armenian shows the same patterns for the non-use of [arɑ͡tʃʰin] in higher numbers (Dum-Tragut 2009: 120). For example, 21st in Standard Eastern Armenian is simply [jeresun-mek-erortʰ] and not *jeresun-arɑ͡tʃʰin.

Different behavior is found for complex ordinals where the ones digit is 2–4. Consider the numeral 2 [eɹku]. Its ordinal is [jek-ɹoɹtʰ] with special root-suffix allomorphs. NK reports that she uses the same allomorphs for both simplex ordinals like 2 and complex ordinals like 32: [jeɹesun-jek-ɹoɹtʰ] (Table 5.11). Such patterns are typologically called internal-marking (Stump 2010), metaphorically meaning that the complex ordinal is treated like an endocentric compound.

Table 5.11: Allomorphy of numerals 2–4 in complex ordinals in Iranian Armenian from NK

2	eɾˈku	2	էրկու
2nd	ˈjek-ɾoɾtʰ	2-ORD	երկրորդ
22	kʰsɒn-eɾˈku	20-2	քսան էրկու
22nd	kʰsɒn-ˈjek-ɾoɾtʰ	20-2-ORD	քսան երկրորդ
32	jeɾesun-eɾˈku	30-2	երեսուն էրկու
32nd	jeɾesun-ˈjek-ɾoɾtʰ	30-2-ORD	երեսուն երկրորդ
42	kʰɒrɒsun-eɾˈku	40-2	քառասուն էրկու
42nd	kʰɒrɒsun-ˈjek-ɾotʰ	40-2-ORD	քառասուն երկրորդ
3	jeˈɾekʰ	3	երեք
3rd	ˈje-ɾoɾtʰ	3-ORD	երրորդ
23	kʰsɒn-jeˈɾekʰ	20-3	քսան երեք
23rd	kʰsɒn-ˈje-ɾoɾtʰ	20-3-ORD	քսան երրորդ
33	jeɾesun-jeˈɾekʰ	30-3	երեսուն երեք
33rd	jeɾesun-ˈje-ɾoɾtʰ	30-3-ORD	երեսուն երրորդ
43	kʰɒrɒsun-jeˈɾekʰ	40-3	քառասուն երեք
43rd	kʰɒrɒsun-ˈje-ɾoɾtʰ	40-3-ORD	քառասուն երրորդ
4	t͡ʃʰoɾs	4	չորս
4th	t͡ʃʰo-ɾoɾtʰ	4-ORD	չորրորդ
24	kʰsɒn-t͡ʃʰoɾs	20-4	քսան չորս
24th	kʰsɒn-t͡ʃʰo-ɾoɾtʰ	20-4-ORD	քսան չորրորդ
34	jeɾesun-t͡ʃʰoɾs	30-4	երեսուն չորս
34th	jeɾesun-t͡ʃʰo-ɾoɾtʰ	30-4-ORD	երեսուն չորրորդ
44	kʰɒrɒsun-t͡ʃʰoɾs	40-4	քառասուն չորս
44th	kʰɒrɒsun-t͡ʃʰo-ɾoɾtʰ	40-4-ORD	քառասուն չորրորդ

Standard Eastern Armenian crucially differs from NK's IA ideolect in this regard. In SEA, a numeral like 2 [jerku] cannot percolate its irregular form [jerk-rortʰ] to higher numerals. Thus, the ordinal of 32 in SEA is [jeresun-erku-erortʰ] with the default ordinal suffix, and not *jeresun-erk-rortʰ with the special allomorphs (Սարգսյան 1985: 209, Hagopian 2005: 308). For discussion on such ordinal variation in Armenian, see Dolatian (2023b).

NK informs us that, because of this difference between Standard Eastern Armenian and Iranian Armenian, her colleagues and family gave her contradictory judgments on the correct formation of complex ordinals like 32. Some recommended the use of the SEA-style ordinal with the default ordinal suffix /-e.ɹo.ɹtʰ/ (like [je.ɹesun-e.ɹku-e.ɹo.ɹtʰ]), while she and her friends preferred the use of the irregular ordinal suffix /-ɹo.ɹtʰ/ (like [je.ɹesun-jek-ɹo.ɹtʰ]). Anooshik Melikian (AM, an Iranian Armenian speaker from Tehran) likewise reports that NK's colloquial constructions are attested across educated and non-educated speakers in Tehran. The use of the SEA-style construction is obviously due to the prestige of SEA, as a form of prescriptivism.

5.5 Other function words

The following are lists of function words that we have elicited which do not fit neatly into the previous sections. As of writing this grammar, we have not been able to study these function words extensively.

Iranian Armenian uses the adverbial function words in Table 5.12 to indicate location, e.g., the equivalent of English 'here' and 'there'. As with demonstratives, these locational words distinguish between proximal, medial, and distal locations. We specify the source of the items.

Table 5.12: Location adverbs in Iranian Armenian

Proximal	esteʁ (KM, NK), ste (AS), steʁ (AS) էստեղ, ստեղ, ստէ	'this place'
Medial	etteʁ (AS, NK) էդտեղ	'that place'
Distal	əndeʁ (AS), ənde (AS), ənne (NK, KM), ənneʁ (KM) ընտեղ, ընտէ, ըննէ, ըննեղ	'that place yonder'

All these words like [esteʁ] 'this place' are morphologically derived from a demonstrative like [es] 'this' and the word 'place' [teʁ]. Note how the [t] becomes [d] after the nasal in [əndeʁ] 'that place yonder'. Post-nasal voicing seems limited to such function words.

To illustrate, the following sentence shows a location adverb (15).

(15) gən-ɒ ənne
     go-TH there'
     'Go over there.'   (NK)
     Գնա ըննէ:

We likewise elicited the following adverbs of manner (Table 5.13).

Table 5.13: Manner adverbs in Iranian Armenian from AS

Proximal	esents͡ʰ, sents͡ʰi	էսէնց, սէնցի	'like this'
Medial	etents͡ʰ, tents͡ʰi	էտէնց, տէնցի	'like that'
Distal	nents͡ʰi	նէնցի	'like that yonder'

An additional adverb of manner is [hents͡ʰ], which has a broad range of uses, often translatable to the English word 'just' (16).

(16) a. hents͡ʰ et
         just   that
         'That's it'   (NK)
         Հէնց էդ:
     b. hents͡ʰ himɒ
         just   now
         'Right now'   (NK)
         Հէնց հիմա:

Iranian Armenian has a modal word [piti] that roughly translates to 'must' (17). It is used to create a debitive or obligative mood (Dum-Tragut 2009: 263).

(17) a. piti etʰ-ɒ-m
         must go-TH-1SG
         'I have to go.'   (NK)
         Պիտի էթամ:
     b. piti ut-e-m
         must eat-TH-1SG
         'I have to eat.'   (NK)
         Պիտի ուտեմ:

This word is related to the syntactic construction [petʰk ɒ] which is used to mean 'it is needed' or 'it is necessary' (18).

(18) a. petk^h ɒ
    need AUX
    'It is needed.'   (NK)
    Պէտք ա:

  b. petk^h ɒ ut-e-m
    need AUX eat-TH-1SG
    'I have to eat.'   (NK)
    Literally: 'It is needed that I eat.'
    Պէտք ա ուտեմ:

6 Verbal morphology

In Iranian Armenian, regular verbs are divided into simple verbs and complex verbs. In their infinitive citation form, simple verbs consist of a root, theme vowel, and infinitive suffix. Of these simple verbs, there are two conjugation classes based on the theme vowel. Complex verbs include a valency-changing morpheme. These include passives, causatives, and inchoatives. In contrast, irregular verbs can be divided into four categories: nasal-infixed verbs, suppletive verbs, defective verbs, and miscellaneous verbs.

When comparing Iranian Armenian with other Armenian lects, Iranian Armenian is close to Standard Eastern Armenian. Like Standard Eastern, Iranian Armenian widely uses periphrasis for various inflectional paradigm cells. Periphrasis is used for the indicative present, indicative past imperfective, and various complex tenses (present perfect, past perfect, future). Periphrasis involves the use of a non-finite converb (which carries lexical meaning) alongside an inflected auxiliary that carries tense/agreement marking. Synthesis is used for less frequent inflectional cells, such as subjunctives, conditionals, futures, and imperatives. The most common synthetic form is the past perfective, also called the aorist.

There is a larger literature on the verbal morphology of other Armenian lects. For Standard Western Armenian morphotactics, see Donabédian (1997), Boyacioglu (2010), Boyacioglu & Dolatian (2020), Dolatian & Guekguezian (2022b,a), and Karakaş et al. (2021). For Standard Eastern Armenian, most work on verbal morphology is on verbal semantics (Kozintseva 1995, Dum-Tragut 2009, Daniel & Khurshudian 2015, Plungian 2018). For Iranian Armenian, we focus on providing complete paradigms for the different conjugation classes. We provide a complete segmentation of all inflectional morphology.

For reference, Iranian Armenian shows the following significant differences from Standard Eastern Armenian in terms of verbal morphology.

- The 1SG marker /-m/ is used in both the present and past paradigms (§6.2.2).

- The present 3SG auxiliary is /ɒ/ in Iranian Armenian, /e/ in Standard Eastern (§6.2.1). The form [ɑ] is also attested in Colloquial Eastern Armenian.

- Iranian Armenian deletes the auxiliary /e/ or theme vowel /e/ before the past marker /i/ (§6.2.2, §6.4.2).

- There is optional leveling of the negated copula and negated auxiliary (§6.2.3).

- The perfective converb suffix displays liquid-zero alternations, briefly illustrated in §6.3.2, discussed more in §3.3.

- The past perfective or aorist system has been significantly altered, by promoting the past morph /-ɒ/ from a restricted marked allomorph to an elsewhere allomorph (§6.4.1).

- The imperative 2SG suffix differs across the lects (§6.4.3).

- Some irregular verbs in Standard Eastern have become leveled or lost in Iranian Armenian (§6.7).

For contrast, we often show the verbal paradigms of both Standard Eastern Armenian and Iranian Armenian. This chapter provides complete paradigms for the simplex verbs, and partial paradigms for complex and irregular verbs. Complete paradigms are found in our online archive.[1]

Across Armenian varieties, the conjugation classes utilize different stems when forming the different paradigm cells. These are often called the present stem and the past/aorist stem. The aorist stem can be formed via various morphological strategies, such as root allomorphy and affix deletion. The aorist stem can include either an overt aorist suffix -$\widehat{ts^h}$- or a covert aorist suffix -∅-. Due to space limitations, we do not explicitly discuss the formation of present vs. aorist stems in Iranian Armenian. Our paradigms indicate the use of the aorist stem and aorist suffix -$\widehat{ts^h}$/∅- in both the past perfective and other paradigm cells as AOR. When used in the past perfective, the aorist morpheme contributes perfective meaning; but it is used meaninglessly as a morphomic element in other paradigm cells (cf. Aronoff 1994). For discussion of the formation of aorist stems in Standard Armenian, see Dolatian & Guekguezian (2022a).

6.1 Simple verbs and their classes

Like in Standard Eastern Armenian, regular simple verbs in Iranian Armenian are classified into two classes based on the choice of theme vowel: -e-, -ɒ- (Table 6.1). We call these classes E-Class and A-Class. The citation form is the infinitive, called the [ɑnoɾoʃ deɾbɑj] անորոշ դերբայ 'indefinite participle' in Standard Eastern Armenian.

---

[1]https://github.com/jhdeov/iranian_armenian

Table 6.1: Simple infinitives from the two regular classes

E-Class		A-Class		
jeɹkʰ-e-l	ɒpɹ-e-l	kɒɹtʰ-ɒ-l	χos-ɒ-l	√-TH-INF
'to sing'	'to live'	'to read'	'to speak'	
երգել	ապրել	կարդալ	խոսալ	

Standard Eastern Armenian uses the same conjugation classes. In general, a given verb belongs to the same conjugation class in both lects. There are some exceptions though. For example, the verb 'to speak' uses the root *χos-*. In Iranian Armenian, this verb belongs to the A-Class: *χos-ɒ-l* 'to speak'. In contrast in Standard Eastern Armenian, this verb belongs to the E-Class: *χos-e-l*.[2]

In terms of morphological structure, we treat theme vowels as meaningless empty morphs (Aronoff 1994). The choice of theme vowel is root-conditioned and meaningless. For a theoretical analysis of Armenian theme vowels, see Guekguezian & Dolatian (forthcoming). Their Standard Western Armenian analysis can easily extend to Iranian Armenian.

Having set up the basic classes, the next sections describe verbal inflection. Like Standard Eastern Armenian, verbal inflection in Iranian Armenian is highly periphrastic. Before we describe these periphrastic forms, we first describe the auxiliary system in Iranian Armenian.

6.2 Auxiliaries

The verb 'to be' acts as both a copula in predicate sentences (1a), and as an auxiliary in periphrastic forms (1b).

(1) a. mɒɹtʰ-ə təχuɹ ɒ
         man-DEF sad   AUX.PRS.3SG
         'The man is sad.'   (NK)
         Մարդը տխուր ա:

---

[2]It is possible that these few deviations have a diachronic reason. Modern Standard Eastern and Iranian Armenian utilize only two theme vowels: *-e-* and *-a/ɒ-*. But Classical Armenian had two additional theme vowels *-i-* and *-u-*. Reflexes of verbs with these theme vowels are assigned to one of the surviving classes, usually to the E-Class. For example, 'to speak' was an I-Class verb in Classical Armenian: *χos-i-l*. The fact that this verb became E-Class in Standard Eastern Armenian, but A-Class in Iranian Armenian suggests that more deviations would be found in the reflexes of Classical verbs with obsolete theme vowels.

b. mɒɹtʰ-ə jeɹkʰ-um   ɒ
   man-DEF sing-IMPF.CVB AUX.PRS.3SG
   'The man is singing.'   (NK)
   Մարդը երգում ա:

In this section, we gloss the present 3SG auxiliary [ɒ] as 'AUX.PRS.3SG' for explanation. But throughout the rest of the grammar, we usually just gloss it as AUX.

In periphrastic constructions, the verb is in a converb form, e.g., the imperfective converb in (1b). Before discussing these converbs, we first lay out the paradigm of the auxiliary. The name of the auxiliary is [oʒɑndɑk bɑj] oժանդակ բայ 'helper verb' in Standard Eastern Armenian.

6.2.1 Present auxiliary

We show the present tense paradigm of the auxiliary in Table 6.2. Because the auxiliary can also function as a copula, we gloss both as AUX. In the present tense, the auxiliary consists of the auxiliary's marker -*e*-, and then a fused tense-agreement marker (T/AGR or just AGR). In the 3SG, there is no T/Agr marker. Instead, the inflected auxiliary is just the auxiliary marker /e/ in Standard Eastern Armenian. In contrast, in Iranian Armenian, the 3SG present uses an allomorph /ɒ/ of the auxiliary.

Table 6.2: Paradigm of the present auxiliary and copula in Standard Eastern and Iranian Armenian

	Standard Eastern		Iranian Armenian	
1SG	e-m	եմ	e-m	եմ
	'I am'		'I am'	
2SG	e-s	ես	e-s	ես
3SG	e	է	ɒ	ա
1PL	e-ŋkʰ	ենք	e-ŋkʰ	ենք
2PL	e-kʰ	եք	e-kʰ	էք
3PL	e-n	են	e-n	են
	AUX-AGR			

The Iranian Armenian 3SG form /ɒ/ is likely diachronically derived from an earlier /e/ form. In fact, the 3SG auxiliary /ɒ/ is found in the colloquial speech of Standard Eastern speakers in Armenia as /ɑ/. For Iranian Armenian, the low-vowel form /ɒ/ form is simply grammaticalized as the only realization of the present 3SG auxiliary.

We utilize the following rules for Iranian Armenian (Rule 2). Tense and agreement are expressed via a single marker in the present.

Rule 2: Rules for marking present agreement

1SG	↔	-*m*
2SG, present	↔	-*s*
3SG, present	↔	-Ø
1PL	↔	-*nkʰ*
2PL	↔	-*kʰ*
3PL	↔	-*n*

Note that the 1PL suffix is underlyingly /-nkʰ/ and the nasal assimilates in place to become [-ŋkʰ] (§2.1.3). This plural morpheme is a reflex of Classical *-m-kʰ*. Compare modern [eŋkʰ] against Classical եմք <emkʼ> (Thomson 1989: 26).

The markers of the 1SG and the plurals do not specify tense. As we see later, these markers are used throughout Iranian Armenian for these person-number combinations.

As for the auxiliary itself (Rule 3), it has allomorphs /e/ and /ɒ/. For the present 3SG, the auxiliary is expressed by /ɒ/ without an extra tense marker. We later revise the marker rules for the auxiliary.

Rule 3: Rules for the form of the auxiliary verb 'to be' in the present (to be revised)

'be' or AUX	↔	ɒ-	/ _ PRS.3SG
		e-	/ elsewhere

6.2.2 Past auxiliary

For the present auxiliary, Standard Eastern and Iranian Armenian have few differences. But in the past form of the auxiliary, we find two major differences between the two lects. In Table 6.3, we provide zero markers for easier illustration. Note the glide is epenthetic.

Table 6.3: Paradigm of the past auxiliary in Standard Eastern and Iranian Armenian

	Without zero markers				With zero markers	
	SEA		IA		SEA	IA
1SG	ej-i 'I was'	t͡ʃʰ	i-m 'I was'	hʊ	ej-i-∅	∅-i-m
2SG	ej-i-ɾ	t͡ʃʰɲ	i-ɭ	hɲ	ej-i-ɾ	∅-i-ɭ
3SG	e-ɾ	t͡ʃɲ	e-ɭ	t͡ʃɲ	e-∅-ɾ	e-∅-ɭ
1PL	ej-i-ŋkʰ	t͡ʃʰʊɞ	i-ŋkʰ	hʊɞ	ej-i-ŋkʰ	∅-i-ŋkʰ
2PL	ej-i-kʰ	t͡ʃʰɞ	i-kʰ	hɞ	ej-i-kʰ	∅-i-kʰ
3PL	ej-i-n	t͡ʃʰʊ	i-n	hʊ	ej-i-n	∅-i-n
					AUX-PST-AGR	

Consider first the non-3SG forms. In Standard Eastern Armenian, the past form of the auxiliary is made up of three overt morphs: the auxiliary *e*, a past suffix *-i*, and then agreement. Tense and agreement are thus separate suffixes in the past. Vowel hiatus between the auxiliary and past suffix triggers glide epenthesis: 1PL /e-i-nkʰ/ → [ej-i-ŋkʰ]. In contrast, in Iranian Armenian, the auxiliary morpheme is covert in these contexts. Outside of the 3SG, there are only two overt morphs and these are the past suffix and the agreement suffix. For example, 1PL is [ej-i-ŋkʰ] in Standard Eastern but [i-ŋkʰ] in Iranian Armenian.

We analyze this difference as due to a morpheme-specific rule of vowel deletion in hiatus (Rule 4). This rule will delete the vowel *e* before the past morpheme *-i*. We call this rule *e-deletion*. The target of this rule is just a segment, while the trigger is a specific morph.

Rule 4: *e*-Deletion: Rule for deleting /e/ before past /i/

$$/e/ \; \rightarrow \; ∅ \; / \_ \, i$$

where *i* is the past suffix

In morphological theory, the use of morpheme-specific phonological processes is controversial (Pater 2007, Siddiqi 2009, Haugen & Siddiqi 2016, Haugen 2016, Embick & Shwayder 2018). There are two pieces of evidence for treating the absence of the auxiliary *-e-* as morpheme-specific phonology instead of allomorphy. First, in the 3SG, the past suffix is covert, and the auxiliary is overt: *e-∅-ɬ* instead of **∅-i-ɬ* or **∅-∅-ɬ*. It thus seems that the absence of the auxiliary is conditioned by making the past suffix an overt vowel. Second, we will see in the subjunctive past (§6.4.2) that the *-e-* theme vowel likewise deletes before the past *-i-* suffix. In sum, the above rule was possibly developed in Iranian Armenian as a morpheme-specific rule for repairing vowel hiatus.

Outside of Iranian Armenian, there are other Armenian dialects where the past auxiliary has this reduced form. For example, in 1911, the dialect of Armenian spoken in Yerevan had past auxiliaries like 3PL [∅-i-n] (Աճառեան 1911: 43; translated by Dolatian submitted). Such auxiliary forms were lost in Yerevan, due to the language shift from (Old) Yerevan Armenian to Standard Eastern Armenian. But they remain as grammaticalized in Iranian Armenian.

The second difference between the lects concerns the 1SG. In Standard Eastern, the Agr morph is covert: *e-i-∅* 'I was'. In Iranian Armenian, the Agr morph is an overt /m/: *∅-i-m*. This /m/ morph is the same suffix used in the present 1SG [e-m]. Thus this morph /m/ has a more general distribution in Iranian Armenian than in Standard Eastern. We list the rules for the 1SG below for the two lects for the two tenses (Rule 5).

The use of *-m* as a general 1SG marker is rather common in Armenian lects in Iran (Ջահուկյան 1972: p. 103, feature 100.6). See Vaux (2022b: 55–56) for useful maps on the spread of this phenomenon across Iran. For the spread of the *-m* morph, it is possible that a contributing factor is that Persian uses a morph *-æm* as a generalized 1SG marker for both the present and past (Mahootian 2002: 229ff).

Rule 5: Rules for the 1SG in the two lects

Standard Eastern	1SG	↔	*-∅*	/ in the past
			-m	/ elsewhere
Iranian Armenian	1SG	↔	*-m*	

We list below the additional rules that are needed for the Iranian Armenian 3SG (Rule 6). The past morph is covert in the 3SG: [e-∅-ɬ], while an overt /-i/

elsewhere. We do not need to list any rules for plural Agr, because they are the same as for the present (§6.2.1).

Rule 6: Rules for past tense and agreement in 3SG

PST	↔	-∅	/ in 3SG
		-i	/ elsewhere
singular non-1st person	↔	-ɫ	/ in the past

The past 2SG and 3SG are syncretic for the agreement suffix (Karakaş et al. 2021). They both use the morph -ɫ. The two paradigm cells are distinguished by tense being overt in the 2SG, but covert in the 3SG: ∅-*i*-ɫ 'you were' vs. *e*-∅-ɫ 'he was'.

6.2.3 Negation

The previous subsections described the inflection of the auxiliary in the positive. Negation is straightforwardly marked by adding the negation prefix $\widehat{tʃ^h}$-. However, we see some divergences in the present 3SG.

Table 6.4 shows the paradigm for the negated present auxiliary for Standard Eastern and Iranian Armenian. For all but the present 3SG, negation is marked by adding the negation prefix $\widehat{tʃ^h}$- to the auxiliary.

Table 6.4: Paradigm of negated present auxiliary in Standard Eastern and Iranian Armenian

Present: (NEG)-AUX-AGR							
	Standard Eastern				Iranian Armenian		
	Positive		Negaive		Positive		Negaive
1SG	e-m	եմ	$\widehat{tʃ^h}$-e-m	չեմ	e-m	եմ	$\widehat{tʃ^h}$-e-m	չեմ
2SG	e-s	ես	$\widehat{tʃ^h}$-e-s	չես	e-s	ես	$\widehat{tʃ^h}$-e-s	չես
3SG	e-∅	է	$\widehat{tʃ^h}$-i-∅	չի	ɒ-∅	ա	$\widehat{tʃ^h}$-i-∅	չի
1PL	e-ŋkʰ	ենք	$\widehat{tʃ^h}$-e-ŋkʰ	չենք	e-ŋkʰ	ենք	$\widehat{tʃ^h}$-e-ŋkʰ	չենք
2PL	e-kʰ	եք	$\widehat{tʃ^h}$-e-kʰ	չեք	e-kʰ	եք	$\widehat{tʃ^h}$-e-kʰ	չեք
3PL	e-n	են	$\widehat{tʃ^h}$-e-n	չեն	e-n	են	$\widehat{tʃ^h}$-e-n	չեն

Table 6.5 shows the paradigm of the negated past auxiliary. Negation is marked by adding the negation prefix.

Table 6.5: Paradigm of negated past auxiliary in Standard Eastern and Iranian Armenian

Past: (NEG)-AUX-PST-AGR								
	Standard Eastern				Iranian Armenian			
	Positive		Negaive		Positive		Negaive	
1SG	ej-i-∅	էի	t͡ʃʰ-ej-i-∅	չէի	∅-i-m	իմ	t͡ʃʰ-∅-i-m	չիմ
2SG	ej-i-r	էիր	t͡ʃʰ-ej-i-r	չէիր	∅-i-ɭ	իր	t͡ʃʰ-∅-i-ɭ	չիր
3SG	e-∅-r	էր	t͡ʃʰ-e-∅-r	չէր	e-∅-ɭ	էր	t͡ʃʰ-e-∅-ɭ	չէր
1PL	ej-i-ŋkʰ	էինք	t͡ʃʰ-ej-i-ŋkʰ	չէինք	∅-i-ŋkʰ	ինք	t͡ʃʰ-∅-i-ŋkʰ	չինք
2PL	ej-i-kʰ	էիք	t͡ʃʰ-ej-i-kʰ	չէիք	∅-i-kʰ	իք	t͡ʃʰ-∅-i-kʰ	չիք
3PL	ej-i-n	էին	t͡ʃʰ-ej-i-n	չէին	∅-i-n	ին	t͡ʃʰ-∅-i-n	չին

Differences emerge in the present 3SG. When used as a verbal auxiliary in Table 6.6, the positive form is /ɒ/ in Iranian Armenian, and /e/ in Standard Eastern. The negative form is /t͡ʃʰ-i/ for both lects. The negative auxiliary is placed before the verb.[3]

Table 6.6: Forms of negative auxiliary across Standard Eastern and Iranian Armenian

	Positive			Negaive		
SEA	jerkʰ-um	e	երգում է:	t͡ʃʰ-i	jerkʰ-um	չի երգում:
IA	je.ɭkʰ-um	ɒ	երգում ա:	t͡ʃʰ-i	je.ɭkʰ-um	չի երգում:
Gloss:	singing	is		NEG-is	singing	
	'He is singing.'			'He isn't singing.'		

But when used as a copula, we find more significant dialectal differences in Table 6.7. In both the positive and negative, the copula is placed after the predicate. The positive form is /ɒ/ in Iranian Armenian and /e/ in Standard Eastern, as expected. When negated, Standard Eastern uses /t͡ʃʰ-e/. In Iranian Armenian, speakers can use either /t͡ʃʰ-e/ or /t͡ʃʰ-i/. We call the use of /t͡ʃʰ-e/ the un-leveled form, while the use of /t͡ʃʰ-i/ is the leveled form. Such variation is also documented for Colloquial Eastern Armenian (Dum-Tragut 2009: 216).

---

[3]The complete gloss for the copula and auxiliary in the tables is AUX.PRS.3SG. The complete gloss for the verb 'singing' is sing-IMPF.CVB.

Table 6.7: Forms of negative copula across Standard Eastern and Iranian Armenian

	Positive			Negaive		
SEA	uɾɑχ	e	Ուրախ է:	uɾɑχ	t͡ʃʰ-e	Ուրախ չէ:
IA (un-leveled)	uɾɒχ	ɒ	Ուրախ ա:	uɾɒχ	t͡ʃʰ-e	Ուրախ չէ:
IA (leveled)	uɾɒχ	ɒ	Ուրախ ա:	uɾɒχ	t͡ʃʰ-i	Ուրախ չի:
Gloss:	happy	is		happy	NEG-is	
	'He is happy.'			'He isn't happy.'		

The above patterns require the following rules (Rule 7). For Standard Eastern, the verb 'to be' surfaces as /i/ only when it is an auxiliary, negative, and present 3SG. In all other contexts (including as a copula), it surfaces as the elsewhere morph /e/.

Rule 7: Rules for the auxiliary verb 'to be' in Standard Eastern

> 'be' or AUX ↔ i- / NEG _ PRS.3SG, used as verbal auxiliary
> (not a copula)
> e- / elsewhere

For Iranian Armenian, matters are slightly more complicated. Some speakers can use /i/ in the negative of both the auxiliary and the copula. All speakers use the form /ɒ/ in the positive of both the auxiliary and copula. This simpler leveled system uses the rules below (Rule 8). The rule for /i/ simply does not reference the auxiliary vs. copula status of the verb. The verb surfaces as [ɒ] in the positive present 3SG, and as [e] elsewhere.

Rule 8: Rules for the auxiliary verb 'to be' in Iranian Armenian with full leveling

> 'be' or AUX ↔ i- / NEG _ PRS.3SG
> ɒ- / _ PRS.3SG
> e- / elsewhere

As for the speakers who have not leveled the negative copula towards the negative auxiliary, they need the more complicated system below (Rule 9). These speakers use /i/ for the negative auxiliary, /ɒ/ for the positive verb, and /e/ elsewhere.

Rule 9: Rules for the auxiliary verb 'to be' without leveling

'be' or AUX ↔ i-   / NEG _ PRS.3SG, used as auxiliary verb
                        (not as copula)
              ɒ-   / _ PRS.3SG
              e-   / elsewhere

6.3 Periphrastic structures

Iranian Armenian uses periphrasis to realize most tense-aspect-mood combinations. These periphrastic forms all utilize a special form of the verb called the converb. Tense and agreement are marked on the auxiliary. The auxiliary follows the converb in the positive, and it precedes the converb in the negative.[4] Note that the future is marked with both synthetic and periphrastic constructions, discussed in §6.5.

Throughout this grammar, we reserve the term "converb" for non-finite verb forms that are restricted to verbal periphrasis. We use the term "participle" for non-finite verb forms that can be used outside of periphrasis. This seems to be the intuition behind the use of these terms in the Eastern Armenian National Corpus.[5]

6.3.1 Indicative present and past imperfective

The first periphrastic construction that we describe is the indicative imperfective forms, called [sahmanakan jeʁanak] սահմանական եղանակ in Standard Eastern Armenian. This construction is used in the indicative present and the indicative past imperfective (also called the past imperfect). This construction is formed identically in Standard Eastern and Iranian Armenian.

The verb is in a converb form called the imperfective converb (2). Some grammars also use the term present participle (Dum-Tragut 2009: 219). In Standard

---

[4]The auxiliary can further move around the sentence because of focus and other syntactic factors (§3.3.1).
[5]eanc.net/

Eastern Armenian, this converb is called [aŋkɑtɑɾ deɾbɑj] անկատար դերբայ. Given the infinitive for a verb like *jeɹkʰ-e-l* 'to sing', the imperfective converb is formed by replacing the theme vowel and infinitive with the suffix *-um*: *jeɹkʰ-um*. Tense and subject agreement are marked on the auxiliary. The present auxiliary is used to form the indicative present; the past auxiliary is used to form the indicative past imperfective.

(2) a. jeɹkʰ-um   e-ŋkʰ
         sing-IMPF.CVB AUX-1PL
         'We are singing.'   (NK)
         երգում ենք:

     b. jeɹkʰ-um   Ø-i-ŋkʰ
         sing-IMPF.CVB AUX-PST-1PL
         'We were singing.'   (NK)
         երգում իևք:

Negation is marked by placing the negated form of the auxiliary before the converb (3).

(3) a. t͡ʃʰ-e-ŋkʰ   jeɹkʰ-um
         NEG-AUX-1PL sing-IMPF.CVB
         'We are not singing.'   (NK)
         Չենք երգում:

     b. t͡ʃʰ-Ø-i-ŋkʰ   jeɹkʰ-um
         NEG-AUX-PST-1PL sing-IMPF.CVB
         'We were not singing.'   (NK)
         Չինք երգում:

The two conjugation classes (E-Class and A-Class) do not differ in constructing the imperfective converb, e.g., the converb of *kɒɹtʰ-ɒ-l* 'to read' is *kɒɹtʰ-um*. All tense-number-person combinations are straightforwardly marked by using the appropriate inflected auxiliary. The complete paradigm is given in Table 6.8. For clarity of presentation, we do not segment the internal structure of the auxiliary.

The imperfective converb suffix is simply *-um*. If we assume that the theme vowels /e, ɒ/ are underlyingly present, then we need a rule that deletes the theme vowels before the converb suffix, as a type of morpheme-specific vowel hiatus repair (Rule 10). For example, /jeɹkʰ-e-um/ → [jeɹkʰ-Ø-um].

Rule 10: Deleting theme vowels before the converb suffix

$$V \rightarrow \emptyset \ / \ \_ V_2 \quad \text{(where } V_2 \text{ is part of a converb suffix)}$$

Table 6.8: Paradigm for indicative present and indicative past imperfective for E-Class [jeɹkʰ-e-l] 'to sing'

	Positive			Negaive			
	Indc. present		Indc. past imperf.		Indc. present		Indc. past imperf.
1SG	jeɹkʰ-um	em	jeɹkʰ-um	im	t͡ʃʰ-em	jeɹkʰ-um	t͡ʃʰ-im	jeɹkʰ-um
	'I am singing'		'I was singing'		'I am not singing'		'I was not singing'	
	երգում	եմ	երգում	իմ	չեմ	երգում	չիմ	երգում
2SG	jeɹkʰ-um	es	jeɹkʰ-um	iɹ	t͡ʃʰ-es	jeɹkʰ-um	t͡ʃʰ-iɹ	jeɹkʰ-um
	երգում	ես	երգում	իր	չես	երգում	չիր	երգում
3SG	jeɹkʰ-um	ɒ	jeɹkʰ-um	eɹ	t͡ʃʰ-i	jeɹkʰ-um	t͡ʃʰ-eɹ	jeɹkʰ-um
	երգում	ա	երգում	էր	չի	երգում	չէր	երգում
1PL	jeɹkʰ-um	eŋkʰ	jeɹkʰ-um	iŋkʰ	t͡ʃʰ-eŋkʰ	jeɹkʰ-um	t͡ʃʰ-iŋkʰ	jeɹkʰ-um
	երգում		երգում	ինք	չենք	երգում	չինք	երգում
2PL	jeɹkʰ-um	ekʰ	jeɹkʰ-um	ikʰ	t͡ʃʰ-ekʰ	jeɹkʰ-um	t͡ʃʰ-ikʰ	jeɹkʰ-um
	երգում	էք	երգում	իք	չէք	երգում	չիք	երգում
3PL	jeɹkʰ-um	en	jeɹkʰ-um	in	t͡ʃʰ-en	jeɹkʰ-um	t͡ʃʰ-in	jeɹkʰ-um
	երգում	են	երգում	ին	չեն	երգում	չին	երգում
	√-IMPF.CVB AUX				NEG-AUX √-IMPF.CVB			

6.3.2 Present perfect and pluperfect

The next periphrastic construction that we discuss is the periphrastic perfective. Like the other periphrastic forms, this construction utilizes a special converb and the inflected auxiliary. The converb is called the perfective converb. Some grammars also use the term perfect participle (Dum-Tragut 2009: 213) or past participle (Աճառեան 1911, Dolatian submitted). It is called [vaʁakataɹ deɹbaj] վաղակատար դերբայ in Standard Eastern Armenian.

The perfective converb has subtle differences across the two lects (Table 6.9). In Standard Eastern Armenian, the perfective converb is formed by adding the suffix *-el*. The theme vowel is deleted thanks to the vowel-hiatus rule in Rule 10. In Iranian Armenian, this suffix is *-el* or *-eɹ*. AS and NK report that *-eɹ* form is more common among younger generations than older ones.[6]

Table 6.9: Liquid quality of the perfective converb in Standard Eastern and Iranian Armenian for E-Class 'to sing'

	Infinitive	Perfective converb
Standard Eastern	jeɾkʰ-e-l	jeɾkʰ-el
Iranian Armenian	jeɹkʰ-e-l	jeɹkʰ-el
		jeɹkʰ-eɹ
	√-TH-INF	√-PERF.CVB
	երգել	երգել, երգեր

For the same speaker, the choice of liquid can vary between [-el] or [-eɹ] without semantic motivation (4). It is possible that [-el] feels more formal for our speakers.

(4) es jeɹkʰ-ə   voɹ mɒm-itsʰ sovoɹ-eɹ/el   e-m
     this song-DEF that mom-ABL learn-PERF.CVB AUX-1SG
     'This song that I learned from my mom.'   (NK)
     Էս երգը որ մամից սովորեր/սովորել եմ:

In some social phrases, AS reports that the liquid is conventionally a lateral (5).

(5) kɒɹot-el   =e-m   kʰez
     miss-PERF.CVB =AUX-1SG you.SG.DAT
     'I've missed you.'   (AS)
     Կարոտել եմ քեզ:

Diachronically, the rhotic form [-eɹ] may have developed from the lateral form [-el]. This development has been attested in other Armenian lects (Գրիգորյան 2018).

AS reports that some archaic registers use the form [-i], such as (6). We found this sentence in our transcribed sample text, uttered by an actor who was putting on an archaic accent.

---

[6]The variation has some connections with geography. Osik Movses, an Iranian Armenian speaker from Tehran, informs us that some Tehran neighborhoods use the [-eɹ] form because these speakers' ancestors originate from villages that used such a form.

(6) vɒksɒn e-n   t͡ʃɒɹ-i
     vaccine AUX-3PL find-PERF.CVB
     'They've found a vaccine.'
     <vaccine> են ճարի:

Iranian Armenian has grammaticalized a process of liquid deletion for the perfective converb suffix [-eɹ] or [-el] (Table 6.10). When this suffix is used in the
positive before the inflected auxiliary, the liquid surfaces. But when the auxiliary
has shifted leftward as in negation, the suffix's liquid is deleted, and sometimes
pronounced as [h].

Table 6.10: Perfective converb in Standard Eastern and Iranian Armenian for the E-Class verb 'to sing'

		Positive present perfect 1SG		Negative present perfect 1SG	
SEA		jeɾkʰ-el	em	t͡ʃʰ-em	jeɾkʰ-el
		երգել եմ:		չեմ երգել:	
IA		jeɹkʰ-el	em	t͡ʃʰ-em	jeɹkʰ-e
		երգել եմ:		չեմ երգէ:	
		jeɹkʰ-eɹ	em	t͡ʃʰ-em	jeɹkʰ-eh
		երգեր եմ:		չեմ երգէ:	
		√-PERF.CVB	AUX	NEG-AUX	√-PERF.CVB
		'I have sung.'		'I have not sung.'	

The behavior of the perfective suffix in Iranian Armenian suggests that the
final liquid is a floating segment or latent segment: *-e(l)* or *-e(ɹ)* (cf. ghost consonants: Tranel 1996, Côté 2011, Zimmermann 2019). The above paradigm suggests
that the liquid is licensed when it is followed by the auxiliary. The conditions for
surfacing or deleting this liquid are discussed in §3.3. For now, we just provide
the relevant rules (Rule 11).

Rule 11: Rule for the perfective converb

PERF.CVB ↔ -e(l) / (older speakers)
              -e(ɹ) / (some younger speakers)

The above data concerns constructing the perfective converb for the E-Class. In the A-Class, the same suffix is used. However, a meaningless affix $-\widehat{ts^h}$- is added between the theme vowel and the converb suffix (Table 6.11).

Table 6.11: Perfective converb in Standard Eastern and Iranian Armenian for the E-Class vs. A-Class verb

	E-Class		A-Class	
	Infinitive	Pfv. converb	Infinitive	Pfv. converb
	երգել	երգել, երգեր	կարդալ	կարդացել, կարդացեր
SEA	jeɾkʰ-e-l	jeɾkʰ-el	kaɾtʰ-a-l	kaɾtʰ-a-t͡sʰ-el
IA	jeɹkʰ-e-l	jeɹkʰ-el	kɒɹtʰ-ɒ-l	kɒɹtʰ-ɒ-t͡sʰ-el
		jeɹkʰ-eɹ		kɒɹtʰ-ɒ-t͡sʰ-eɹ
	√-TH-INF	√-PERF.CVB	√-TH-INF	√-TH-AOR-PERF.CVB

In the traditional literature on Armenian, the meaningless $-\widehat{ts^h}$- is called the aorist suffix. We gloss the additional meaningless suffix $\widehat{ts^h}$ as AOR. The suffix is used to mark synthetic past perfective verbs for the A-Class, but it is also used meaninglessly in other constructions. In the case of the perfective converb, this $-\widehat{ts^h}$- is being used morphomically. The use of this suffix in the A-Class perfective converb is treated as using an aorist stem. Such a stem is morphomic (Aronoff 1994). For a discussion and analysis of aorist stems in Armenian, see Dolatian & Guekguezian (2022a). In this grammar, we do not provide rules for generating this meaningless aorist suffix. For descriptive purposes, the full paradigm is given in Table 6.12 for the E-Class.

When the perfective converb is used with the present auxiliary, the construction denotes the present perfect. If we use the past auxiliary, then the construction denotes the pluperfect. The paradigm for the A-Class 'to read' is analogously constructed with the converb [kɒɹtʰ-ɒ-t͡sʰ-el]. We do not segment the auxiliary. As before, the auxiliary shifts its position in the negated form.

6.3.3 Simultaneous converb

Standard Eastern Armenian has an additional periphrastic construction that uses the simultaneous converb (Table 6.13), also called the processual participle (Dum-Tragut 2009: 205). The converb is called [hamakataɾ deɾbaj] համակատար դերբայ in Standard Eastern Armenian. This converb is built by adding the suffix *-is* to infinitives. This construction is quite infrequent in Standard Eastern Armenian.

Table 6.12: Paradigm for the present perfect and the pluperfect for E-Class [je.ɻkʰ-e-l] 'to sing'

	Positive		Negaive	
	Present perfect	Pluperfect	Present perfect	Pluperfect
1SG	je.ɻkʰ-el em je.ɻkʰ-eɻ em 'I have sung' երգել եմ երգեր եմ	je.ɻkʰ-el im je.ɻkʰ-eɻ im 'I had sung' երգել իմ երգեր իմ	tʃʰ-em je.ɻkʰ-e 'I haven't sung' չեմ երգե չեմ երգե	tʃʰ-im je.ɻkʰ-e 'I hadn't sung' չիմ երգե չիմ երգե
2SG	je.ɻkʰ-el es je.ɻkʰ-eɻ es երգել ես երգեր ես	je.ɻkʰ-el iɻ je.ɻkʰ-eɻ iɻ երգել իր երգեր իր	tʃʰ-es je.ɻkʰ-e չես երգե չես երգե	tʃʰ-iɻ je.ɻkʰ-e չիր երգե չիր երգե
3SG	je.ɻkʰ-el ɒ je.ɻkʰ-eɻ ɒ երգել ա երգեր ա	je.ɻkʰ-el eɻ je.ɻkʰ-eɻ eɻ երգել էր երգեր էր	tʃʰ-i je.ɻkʰ-e չի երգե չի երգե	tʃʰ-eɻ je.ɻkʰ-e չէր երգե չէր երգե
1PL	je.ɻkʰ-el eŋkʰ je.ɻkʰ-eɻ eŋkʰ երգել ենք երգեր ենք	je.ɻkʰ-el iŋkʰ je.ɻkʰ-eɻ iŋkʰ երգել ինք երգեր ինք	tʃʰ-eŋkʰ je.ɻkʰ-e չենք երգե չենք երգե	tʃʰ-iŋkʰ je.ɻkʰ-e չինք երգե չինք երգե
2PL	je.ɻkʰ-el ekʰ je.ɻkʰ-eɻ ekʰ երգել եք երգեր եք	je.ɻkʰ-el ikʰ je.ɻkʰ-eɻ ikʰ երգել իք երգեր իք	tʃʰ-ekʰ je.ɻkʰ-e չեք երգե չեք երգե	tʃʰ-ikʰ je.ɻkʰ-e չիք երգե չիք երգե
3PL	je.ɻkʰ-el en je.ɻkʰ-eɻ en երգել են երգեր են	je.ɻkʰ-el in je.ɻkʰ-eɻ in երգել ին երգեր ին	tʃʰ-en je.ɻkʰ-e չեն երգե չեն երգե	tʃʰ-in je.ɻkʰ-e չին երգե չին երգե
	√-PERF.CVB AUX		NEG-AUX √-PERF.CVB	

For Iranian Armenian, NK reports that she never uses this participle, while KM reports that she does use it. AS reports that his consultants never use it. We do not report further on this converb because of the the limited data available to us.

Table 6.13: Forming the simultaneous converb

E-Class 'to sing'		A-Class 'to read'	
Infinitive	Simultaneous converb	Infinitive	Simultaneous converb
jeɹkʰ-e-l	jeɹkʰ-e-l-is	kɒɹtʰ-ɒ-l	kɒɹtʰ-ɒ-l-is
√-TH-INF	√-TH-INF-SIM.CVB	√-TH-INF	√-TH-INF-SIM.CVB
երգել	երգելիս	կարդալ	կարդալիս

6.4 Synthetic forms

A large chunk of Iranian Armenian verbal inflection is handled via periphrasis. There are however some pockets of synthetic constructions. These include the aorist (past perfective), subjunctives, and imperatives. Prohibitives are derived from imperatives via the addition of a particle. Note that the future is marked with both synthetic and periphrastic constructions, discussed in §6.5.

6.4.1 Past perfective or aorist form

Impressionistically, the past perfective or aorist is the most common synthetic construction. It is used to denote the simple past. But as the examples in Table 6.14 illustrate, the two classes use markedly different affixes to generate the past perfective. The past perfective of the A-Class is formed in essentially the same way for the two lects, while the E-Class uses a markedly different construction.

The name of the past perfective is [antsʰjal katarjal] անցյալ կատարյալ in Standard Eastern Armenian.

We first describe the A-Class in Iranian Armenian, whose past perfective is formed essentially the same in Standard Eastern. The past perfective is formed by taking the stem of the A-Class (root and theme vowel), and adding the aorist suffix -tsʰ-. The -tsʰ- is a marker of perfectivity (Donabédian 2016). We then add the past marker /i/ and agreement markers. For brevity, we say that A-Class verbs use the /-tsʰ-i/ template for marking the past perfective. We gloss -tsʰ- as -AOR- both in the past perfective (where it is meaningful) and in non-past paradigms, as in the perfective converb of the A-Class (§6.3.2).

Table 6.14: Past perfective 1PL for E-Class and A-Class

| | E-Class | | A-Class | |
	IA	SEA	IA	SEA
Infinitive	jeɹkʰ-e-l	jeɾkʰ-e-l	kɒɹtʰ-ɒ-l	kaɾtʰ-a-l
	√-TH-INF	√-TH-INF	√-TH-INF	√-TH-INF
	'to sing'	'to sing'	'to read'	'to read'
	երգել	երգել	կարդալ	կարդալ
Past Pfv.	jeɹkʰ-ɒ-ŋkʰ	jeɾkʰ-e-t͡sʰ-i-ŋkʰ	kɒɹtʰ-ɒ-t͡sʰ-i-ŋkʰ	kaɾtʰ-a-t͡sʰ-i-ŋkʰ
	√-PST-1PL	√-TH-AOR-PST-1PL	√-TH-AOR-PST-1PL	√-TH-AOR-PST-1PL
	'we sang'	'we sang'	'we read (past)'	'we read (past)'
	երգանք	երգեցինք	կարդացինք	կարդացինք

The complete paradigm is shown in Table 6.15 for the A-Class in Standard Eastern and Iranian Armenian. Negation is formed by adding the prefix $\widehat{tʃ}$-, which surfaces with a schwa before consonant-initial verbs. The only morphological difference between the two lects is that the 1SG marker /-m/ is used in Iranian Armenian (§6.2.2), while Standard Eastern uses a zero suffix.

Table 6.15: Paradigm of past perfective of A-Class [kɒɹtʰ-ɒ-l] 'to read' in Standard Eastern and Iranian Armenian

| | Positive | | Negative | |
	SEA	IA	SEA	IA
1SG	kaɾtʰ-a-t͡sʰ-i	kɒɹtʰ-ɒ-t͡sʰ-i-m	t͡ʃʰə-kaɾtʰ-a-t͡sʰ-i	t͡ʃʰə-kɒɹtʰ-ɒ-t͡sʰ-i-m
	'I read (past)'	'I read (past)'	'I did not read'	'I did not read'
	կարդացի	կարդացիմ	չկարդացի	չկարդացիմ
2SG	kaɾtʰ-a-t͡sʰ-i-ɾ	kɒɹtʰ-ɒ-t͡sʰ-i-ɭ	t͡ʃʰə-kaɾtʰ-a-t͡sʰ-i-ɾ	t͡ʃʰə-kɒɹtʰ-ɒ-t͡sʰ-i-ɭ
	կարդացիր	կարդացիր	չկարդացիր	չկարդացիր
3SG	kaɾtʰ-a-t͡sʰ	kɒɹtʰ-ɒ-t͡sʰ	t͡ʃʰə-kaɾtʰ-a-t͡sʰ	t͡ʃʰə-kɒɹtʰ-ɒ-t͡sʰ
	կարդաց	կարդաց	չկարդաց	չկարդաց
1PL	kaɾtʰ-a-t͡sʰ-i-ŋkʰ	kɒɹtʰ-ɒ-t͡sʰ-i-ŋkʰ	t͡ʃʰə-kaɾtʰ-a-t͡sʰ-i-ŋkʰ	t͡ʃʰə-kɒɹtʰ-ɒ-t͡sʰ-i-ŋkʰ
	կարդացինք	կարդացինք	չկարդացինք	չկարդացինք
2PL	kaɾtʰ-a-t͡sʰ-i-kʰ	kɒɹtʰ-ɒ-t͡sʰ-i-kʰ	t͡ʃʰə-kaɾtʰ-a-t͡sʰ-i-kʰ	t͡ʃʰə-kɒɹtʰ-ɒ-t͡sʰ-i-kʰ
	կարդացիք	կարդացիք	չկարդացիք	չկարդացիք
3PL	kaɾtʰ-a-t͡sʰ-i-n	kɒɹtʰ-ɒ-t͡sʰ-i-n	t͡ʃʰə-kaɾtʰ-a-t͡sʰ-i-n	t͡ʃʰə-kɒɹtʰ-ɒ-t͡sʰ-i-n
	կարդացին	կարդացին	չկարդացին	չկարդացին
	√-TH-AOR-PST-AGR		NEG-√-TH-AOR-PST-AGR	

For illustration, Table 6.16 provides a fuller segmentation that shows zero markers for the positive. For contrast, we also repeat the paradigm of the past auxiliary.

Table 6.16: Full segmentation of past perfective for A-Class [kɒɹtʰ-ɒ-l] 'to read' and past auxiliary

	Past Pfv. with zero markers		Past auxiliary	
1SG	kɒɹtʰ-ɒ-t͡sʰ-i-m	կարդացիմ	Ø-i-m	իմ
2SG	kɒɹtʰ-ɒ-t͡sʰ-i-ɹ	կարդացիր	Ø-i-ɹ	իր
3SG	kɒɹtʰ-ɒ-t͡sʰ-Ø-Ø	կարդաց	e-Ø-ɹ	էր
1PL	kɒɹtʰ-ɒ-t͡sʰ-i-ŋkʰ	կարդացինք	Ø-i-ŋkʰ	ինք
2PL	kɒɹtʰ-ɒ-t͡sʰ-i-kʰ	կարդացիք	Ø-i-kʰ	իք
3PL	kɒɹtʰ-ɒ-t͡sʰ-i-n	կարդացին	Ø-i-n	ին
	√-TH-AOR-PST-AGR		AUX-PST-AGR	

For the past perfective in the 3SG, both the past suffix and the agreement suffix are covert. Elsewhere for the A-Class, the past suffix is /i/ in the past perfective, just as in past auxiliaries. Outside of the 3SG, the agreement morphs likewise match the morphs used in the past auxiliary: *i-ŋkʰ* 'we were'. We list below some other example A-Class words in the past perfective that we have collected (Table 6.17).

Table 6.17: Past perfective form of some A-Class verbs

Infinitive		Past perfective		
IA		IA	SEA	
ʒəpt-ɒ-l ժպտալ	'to smile'	ʒəpt-ɒ-t͡sʰ-i-ɹ ժպտացիր	ʒəpt-a-t͡sʰ-i-r ժպտացիր	'You.SG smiled'
hɒvɒt-ɒ-l հավատալ	'to believe'	hɒvɒt-ɒ-t͡sʰ-i-m հավատացիմ	havat-a-t͡sʰ-i-Ø հավատացի	'I believed'
√-TH-INF		√-TH-AOR-PST-AGR		

For the E-Class, the past perfective has a more complicated construction. In Standard Eastern, the past perfective is formed in the same way as for the A-Class, except for a difference in theme vowel: [jeɹkʰ-e-t͡sʰ-i-ŋkʰ] 'we sang'. Thus the Standard Eastern E-Class uses the template /-t͡sʰ-i/. In contrast, the Iranian Armenian form drops the theme vowel and the aorist, and uses a different past allomorph /ɒ/: [jeɹkʰ-ɒ-ŋkʰ] 'we sang'. For brevity, we say that the Iranian Armenian E-Class uses the template /-∅-ɒ/ where -∅ is a covert perfective or aorist marker.

The paradigm is given below for both lects (Table 6.18). The negative is formed by just adding the negation prefix t͡ʃʰə-. In order to save space we do not show zero morphs. In the 3SG of the E-Class, Iranian Armenian uses an overt /ɒ/ morph for past, and /v/ for agreement. Standard Eastern uses covert nodes for both. The 1SG uses an overt agreement morph /m/ in Iranian Armenian, but covert in Standard Eastern.

Table 6.18: Paradigm of past perfective of E-Class 'to sing' in both lects

	Standard Eastern		Iranian Armenian	
	Positive	Negative	Positive	Negative
1SG	jerkʰ-e-t͡sʰ-i	t͡ʃʰə-jerkʰ-e-t͡sʰ-i	jeɹkʰ-ɒ-m	t͡ʃʰə-jeɹkʰ-ɒ-m
	'I sang'	'I did not sing'	'I sang'	'I did not sing'
	երգեցի	չերգեցի	երգամ	չերգամ
2SG	jerkʰ-e-t͡sʰ-i-r	t͡ʃʰə-jerkʰ-e-t͡sʰ-i-r	jeɹkʰ-ɒ-ɹ	t͡ʃʰə-jeɹkʰ-ɒ-ɹ
	երգեցիր	չերգեցիր	երգար	չերգար
3SG	jerkʰ-e-t͡sʰ	t͡ʃʰə-jerkʰ-e-t͡sʰ	jeɹkʰ-ɒ-v	t͡ʃʰə-jeɹkʰ-ɒ-v
	երգեց	չերգեց	երգաւ	չերգաւ
1PL	jerkʰ-e-t͡sʰ-i-ŋkʰ	t͡ʃʰə-jerkʰ-e-t͡sʰ-i-ŋkʰ	jeɹkʰ-ɒ-ŋkʰ	t͡ʃʰə-jeɹkʰ-ɒ-ŋkʰ
	երգեցիինք	չերգեցինք	երգանք	չերգանք
2PL	jerkʰ-e-t͡sʰ-i-kʰ	t͡ʃʰə-jerkʰ-e-t͡sʰ-i-kʰ	jeɹkʰ-ɒ-kʰ	t͡ʃʰə-jeɹkʰ-ɒ-kʰ
	երգեցիք	չերգեցիք	երգաք	չերգաք
3PL	jerkʰ-e-t͡sʰ-i-n	t͡ʃʰə-jerkʰ-e-t͡sʰ-i-n	jeɹkʰ-ɒ-n	t͡ʃʰə-jeɹkʰ-ɒ-n
	երգեցին	չերգեցին	երգան	չերգան
	(NEG)-√-TH-AOR-PST-AGR		(NEG)-√-PST-AGR	

To showcase the widespread difference between Standard Eastern and Iranian Armenian for the E-Class perfective, Table 6.19 lists some frequent E-Class verbs, and an example past perfective form.

Table 6.19: Past perfective form of some E-Class verbs

Infinitive		Past perfective form			
Iranian Armenian		Iranian Armenian		Standard Eastern Armenian	
χəm-e-l	խմել	χəm-ɒ-m	խմամ	χəm-e-t͡sʰ-i	խմեցի	'I drank'
t͡sɒk-e-l	ծակել	t͡sɒk-ɒ-ɹ	ծակար	t͡sak-e-t͡sʰ-i-r	ծակեցիր	'you.sg made a hole'
t͡sɒχ-e-l	ծախել	t͡sɒχ-ɒ-v	ծախավ	t͡sɒχ-e-t͡sʰ	ծախեց	'he sold'
voɹoʃ-e-l	որոշել	voɹoʃ-ɒ-v	որոշավ	voroʃ-e-t͡sʰ	որոշեց	'he decided'
kɒnt͡ʃʰ-e-l	կանչել	kɒnt͡ʃʰ-ɒ-v	կանչավ	kant͡ʃʰ-e-t͡sʰ	կանչեց	'he called'
mekn-e-l	մեկնել	mekn-ɒ-v	մեկնավ	mekn-e-t͡sʰ	մեկնեց	'he went away'
bərn-e-l	բռնել	bərn-ɒ-v	բռնավ	bərn-e-t͡sʰ	բռնեց	'he caught'
kɒŋg(ə)n-e-l	կանգնել	kɒŋg(ə)n-ɒ-v	կանգնավ	kaŋgn-e-t͡sʰ	կանգնեց	'he stood'
kʰɒjl-e-l	քայլել	kʰɒjl-ɒ-v	քայլավ	kʰajl-e-t͡sʰ	քայլեց	'he walked'
uʁɒɹk-e-l	ուղարկել	uʁɒɹk-ɒ-ŋkʰ	ուղարկանք	uʁark-e-t͡sʰ-i-ŋkʰ	ուղարկեցինք	'we sent'
ɒpɹ-e-l	ապրել	ɒpɹ-ɒ-kʰ	ապրաք	apr-e-t͡sʰ-i-kʰ	ապրեցիք	'you.PL lived'
gəɹ-e-l	գրել	gəɹ-ɒ-n	գրան	gər-e-t͡sʰ-i-n	գրեցին	'they wrote'
√-TH-INF		√-PST-2SG		√-TH-AOR-PST-AGR		

In terms of morphological structure, we assume that the Iranian Armenian past perfective of the E-Class contains a covert aorist perfective suffix to license perfective meaning. The theme vowel is then deleted before the /ɒ/ vowel as a morpheme-specific rule of vowel-hiatus repair (Rule 12).

We show below the underlying and surface structure of the past perfective 1PL for both the A-Class and E-Class in Iranian Armenian (Table 6.20). The aorist suffix marks perfective aspect ASP.

Rule 12: Delete theme vowels before the past suffix /ɒ/

$$/e/ \quad \rightarrow \quad \emptyset \quad / \_ \, ɒ$$

(where /e/ is a theme vowel, and /ɒ/ is a past marker)

Before we provide complete rules for these morphemes in Iranian Armenian, readers might wonder about the origin of this /ɒ/ morph. In Standard Eastern, the cognate of this morph is the past morph /a/. This /a/ is restricted to certain irregular classes and in some regular complex verbs such as inchoatives. In fact, the /a/ morph is treated as the restricted or marked past allomorph in Standard Eastern and in Western Armenian (Dolatian & Guekguezian 2022b, Karakaş et al. 2021), while /i/ is the elsewhere morph. In contrast, in Iranian Armenian, the /ɒ/ morph has developed a larger distribution, while /i/ shrank in its distribution.

Table 6.20: Underlying and surface structure of past perfective 1PL in Iranian Armenian

A-Class Underlying and surface	E-Class Underlying	Surface
'we read' /kɒɹtʰ-ɒ-t͡sʰ-i-ŋkʰ/	'we sang' /jeɹkʰ-e-∅-ɒ-ŋkʰ/	→ [jeɹkʰ-∅-∅-ɒ-ŋkʰ]

A-Class tree:

AGR
- T
  - ASP
    - TH
      - √ — TH
    - AOR
  - T
- AGR

√ TH AOR T AGR
kɒɹtʰ -ɒ -t͡sʰ -i -ŋkʰ

E-Class Underlying tree:

AGR
- T
  - ASP
    - TH
      - √ — TH
    - AOR
  - T
- AGR

√ TH AOR T AGR
jeɹkʰ -e -∅ -ɒ -ŋkʰ

Surface tree:

AGR
- T
  - ASP
    - TH
      - √ — TH
    - AOR
  - T
- AGR

√ TH AOR T AGR
jeɹkʰ -∅ -∅ -ɒ -ŋkʰ

Similarly for the aorist/perfective suffix, the morph /t͡sʰ/ is the elsewhere morph in Standard Eastern, while a covert -∅ is restricted to some irregular verbs.

Table 6.21 illustrates the distribution of these four morphs. For Standard Eastern, the perfective-past sequence of morphs is /-t͡sʰ-i/ for E-Class and A-Class verbs, while this sequence is /-∅-ɑ/ for suppletive verbs like *ut-e-l* 'to eat'. In contrast, for Iranian Armenian, the /∅-ɒ/ sequence is now generalized to the perfective of E-Class, while /-t͡sʰ-i/ shrank in its distribution. We show the deleted theme vowels and covert aspect.

It is a separate diachronic question to determine what caused these changes. One possible source is that the /ɑ/ morph is used in high-frequency irregular and suppletive verbs in Standard Eastern Armenian. Iranian Armenian speakers thus generalized the distribution of /ɑ, ɒ/ from high-frequency verbs to regular verbs, as illustrated above. Such a diachronic change is attested across different Armenian lects of Iran (Աճառյան 1961: 201, Martirosyan 2018) and Colloquial Eastern Armenian in Yerevan (Dum-Tragut 2009: 230 citing Ղարագյուլյան 1981: 98, Ավետյան 2020). Tehrani Iranian Armenian is special in how wide-scale this change is.[7]

---

[7]Some dialectological sources are more vague because they conflate the use of a zero perfective -∅ with a past /-ɑ, -ɒ/ (Ջահուկյան 1972: p. 102, feature 95).

Table 6.21: Past perfective 1PL for E-Class, A-Class, and suppletive verbs

	A-Class 'we read'	E-Class 'we sang'	Suppletive 'we ate'
SEA	karᵗʰ-a-t͡sʰ-i-ŋkʰ $\sqrt{}$-TH-AOR-PST-1PL կարդացինք	jeɾkʰ-e-t͡sʰ-i-ŋkʰ $\sqrt{}$-TH-AOR-PST-1PL երգեցինք	keɾ-∅-∅-**a**-ŋkʰ $\sqrt{}$-TH-AOR-PST-1PL կերանք
IA	kɒɹtʰ-ɒ-t͡sʰ-i-ŋkʰ $\sqrt{}$-TH-AOR-PST-1PL կարդացինք	jeɹkʰ-∅-∅-**ɒ**-ŋkʰ $\sqrt{}$-TH-AOR-PST-1PL երգանք	keɹ-∅-∅-**ɒ**-ŋkʰ $\sqrt{}$-TH-AOR-PST-1PL կերանք

We leave a full-scale diachronic investigation to future work. For now, we focus on a synchronic analysis of Iranian Armenian.[8] The generalization is that in Standard Eastern, the default template for the past perfective is /-t͡sʰ-i/, while it is /-∅-ɒ/ in Iranian Armenian. In auxiliaries and in the subjunctive past (§6.4.2), the past is uniformly just /-i/ for all classes (Table 6.22); it is zero for the 3SG.

Table 6.22: Infinitive and subjunctive past forms

		A-Class 'to read'	E-Class 'to sing'	Suppletive 'to eat'	
Inf.	SEA	karᵗʰ-a-l	jeɾkʰ-e-l	ut-e-l	$\sqrt{}$-TH-INF
	IA	kɒɹtʰ-ɒ-l	jeɹkʰ-e-l	ut-e-l	$\sqrt{}$-TH-INF
		կարդալ	երգել	ուտել	
Sbjv. Past 3PL	SEA	karᵗʰ-aj-i-n	jeɾkʰ-ej-i-n	ut-ej-i-n	$\sqrt{}$-TH-PST-3PL
	IA	kɒɹtʰ-ɒj-i-n	jeɹkʰ-∅-i-n	ut-∅-i-n	$\sqrt{}$-TH-PST-3PL
		կարդային	երգեին, երգին	ուտեին, ուտին	
Sbjv. Past 3SG	SEA	karᵗʰ-a-∅-r	jeɾkʰ-e-∅-r	ut-e-∅-r	$\sqrt{}$-TH-PST-3SG
	IA	kɒɹtʰ-ɒ-∅-ɹ	jeɹkʰ-e-∅-ɹ	ut-e-∅-ɹ	$\sqrt{}$-TH-PST-3SG
		կարդար	երգէր, երգէր	ուտէր, ուտէր	

---

[8]For the perfective of the A-Class, one could argue that the reason why the aorist -t͡sʰ- and past suffix /i/ are used is to maintain a contrast between a past perfective 1PL form like [kɒɹtʰ-ɒ-t͡sʰ-i-ŋkʰ] 'we read.PST' (where /ɒ/ is the past morph) vs. a subjunctive present form kɒɹtʰ-ɒ-ŋkʰ and subjunctive past [kɒɹtʰ-ɒj-i-ŋkʰ] 'if we read.PST' (where /ɒ/ is the theme vowel). See §6.4.2 for a fuller discussion of subjunctives.

These generalizations are formalized below, based on the A-Class, suppletive 'to eat', and E-Class. For illustration, we use rules that realize templates of morphemes like AOR-PST because the exponents for the two morpheme slots are highly correlated.

For the past perfective, this paradigm cell uses the morpheme template AOR-PST (Rule 13). In Standard Eastern Armenian, this template is realized as /-∅-ɑ/ for a handful of irregular verbs like 'to eat', while it is /-t͡sʰ-i/ elsewhere for the E-Class and A-Class. In contrast, in Iranian Armenian, the template /-t͡sʰ-i/ is for the A-Class, and /-∅-ɒ/ is elsewhere.

Rule 13: Rules for exponing the template /AOR-PST/ in the past perfective for the E-Class, A-Class, and suppletive 'to eat'

- Standard Eastern: AOR-PST → -∅-ɑ   / √eat TH _
  -t͡sʰ-i   / elsewhere

- Iranian Armenian: AOR-PST → -t͡sʰ-i   / √A-Class TH _
  -∅-ɒ   / elsewhere

Table 6.23 illustrates the application of the above rules.

Table 6.23: Deriving or exponing the template AOR-PST in the past perfective

	E-Class 'they sang'	A-Class 'they read'	Suppletive 'they ate'
Input	√sing-TH-**AOR-PST**-3PL	√read-TH-**AOR-PST**-3PL	√eat-TH-**AOR-PST**-3PL
SEA	jeɾkʰ-e-t͡sʰ-i-n	kɑɾtʰ-ɑ-t͡sʰ-i-n	keɾ-∅-**∅-ɑ**-n
IA	jeɹkʰ-∅-**∅-ɒ**-n	kɒɹtʰ-ɒ-t͡sʰ-i-n	keɹ-∅-**∅-ɒ**-n

In the past auxiliary and subjunctive past, there is no perfective or aorist morpheme AOR. Instead, the template is just PST. This morpheme is realized in the same way in both dialects as just /i/ for all but the 3SG. We illustrate a rule below (Rule 14). It is /-∅/ for the 3SG, and /-i/ elsewhere.

Table 6.24 illustrates the application of the above rules.

Rule 14: Rules for exponing the template /PST/ in the past auxiliary and subjunctive past

Standard Eastern		Iranian Armenian	
PST →	-∅ / _ 3SG	PST →	-∅ / _ 3SG
	-i / elsewhere		-i / elsewhere

Table 6.24: Deriving or exponing the template AOR-PST in the past auxiliary or subjunctive past

	A-Class 'if he were reading'	A-Class 'if they were reading'
Input	√read-TH-**PST**-3SG	√read-TH-**PST**-3PL
SEA	kaɾtʰ-a-∅-ɾ	kaɾtʰ-aj-i-n
IA	kɒɹtʰ-ɒ-∅-ɹ	kɒɹtʰ-ɒj-i-n

If we try to decompose the template AOR-PST into two separate realizations, so that we can unite the rules for the perfective and non-perfective (sbjv. past), then it is difficult to write a coherent set of rules to expone the past morpheme (Rule 15). For Standard Eastern Armenian, the past morpheme is /-a/ for irregular perfectives, /-∅/ for 3SG, and /-i/ elsewhere (regular perfectives and non-3SG non-perfectives). For Iranian Armenian, the past morpheme is /-∅/ for A-Class 3SG perfectives, /-∅/ for 3SG non-perfectives, /-i/ for A-Class non-3SG perfectives, /-ɒ/ for other perfectives (for other classes), and then /-i/ again for non-3SG non-perfectives. We use the notation ¬AOR to denote non-perfective contexts (cf. Siddiqi 2009: 49).

Table 6.25 illustrates the application of the above rules for Iranian Armenian.

The rules are quite convoluted. But the core generalization is that in the past perfective, the default template is /-t͡sʰ-i/, while /-∅-a/ is the restricted or marked template. Iranian Armenian instead does the reverse, with /-∅-ɒ/ as default while /-t͡sʰ-i/ is restricted or marked. When there is no aorist morpheme, the past morpheme reverts back to /-i/ as the elsewhere form. We next discuss subjunctives, where we again find the past marker /-i/.

Rule 15: Rules for exponing the morpheme PST in the past auxiliary, subjunctive past, and past perfective for E/A-Class and 'to eat'

Standard Eastern		Iranian Armenian		
PST	→	-ɑ	/ √eat AOR _	PST →	-∅	/ √A-Class TH AOR _ 3SG
		-∅	/ _ 3SG		-∅	/ ¬AOR _ 3SG
		-i	/ elsewhere		-i	/ √A-Class TH AOR _
					-ᴅ	/ AOR _
					-i	/ ¬AOR _

Table 6.25: Deriving or exponing the past morpheme in Iranian Armenian

A-Class	'to read'	perfective 3SG	√read-TH-AOR-**PST**-3SG	kɒɹtʰ-ᴅ-ts͡ʰ-∅-∅
E-Class	'to sing'	sbjv. past 3SG	√sing-TH-**PST**-3SG	jeɹkʰ-e-∅-ɹ
A-Class	'to read'	perfective 3PL	√read-TH-AOR-**PST**-3PL	kɒɹtʰ-ᴅ-ts͡ʰ-i-n
E-Class	'to sing'	perfective 3PL	√sing-TH-AOR-**PST**-3SG	jeɹkʰ-∅-∅-ᴅ-n
E-Class	'to sing'	sbjv. past 3PL	√sing-TH-**PST**-3PL	jeɹkʰ-∅-i-n

6.4.2 Subjunctive

The subjunctive is a synthetic construction. It includes present and past subjunctives. In brief, these synthetic subjunctive forms differ from the periphrastic indicative forms by placing T/Agr suffixes on the verb itself instead of on the auxiliary. We illustrate below for the A-Class verb [kɒɹtʰ-ᴅ-l] 'to read' in Iranian Armenian (Table 6.26).

Diachronically, the modern subjunctive construction is a reflex of the Classical indicative (Vaux 1995). Subjunctive forms can also combine with other particles to create more nuanced meanings. For example, subjunctives can combine with the debitive proclitic [piti] to create the debitive mood (§5.5).

We discuss the two types of subjunctives below.

Table 6.26: Synthetic subjunctives vs. periphrastic indicatives for the 1PL in Iranian Armenian

	Present 1PL		Past PL	
Indicative	kɒɹtʰ-um	e-ŋkʰ	kɒɹtʰ-um	Ø-i-ŋkʰ
	√-IMPF.CVB	AUX-1PL	√-IMPF.CVB	AUX-PST-1PL
	'we read'		'we were reading'	
	կարդում ենք		կարդում ինք	
Subjunctive	kɒɹtʰ-ɒ-ŋkʰ		kɒɹtʰ-ɒj-i-ŋkʰ	
	√-TH-1PL		√-TH-PST-1PL	
	'(if) we read'		'(if) we were reading'	
	կարդանք		կարդայինք	

6.4.2.1 Subjunctive with present-tense agreement

We first discuss the present subjunctive. When the finite verb uses present-tense agreement morphemes, the construction has been called "subjunctive present" (Minassian 1980: 190, Hagopian 2005: 160), "subjunctive future" (Bardakjian & Vaux 1999: 174, Sakayan 2007: 150, Dum-Tragut 2009: 239), "present optative" (Fairbanks & Stevick 1975: 149). We label this construction as just the "subjunctive present", in order to emphasize the connection between the indicative and subjunctive forms.

Paradigms for the E-Class are in Table 6.27 and for the A-Class in Table 6.28. Negation is marked by adding the prefix /tʃʰ-/, which triggers schwa epenthesis before a consonant. We juxtapose these subjunctive forms with their indicative periphrastic forms. For illustration, we also provide the Standard Eastern subjunctive present which does not morphologically differ from Iranian Armenian. As before, we treat the present tense suffix as fused with the agreement suffix.

For all but the 3SG, the distribution of the Agr suffixes follows straightforwardly. The same Agr suffixes as used in the present auxiliary are placed onto the subjunctive verb. In the A-Class, we see that the 3SG morph is covert in the present subjunctive: [kɒɹtʰ-ɒ-Ø] √read-TH-3SG 'he reads'. Similarly, the present 3SG auxiliary is just /ɒ-Ø/. But for the E-Class, the /e/ theme vowel is replaced by /i/: [jeɹkʰ-i-Ø] 'he sings' instead of *jeɹkʰ-e-Ø.

In terms of explanation, this apparent allomorphy has multiple options (Rule 16).

Table 6.27: Paradigm of subjunctive present in simple E-Class verbs in Standard Eastern and Iranian Armenian

	Iranian Armenian			Standard Eastern
	Sbjv. present		Indc. present	Sbjv. present
	Positive	Negaive	Positive	Positive
1SG	jeɹkʰ-e-m	t͡ʃʰə-jeɹkʰ-e-m	jeɹkʰ-um e-m	jeɾkʰ-e-m
	'(if) I sing'	'(if) I did not sing'	'I sing'	'(if) I sing'
	երգեմ	չերգեմ	երգում եմ	երգեմ
2SG	jeɹkʰ-e-s	t͡ʃʰə-jeɹkʰ-e-s	jeɹkʰ-um e-s	jeɾkʰ-e-s
	երգես	չերգես	երգում ես	երգես
3SG	jeɹkʰ-i	t͡ʃʰə-jeɹkʰ-i	jeɹkʰ-um ɒ	jeɾkʰ-i
	երգի	չերգի	երգում ա	երգի
1PL	jeɹkʰ-e-ŋkʰ	t͡ʃʰə-jeɹkʰ-e-ŋkʰ	jeɹkʰ-um e-ŋkʰ	jeɾkʰ-e-ŋkʰ
	երգենք	չերգենք	երգում ենք	երգենք
2PL	jeɹkʰ-e-kʰ	t͡ʃʰə-jeɹkʰ-e-kʰ	jeɹkʰ-um e-kʰ	jeɾkʰ-e-kʰ
	երգեք	չերգեք	երգում էք	երգեք
3PL	jeɹkʰ-e-n	t͡ʃʰə-jeɹkʰ-e-n	jeɹkʰ-um e-n	jeɾkʰ-e-n
	երգեն	չերգեն	երգում են	երգեն
	(NEG)-√-TH-AGR		√-IMPF.CVB AUX-AGR	√-TH-AGR

Rule 16: Hypothetical rules to explain the subjunctive present 3SG

1. /i/ is the marker of the theme vowel /e/ but it has changed to [i] in the 3SG.

   /jeɹkʰ-e-∅/ → [jeɹkʰ-i-∅]

2. /i/ is the allomorph of the E-Class theme vowel in the present 3SG.

   /jeɹkʰ-i-∅/

3. /i/ is the marker of the E-Class 3SG Agr suffix, and the theme /e/ is deleted before /i/.

   /jeɹkʰ-e-i/ → [jeɹkʰ-∅-i]

4. /i/ is the fused marker of the theme vowel /e/ and 3SG.

/jeɹkʰ-i/ with glossing √-TH.3SG

5. /i/ is the result of autosegmental docking of the theme vowel /e/ and the E-Class 3SG floating feature [+HIGH]

/jeɹkʰ-e-[+ HIGH]/ → [jeɹkʰ-i]

Glossing as [jeɹkʰ-i-∅]

Table 6.28: Paradigm of subjunctive present in simple A-Class verbs in Standard Eastern and Iranian Armenian

	Iranian Armenian			Standard Eastern
	Sbjv. present Positive	Negaive	Indc. present Positive	Sbjv. present Positive
1SG	kɒɹtʰ-ɒ-m '(if) I read' կարդամ	t͡ʃʰə-kɒɹtʰ-ɒ-m '(if) I did not read' չկարդամ	kɒɹtʰ-um e-m 'I read' կարդում եմ	kɑrtʰ-ɑ-m '(If) I read' կարդամ
2SG	kɒɹtʰ-ɒ-s կարդաս	t͡ʃʰə-kɒɹtʰ-ɒ-s չկարդաս	kɒɹtʰ-um e-s կարդում ես	kɑrtʰ-ɑ-s կարդաս
3SG	kɒɹtʰ-ɒ կարդայ	t͡ʃʰə-kɒɹtʰ-ɒ չկարդայ	kɒɹtʰ-um ɒ կարդում ա	kɑrtʰ-ɑ կարդա
1PL	kɒɹtʰ-ɒ-ŋkʰ կարդանք	t͡ʃʰə-kɒɹtʰ-ɒ-ŋkʰ չկարդանք	kɒɹtʰ-um e-ŋkʰ կարդում ենք	kɑrtʰ-ɑ-ŋkʰ կարդանք
2PL	kɒɹtʰ-ɒ-kʰ կարդաք	t͡ʃʰə-kɒɹtʰ-ɒ-kʰ չկարդաք	kɒɹtʰ-um e-kʰ կարդում էք	kɑrtʰ-ɑ-kʰ կարդաք
3PL	kɒɹtʰ-ɒ-n կարդան	t͡ʃʰə-kɒɹtʰ-ɒ-n չկարդան	kɒɹtʰ-um e-n կարդում են	kɑrtʰ-ɑ-n կարդան
	(NEG)-√-TH-AGR		√-IMPF.CVB AUX-AGR	√-TH-AGR

Any of the above options must restrict the relevant change to the E-Class, while the A-Class and auxiliary would use a zero morph for the 3SG. We are partial to a floating feature analysis (cf. Akinlabi 2011) and we use that for illustration. We likewise suspect that such allomorphy is not triggered by classes themselves, but by the identity of the actual theme vowel. That is, the present 3SG is [+HIGH] after the /e/ theme vowel, but a zero -∅ elsewhere (Rule 17).

Rule 17: Rule for the present 3SG agreement suffix

$$\text{PRS.3SG} \quad \leftrightarrow \quad \begin{array}{ll} [\text{+HIGH}] & / \; e_{\text{Th}} \, \_\_ \\ \text{-∅} & / \; \text{elsewhere} \end{array}$$

One reason why we are partial to this floating feature analysis over alternatives involving allomorphs is that in Standard Western Armenian, the present 3SG suffix is uniformly a zero for both the E-Class and the A-Class, e.g., the subjunctive forms [jeɾkʰ-e-∅] '(if) he sings' and [gaɾtʰ-a-∅] '(if) he reads' [√-TH-PRS/1SG]. Thus, it is likely that Standard Eastern and Iranian Armenian are innovative in causing this /e/→[i] change in the present 3SG.

6.4.2.2 Subjunctive with past-tense agreement

Moving on to the past tense, the subjunctive forms again involve placing the T/Agr suffixes directly onto the verb instead of the auxiliary.

When the verb has the tense-agreement morphemes of the past, then the construction has been called the "subjunctive past" in grammars of Standard Eastern Armenian that are written in English (Bardakjian & Vaux 1999: 174, Hagopian 2005: 160, Sakayan 2007: 150, Dum-Tragut 2009: 249). One French grammar uses the "subjunctive imperfect" (Minassian 1980: 191). However, for grammars of Standard Western Armenian, the cognate construction is called either the "subjunctive past" (Sakayan 2000: 113, Hagopian 2005: 143), "subjunctive imperfect" (Riggs 1856: 35, Gulian 1902: 50, Feydit 1948: 107, Kogian 1949: 89, Bardakjian & Thomson 1977: 154, Andonian 1999: 47, Bardakjian & Vaux 2001: 181), "past optative" (Fairbanks 1948: 78, 1958), "hypothetical imperfect" (Boyacioglu 2010). The large set of names for the past-based subjunctive is due to the fact that the Armenian name for it is variably the subjunctive imperfect or subjunctive past.[9] We call this construction the "subjunctive past".

We provide paradigms below for E-Class *jeɾkʰ-e-l* (Table 6.29) and A-Class *kɒɹtʰ-ɒ-l* (Table 6.30). The abstract morphological structure of subjunctive past verbs is the same in Standard Eastern and Iranian Armenian. We show deleted and zero morphs. Negation is again formed by adding [t͡ʃʰ(ə)-].

---

[9]The SEA name for the word "subjunctive" is variably [əɾd͡zakan] ըղձական or [stoɾadasakan] ստորադասական.

Table 6.29: Paradigm of subjunctive past in simple E-Class verbs in Standard Eastern and Iranian Armenian

	Iranian Armenian			Standard Eastern
	Sbjv. past		Indc. past impf.	Sbjv. past
	Positive	Negaive	Positive	Positive
1SG	jeɪkʰ-∅-i-m '(if) I were singing' ɛɾqhմ	tʃʰə-jeɪkʰ-∅-i-m '(if) I were not singing' ʒɛɾqhմ	jeɪkʰ-um ∅-i-m 'I was singing' ɛɾqnմ hմ	jeɾkʰ-ej-i-∅ '(if) I were singing' ɛɾqɛh
2SG	jeɪkʰ-∅-i-ɪ ɛɾqhɾ	tʃʰə-jeɪkʰ-∅-i-ɪ ʒɛɾqhɾ	jeɪkʰ-um ∅-i-ɪ ɛɾqnմ hɾ	jeɾkʰ-ej-i-ɾ ɛɾqɛhɾ
3SG	jeɪkʰ-e-∅-ɪ ɛɾqɛɾ	tʃʰə-jeɪkʰ-e-∅-ɪ ʒɛɾqɛɾ	jeɪkʰ-um e-∅-ɪ ɛɾqnմ ɛɾ	jeɾkʰ-e-∅-ɾ ɛɾqɛɾ
1PL	jeɪkʰ-∅-i-ŋkʰ ɛɾqhuᴘ	tʃʰə-jeɪkʰ-∅-i-ŋkʰ ʒɛɾqhuᴘ	jeɪkʰ-um ∅-i-ŋkʰ ɛɾqnմ huᴘ	jeɾkʰ-ej-i-ŋkʰ ɛɾqɛuᴘ
2PL	jeɪkʰ-∅-i-kʰ ɛɾqhᴘ	tʃʰə-jeɪkʰ-∅-i-kʰ ʒɛɾqhᴘ	jeɪkʰ-um ∅-i-kʰ ɛɾqnմ hᴘ	jeɾkʰ-ej-i-kʰ ɛɾqɛhᴘ
3PL	jeɪkʰ-∅-i-n ɛɾqhu	tʃʰə-jeɪkʰ-∅-i-n ʒɛɾqhu	jeɪkʰ-um ∅-i-n ɛɾqnմ hu	jeɾkʰ-ej-i-n ɛɾqɛhu
	√-TH-PST-AGR	NEG-√-TH-PST-AGR	√-IMPF.CVB AUX-PST-AGR	√-TH-PST-AGR

The markers of tense and agreement in the subjunctive past all follow from the same rules used for auxiliaries.

Morphophonologically, vowel hiatus between the theme vowel and past /i/ causes deletion of the /e/ theme vowel in Iranian Armenian, while [j] is epenthesized after the /ɒ/ theme vowel. In Standard Eastern, the /e/ theme vowel is not deleted; instead [j] is epenthesized to resolve vowel hiatus. We illustrate this below for the 1PL (see the derivation in Table 6.31).

Glide epenthesis is a general rule of hiatus repair in Armenian, while deletion requires morpheme-specific deletion rules (Rule 18).

Rule 18: Delete the /e/ theme vowel before past /i/

$$/e/ \rightarrow \emptyset \; / \_ i$$

(where /e/ is a theme vowel, /i/ is past)

Table 6.30: Paradigm of subjunctive past in simple A-Class verbs in Standard Eastern and Iranian Armenian

	Iranian Armenian			Standard Eastern
	Sbjv. past		Indc. past impf.	Sbjv. past
	Positive	Negaive	Positive	Positive
1SG	kɒɾtʰ-ɒj-i-m 'if) I were reading' կարդայիմ	t͡ʃʰə-kɒɾtʰ-ɒj-i-m '(if) I were not reading' չկարդայիմ	kɒɾtʰ-um ∅-i-m 'I was reading' կարդում իմ	kɑɾtʰ-ɑj-i-∅ '(if) I were reading' կարդայի
2SG	kɒɾtʰ-ɒj-i-ɭ կարդայիր	t͡ʃʰə-kɒɾtʰ-ɒj-i-ɭ չկարդայիր	kɒɾtʰ-um ∅-i-ɭ կարդում իր	kɑɾtʰ-ɑj-i-ɾ կարդայիր
3SG	kɒɾtʰ-ɒ-∅-ɭ կարդար	t͡ʃʰə-kɒɾtʰ-ɒ-∅-ɭ չկարդար	kɒɾtʰ-um e-∅-ɭ կարդում էր	kɑɾtʰ-ɑ-∅-ɾ կարդար
1PL	kɒɾtʰ-ɒj-i-ŋkʰ կարդայինք	t͡ʃʰə-kɒɾtʰ-ɒj-i-ŋkʰ չկարդայինք	kɒɾtʰ-um ∅-i-ŋkʰ կարդում ինք	kɑɾtʰ-ɑj-i-ŋkʰ կարդայինք
2PL	kɒɾtʰ-ɒj-i-kʰ կարդայիք	t͡ʃʰə-kɒɾtʰ-ɒj-i-kʰ չկարդայիք	kɒɾtʰ-um ∅-i-kʰ կարդում իք	kɑɾtʰ-ɑj-i-kʰ կարդայիք
3PL	kɒɾtʰ-ɒj-i-n կարդային	t͡ʃʰə-kɒɾtʰ-ɒj-i-n չկարդային	kɒɾtʰ-um ∅-i-n կարդում ին	kɑɾtʰ-ɑj-i-n կարդային
	√-TH-PST-AGR	NEG-√-TH-PST-AGR	√-IMPF.CVB AUX-PST-AGR	√-TH-PST-AGR

Table 6.31: Vowel hiatus repair in subjunctive past

	A-Class 1PL '(if) we were reading'		E-Class 1PL '(if) we were singing'	
	SEA	IA	SEA	IA
Input Epenthesis Deletion	/kɑɾtʰ-ɑ-i-ŋkʰ/ kɑɾtʰ-ɑj-i-ŋkʰ	/kɒɾtʰ-ɒ-i-ŋkʰ/ kɒɾtʰ-ɒj-i-ŋkʰ	/jeɾkʰ-e-i-ŋkʰ/ jeɾkʰ-ej-i-ŋkʰ	/jeɭkʰ-e-i-ŋkʰ/ jeɭkʰ-∅-i-ŋkʰ
	կարդայինք	կարդայինք	երգեինք	երգինք

131

There is evidence that the Armenian dialects of Iran vary in the application of theme vowel deletion before the past marker /i/. In Standard Eastern Armenian, neither the theme vowel /ɑ/ nor the theme vowel /e/ is deleted before past /-i/. In Tehrani Iranian Armenian, only /e/ is deleted. But in New Julfa Armenian (Isfahan), both theme vowels are deleted (Աճառյան 1940, Vaux in preparation: §275).

As with the past auxiliary (§6.2.2), the deletion of the theme vowel /e/ before past /i/ is not rare among Armenian dialects. Old Yerevan Armenian likewise had such a rule in the subjunctive past (Աճառեան 1911: 42; translated: Dolatian submitted).

6.4.2.3 Eliciting the subjunctive

Before closing this section, we document how we elicited such subjunctives. These subjunctive forms can be elicited in diverse contexts with various meanings (Dum-Tragut 2009: 239ff). In our fieldwork, we used the following sentence where the verb 'to want' selects for a subjunctive clause (7). Note that this sentence is not a control or ECM (exceptional case-marking) construction. The embedded clause can have a different subject than the main clause. The embedded subject can be made overt as a pronoun. The complementizer *voɹ* can be optionally added.

(7) a. uz-um   e-m   (voɹ) (iɹɒŋkʰ) jeɹkʰ-e-n
        want-IMPF.CVB AUX-1SG (that) (they.NOM) sing-TH-3PL
        'I want them to sing.'   (NK)
        Ուզում եմ որ իրանք երգեն:

     b. uz-um   Ø-i-m   (voɹ) (iɹɒŋkʰ) jeɹkʰ-Ø-i-n
        want-IMPF.CVB AUX-PST-1SG (that) (they.NOM) sing-TH-PST-3PL
        'I wanted them to sing.'   (NK)
        Ուզում իմ որ իրանք երգին:

6.4.3 Imperatives and prohibitives

Imperatives and prohibitives are formed almost identically between Standard Eastern and Iranian Armenian. They are restricted to the second person. The markers of imperative and prohibitive morphology depend on verb class. We show the imperative paradigms in Table 6.32. We use zero morphs to represent deleted theme vowels and covert 2SG suffixes.

The imperative is called [həɾɑmɑjɑkɑn jeʁɑnɑk] հրամայական եղանակ in Standard Eastern Armenian. In the imperative 2SG, the A-Class is inflected by adding

Table 6.32: Paradigm of imperatives in Standard Eastern and Iranian Armenian

	E-Class 'to sing'		A-Class 'to read'	
	SEA	IA	SEA	IA
Infinitive	jeɾkʰ-e-l	je.ɭkʰ-e-l	kɑɾtʰ-ɑ-l	kɒrtʰ-ɒ-l
	√-TH-INF		√-TH-INF	
	երգել	երգել	կարդալ	կարդալ
Imperative 2SG Colloquial	jeɾkʰ-∅-iɾ jeɾkʰ-∅-i	je.ɭkʰ-∅-i	kɑɾtʰ-ɑ-∅	kɒ.ɭtʰ-ɒ-∅
	√-TH-IMP.2SG		√-TH-IMP.2SG	
	երգիր	երգի	կարդա	կարդա
Imperative 2PL	jeɾkʰ-∅-ekʰ	je.ɭkʰ-∅-ekʰ	kɑɾtʰ-ɑ-t͡sʰ-ekʰ	kɒ.ɭtʰ-ɒ-t͡sʰ-ekʰ
	√-TH-IMP.2PL		√-TH-AOR-IMP.2PL	
	երգեք	երգեք	կարդացեք	կարդացեք

nothing to the theme vowel in both lects. The imperative 2SG suffix is thus covert for the A-Class: *kɒ.ɭtʰ-ɒ* 'read!'.

But for the E-Class, there is significant cross-dialectal variation. In Standard Eastern Armenian, the theme vowel is deleted, and followed by the overt imperative 2SG suffix *-iɾ*: *jeɾkʰ-iɾ* 'sing!'. In Colloquial Eastern Armenian, the suffix can be optionally reduced to *-i*: *jeɾkʰ-i* (Dum-Tragut 2009: 273, Քամայան 2015: 164, Գրիգորյան 2019). Iranian Armenian uses only *-i*: *je.ɭkʰ-i* 'sing!'. In contrast, in Standard Western Armenian, both the E-Class and A-Class use a covert suffix without a vowel change: *jeɾkʰ-e* 'sing!' երգէ, *gɑɾtʰ-ɑ* 'read!' կարդա.

For the imperative 2PL, the two lects align. The E-Class is inflected by adding the imperative 2PL suffix *-ekʰ* to the root, deleting the theme vowel: *je.ɭkʰ-ekʰ* 'sing.PL'. In the A-Class, the aorist suffix *-t͡sʰ-* is added between the theme vowel and the *-ekʰ*: : *kɒ.ɭtʰ-ɒ-t͡sʰ-ekʰ* 'read.PL'. The use of the aorist here is morphomic and meaningless, and is traditionally analyzed as part of an "aorist stem".[10] For the E-Class, more prescriptive uses of Standard Eastern Armenian utilize the

---

[10] One could argue that the reason why the A-Class imperative 2PL uses the morphomic aorist in [kɒ.ɭtʰ-ɒ-t͡sʰ-ekʰ] 'read.PL' is to prevent ambiguity with the present subjunctive 2PL [kɒ.ɭtʰ-ɒ-kʰ] 'if you.PL read'. Analyzing the use of morphomic aorist as due to contrast-preservation is attractive. However, it would not extend to other paradigm cells for the A-Class like the subject participle, which also uses the morphomic aorist [kɒ.ɭtʰ-ɒ-t͡sʰ-oʁ] 'reader' without any contrasting form [*kɒ.ɭtʰ-oʁ].

aorist stem for the E-Class imperative 2PL as well (Dum-Tragut 2009: 272). But it has become increasingly common to abandon the aorist stem for the E-Class imperative 2PL in Standard Eastern Armenian.

The prohibitive is formed by simply adding the proclitic *mi* before the imperative form: *mi kɒɹtʰ-ɒ* 'don't read!' (Table 6.33).

Table 6.33: Paradigm of prohibitives in Standard Eastern and Iranian Armenian

	E-Class		A-Class	
	SEA	IA	SEA	IA
Infinitive	jeɾkʰ-e-l	jeɹkʰ-e-l	kaɾtʰ-a-l	kɒɾtʰ-ɒ-l
	√-TH-INF		√-TH-INF	
	'to sing'	'to sing'	'to read'	'to read'
	երգել	երգել	կարդալ	կարդալ
Prohibitive 2SG Colloquial	mi jeɾkʰ-∅-iɾ mi jeɾkʰ-∅-i	mi jeɹkʰ-∅-i	mi kaɾtʰ-a-∅	mi kɒɹtʰ-ɒ-∅
	PROH √-TH-IMP.2SG		PROH √-TH-IMP.2SG	
	մի երգիր	մի երգի	մի կարդա	մի կարդա
Prohibitive 2PL	mi jeɾkʰ-∅-ekʰ	mi jeɹkʰ-∅-ekʰ	mi kaɾtʰ-a-t͡sʰ-ekʰ	mi kɒɹtʰ-ɒ-t͡sʰ-ekʰ
	PROH √-TH-IMP.2PL		PROH √-TH-AOR-IMP.2PL	
	մի երգեք	մի երգեք	մի կարդացեք	մի կարդացեք

For illustration, the verbs below show the imperative and prohibitive form of various verbs that we had elicited over the years (Table 6.34). We omit zero morphs for space.

One thing to note though is that our Iranian Armenian speakers frequently prefer to use the negative subjunctive present 2PL in lieu of the prohibitive 2PL (Table 6.35). We suspect this is an influence from Persian. AS reports that Persian often utilizes the subjunctive 2PL in lieu of the negative imperative 2PL. Note how for the E-Class, the surface sequence *-ekʰ* has different morphological parses in the subjunctive vs. the prohibitive.

6.4.4 Participles

Alongside converbs, Iranian Armenian utilizes a set of participles derived from verbs. These participles cannot be used in periphrastic constructions. They are restricted to use as adjectives or nouns. Participle formation in Iranian Armenian is identical to that in Standard Eastern.

Table 6.34: Elicited imperatives and prohibitives

Infinitive			Finite form	Quality	
nəst-e-l	'to sit'	նստել	nəst-i	Imp 2SG	նստի
kʰən-e-l	'to sleep'	քնել	kʰən-i	Imp 2SG	քնի
gəɹ-e-l	'to write'	գրել	gəɹ-i	Imp 2SG	գրի
			mi gəɹ-i	Proh 2SG	մի գրի
			mi gəɹ-ekʰ	Proh 2PL	մի գրեք
bərn-e-l	'to hold/catch'	բռնել	mi bərn-i	Proh 2SG	մի բռնի
			mi bərn-ekʰ	Proh 2PL	մի բռնեք
t͡səχ-e-l	'to smoke'	ծխել	mi t͡səχ-i	Proh 2SG	մի ծխի
			mi t͡səχ-ekʰ	Proh 2PL	մի ծխեք
χɒʁ-ɒ-l	'to play'	խաղալ	mi χɒʁ-ɒ	Proh 2SG	մի խաղա
			mi χɒʁ-ɒ-t͡sʰ-ekʰ	Proh 2PL	մի խաղացեք
mən-ɒ-l	'to remain'	մնալ	mi mən-ɒ	Proh 2SG	մի մնա
			mi mən-ɒ-t͡sʰ-ekʰ	Proh 2PL	մի մնացեք
ʒəpt-ɒ-l	'to smile'	ժպտալ	mi ʒəpt-ɒ	Proh 2SG	մի ժպտա
			mi ʒəpt-ɒ-t͡sʰ-ekʰ	Proh 2PL	մի ժպտացեք

Table 6.35: Negative subjunctive vs. prohibitive 2PL in Iranian Armenian

	Prohibitive 2PL	Negative sbjv. 2PL
E-Class 'to sing'	mi jeɹkʰ-∅-ekʰ	t͡ʃə-jeɹkʰ-e-kʰ
	PROH √-TH-IMP.2PL	NEG-√-TH-2PL
	մի երգեք	չերգեք
A-Class 'to read'	mi kɒɹtʰ-ɒ-t͡sʰ-ekʰ	t͡ʃə-kɒɹtʰ-ɒ-kʰ
	PROH √-TH-AOR-IMP.2PL	NEG-√-TH-2PL
	մի կարդացեք	չկարդաք

There are two types of participles: the subject participle and the resultative participle (Table 6.36). The subject participle uses the suffix [-oʁ]. The resultative participle uses the suffix [-ɒts͡ʰ] in Iranian Armenian, [-ɑts͡] in Standard Eastern.[11] For the E-Class, these suffixes are added directly after the root, deleting the theme vowel. We use zero morphs to show the deleted theme vowel. For A-Class verbs, these suffixes trigger a morphomic aorist suffix -*ts͡ʰ*- between the theme and suffix, i.e., an aorist stem.

Table 6.36: Paradigm of subject and resultative participles

	E-Class		A-Class	
	SEA	IA	SEA	IA
Infinitive	jeɾkʰ-e-l 'to sing' √-TH-INF երգել	jeɹkʰ-e-l	kaɾtʰ-a-l 'to read' √-TH-INF կարդալ	kɒɹtʰ-ɒ-l
Subject participle	jeɾkʰ-∅-oʁ √-TH-SPTCP երգող	jeɹkʰ-∅-oʁ	kaɾtʰ-a-t͡sʰ-oʁ √-TH-AOR-SPTCP կարդացող	kɒɹtʰ-ɒ-t͡sʰ-oʁ
Resultative participle	jeɾkʰ-∅-ɑt͡s √-TH-RPTCP երգած	jeɹkʰ-∅-ɒt͡sʰ	kaɾtʰ-a-t͡sʰ-ɑt͡s √-TH-AOR-RPTCP կարդացած	kɒɹtʰ-ɒ-t͡sʰ-ɒt͡sʰ

In Standard Eastern Armenian, the resultative participle is called [haɾakataɾ deɾbaj] հարակատար դերբայ, and the subject participle is called [jentʰakajakan deɾbaj] ենթակայական դերբայ.

The following are examples with these participles in Iranian Armenian (8).

(8) a. Subject participle
      jeɹkʰ-oʁ-ə   jev kɒɹtʰ-ɒ-t͡sʰ-oʁ-ə
      sing-SPTCP-DEF and read-TH-AOR-SPTCP-DEF
      'the singer and the reader'
      երգողը եւ կարդացողը

---

[11]As explained in §2.1.1, some Iranian Armenian speakers aspirate the resultative suffix as [-ɒt͡sʰ], while some do not. Throughout this section, we aspirate this suffix because our main consultant NK used aspiration.

b. Resultative participle

je.ɹkʰ-ɒtsʰ je.ɹkʰ jev kɒ.ɹtʰ-ɒ-tsʰ-ɒtsʰ   gi.ɹkʰ
sing-RPTCP song and read-TH-AOR-RPTCP book

'a sung song and a read book'

Երգած երգ եւ կարդացած գիրք

6.5 Future: Synthetic and periphrastic constructions

This section discusses the two morphological strategies that are used to mark the future. One strategy is periphrastic with a converb, while the other is synthetic with a prefix. The same strategies are used in both Standard Eastern Armenian and Iranian Armenian.

The existing literature on Armenian is quite inconsistent in how these two categories are classified and analyzed. To minimize these inconsistencies, we discuss them both together here.

6.5.1 Variation in future marking

To mark the simple future in Standard Eastern Armenian, most traditional grammars (both descriptive and pedagogical) report a periphrastic construction (9). Dum-Tragut (2009: 233) labels this as the "simple future". The verb is in a non-finite form called the future converb (with suffix *-u*) while tense-agreement is on an auxiliary. Iranian Armenian has the same periphrastic construction.

(9)   Periphrastic future
      gəɾ-e-l-u   e-m   (SEA)
      gə.ɹ-e-l-uw   e-m   (IA)
      write-TH-INF-FUT.CVB AUX-1SG

      'I will write.'
      Գրելու եմ:

An alternative synthetic construction is to add the prefix *k(ə)-* before a finite subjunctive verb (10). Dum-Tragut (2009: 253) calls this the "conditional future".

(10)   Synthetic future
       kə-gəɾ-e-m   (SEA)
       kə-gə.ɹ-e-m   (IA)
       FUT-write-TH-1SG

       'I will write.'
       Կը գրեմ:

Note that our translations for the periphrastic future (9) and synthetic future (10) are identical. The problem is that it is quite unclear what are the fixed semantic and functional differences between the periphrastic and synthetic future.[12] To quote Dum-Tragut (2009: 253):

> In [SEA], however, [the synthetic future] is more often used to express simple actions in the future and as such has no major semantic differences to the [periphrastic future] and is even more often used [than] the [periphrastic future].

There are some subtle semantic distinctions between the periphrastic and synthetic forms. For example, the synthetic form implies a stronger sense of intentionality or volition. For our consultants, it can denote a wish, a future condition, or an optative. It can be used to denote an action in the immediate future, where the agent has a strong desire to perform the action. The synthetic future has a sense of being more temporally immediate than the periphrastic future. But in general, the two types of futures can be used interchangeably.

The above semantic observations concerning the future contrast strongly with the traditional names that grammars use. The periphrastic future is always labeled as "the future" (Minassian 1980: 182, Fairbanks & Stevick 1975: 209, Bardakjian & Vaux 1999: 71, Hagopian 2005: 94, Sakayan 2007: 124, Dum-Tragut 2009: 233). This shows that these grammarians think that the main function of this construction is to mark the future. In contrast, the synthetic form has multiple names, each of which make the synthetic form seem subordinate to the periphrastic form. It has been called the "conditional present" (Minassian 1980: 192, Hagopian 2005: 160), "hypothetical future" (Sakayan 2007: 224), "future" (Johnson 1954: 85, Fairbanks & Stevick 1975: 93), and "conditional future" (Bardakjian & Vaux 1999: 196, Dum-Tragut 2009: 253). In contrast, in Armenian dialectology, Adjarian (Աճառեան 1911, translated in Dolatian submitted) labels the synthetic future as just the future.[13]

There is thus a mismatch between the names and functions of the two future constructions. Traditional grammars and names treat the periphrastic future as the default, while the synthetic future is argued to be restricted to special types of

---

[12] Sometimes NK would say that the periphrastic construction means 'I will X' while the synthetic one means 'I am going to X'. But then we get the opposite order from AS's consultants.

[13] Among modern grammars written in Armenian, there is also some inconsistency. The periphrastic future has been called the "future" [aparni] ապառնի (Եզեկյան 2007: 292) or the "future present" [aparni nerka] ապառնի ներկա (Սևակ 2009: 295). In contrast, the synthetic is called the "conditional future present" or "(conditional) future" (Եզեկյան 2007: 292, Սևակ 2009: 295). The word for "conditional" can be [jentʰadrakan] ենթադրական or [pajmanakan] պայմանական.

conditional clauses. However, more recent semantic work on Armenian argues that the synthetic future is the default way to mark the future tense (Ավետյան 2022). The periphrastic future is instead an expected (predetermined) future. Personal communication with Avetyan (Ավետյան 2022) then suggests the following two translations for these two types of futures (11).

(11) Alternative translations

    a. Periphrastic future (expected)

        gər-e-l-u   e-m   (SEA)

        gəɹ-e-l-uw   e-m   (IA)

        write-TH-INF-FUT.CVB AUX-1SG

        'I am (going) to write.'

        Գրելու եմ:

    b. Synthetic future (simple)

        kə-gər-e-m   (SEA)

        kə-gəɹ-e-m   (IA)

        FUT-write-TH-1SG

        'I will write.'

        Կը գրեմ:

As can be seen, it is difficult to know how to label these two morphological constructions. The traditional names obfuscate the fact that the synthetic structure is more common than the periphrastic structure, and that the synthetic can be used in non-conditional contexts. But, if we use new names based on semantic functions, then we run the risk that future more in-depth work may contradict our grammar. With new semantically-based names, a future reader might also have trouble seeing the connection between our grammar and past grammars.

As a compromise, we use morphological names for the two types of futures: the periphrastic future and the synthetic future (Fairbanks & Stevick 1975). We gloss the morpheme /-u/ for periphrastic future as -FUT.CVB 'future converb', and the prefix /k-/ for the synthetic future as FUT- 'future'.

The rest of this section discusses in more detail the morphology of these two constructions. More specifically, we discuss their past forms and their negation.

6.5.2 Periphrastic future with a converb

The periphrastic future is made by combining the future converb with an inflected auxiliary. The future converb is formed by taking the infinitive and then adding the suffix -u (Table 6.37). Both the E-Class and A-Class keep their theme vowel. This construction is formed identically in Standard Eastern and Iranian Armenian. The future converb is also called the future participle [ɑpɑrni derbɑj] ապառնի դերբայ in Standard Eastern Armenian (Dum-Tragut 2009: 206).

Table 6.37: Forming the future converb for simple regular verbs

E-Class 'to sing'		A-Class 'to read'	
Infinitive	Future converb	Infinitive	Future converb
je.ɹkʰ-e-l	je.ɹkʰ-e-l-u	kɒ.ɹtʰ-ɒ-l	kɒ.ɹtʰ-ɒ-l-u
√-TH-INF	√-TH-INF-FUT.CVB	√-TH-INF	√-TH-INF-FUT.CVB
երգել	երգելու	կարդալ	կարդալու

The future converb suffix -u likely originates from the genitive/dative suffix -u that is used by some declension classes (traditionally called the second declension). Its use is grammaticalized here as part of the future converb.

The converb can take the present or past auxiliaries to respectively create the simple future or the past future ("future in the past", Dum-Tragut 2009: 235). We show in Table 6.38 the complete paradigm for the E-Class je.ɹkʰ-e-l. The paradigm for the A-Class is analogously constructed with the converb [kɒ.ɹtʰ-ɒ-l-u]. We do not segment the auxiliary.

Vowel hiatus between the converb and the auxiliary triggers the insertion of [w], discussed in §3.1.2.

When the converb is combined with the past auxiliary, the usual name for this construction is the "past future" or "future in the past" (Minassian 1980: 182, Bardakjian & Vaux 1999: 71, Hagopian 2005: 94, Dum-Tragut 2009: 235). Other names include the "future imperfect" (Sakayan 2007: 126) and "past future" (Fairbanks & Stevick 1975: 210).

As before, the auxiliary shifts its position in the negated form.

6.5.3 Synthetic future with a prefix

The synthetic future is derived from subjunctives via prefixation in the positive. But its negative form uses periphrasis with a converb called the connegative (12).

(12) a. kə- kɒ.ɹtʰ -ɒ -ŋkʰ
      FUT- read-TH -1PL
      'We will read.'   (NK)
      Կը կարդանք:

Table 6.38: Paradigm for the periphrastic future and the periphrastic past future for E-Class [jeɹkʰ-e-l] 'to sing'

	Positive				Negaive			
	Future		Past future		Future		Past future	
1SG	jeɹkʰ-e-l-uw	em	jeɹkʰe-l-uw	im	tʃʰ-em	jeɹkʰ-e-l-u	tʃʰ-im	jeɹkʰe-l-u
	'I will sing'		'I was going to sing'		'I will not sing'		'I wasn't going to sing'	
	երգելու	եմ	երգելու	իմ	չեմ	երգելու	չիմ	երգելու
2SG	jeɹkʰ-e-l-uw	es	jeɹkʰ-e-l-uw	iɹ	tʃʰ-es	jeɹkʰ-e-l-u	tʃʰ-iɹ	jeɹkʰ-e-l-u
	երգելու	ես	երգելու	իր	չես	երգելու	չիր	երգելու
3SG	jeɹkʰ-e-l-uw	ɒ	jeɹkʰ-e-l-uw	eɹ	tʃʰ-i	jeɹkʰ-e-l-u	tʃʰ-eɹ	jeɹkʰ-e-l-u
	երգելու	ա	երգելու	էր	չի	երգելու	չէր	երգելու
1PL	jeɹkʰ-e-l-uw	eŋkʰ	jeɹkʰ-e-l-uw	iŋkʰ	tʃʰ-eŋkʰ	jeɹkʰ-e-l-u	tʃʰ-iŋkʰ	jeɹkʰ-e-l-u
	երգելու	ենք	երգելու	ինք	չենք	երգելու	չինք	երգելու
2PL	jeɹkʰ-e-l-uw	ekʰ	jeɹkʰ-e-l-uw	ikʰ	tʃʰ-ekʰ	jeɹkʰ-e-l-u	tʃʰ-ikʰ	jeɹkʰ-e-l-u
	երգելու	էք	երգելու	իք	չէք	երգելու	չիք	երգելու
3PL	jeɹkʰ-e-l-uw	en	jeɹkʰ-e-l-uw	in	tʃʰ-en	jeɹkʰ-e-l-u	tʃʰ-in	jeɹkʰ-e-l-u
	երգելու	են	երգելու	ին	չեն	երգելու	չին	երգելու
	√-TH-INF-FUT.CVB AUX				NEG-AUX √-TH-INF-FUT.CVB			

b. tʃʰ-   e   -ŋkʰ   kɒɹtʰ-ɒ-∅
   NEG- is -1PL   read-TH-CN.CVB
   'We will not read.'   (NK)
   Չենք կարդայ:

In the positive, these synthetic forms are created by adding the prefix *k-* to the subjunctive form (§6.4.2). A schwa is added to repair any consonant clusters created by this prefix. Complications arise when the root starts with [je] (§3.1.1).

When the prefix is added to a subjunctive present verb, it produces a future meaning, but with various nuances (§6.5.1). When this prefix is added to a subjunctive past verb, the meaning is more conditional-oriented. Grammars give many divergent names for this construction: conditional past (Hagopian 2005: 160, Dum-Tragut 2009: 260), conditional imperfect (Minassian 1980: 192, Bardakjian & Vaux 1999: 196), hypothetical past (Sakayan 2007: 225), past future (Fairbanks & Stevick 1975: 132). Because NK translates this construction as 'I would X', we decided to call it the conditional past.

Table 6.39 shows the paradigm of the synthetic future and of the conditional past. We do not provide the Standard Eastern Armenian forms because Standard Eastern Armenian likewise builds this tense from the subjunctive.

Table 6.39: Paradigm of positive synthetic future and the conditional past in Iranian Armenian

	Future		Conditional past	
	E-Class	A-Class	E-Class	A-Class
1SG	kə-jeɹkʰ-e-m 'I will sing.' Կը երգեմ	kə-kɒɹtʰ-ɒ-m 'I will read.' Կը կարդամ	kə-jeɹkʰ-∅-i-m 'I would sing' Կը երգիմ	kə-kɒɹtʰ-ɒj-i-m 'I would read.' Կը կարդայիմ
2SG	kə-jeɹkʰ-e-s Կը երգես	kə-kɒɹtʰ-ɒ-s Կը կարդաս	kə-jeɹkʰ-∅-i-ɹ Կը երգիր	kə-kɒɹtʰ-ɒj-i-ɹ Կը կարդայիր
3SG	kə-jeɹkʰ-i-∅ Կը երգի	kə-kɒɹtʰ-ɒ Կը կարդայ	kə-jeɹkʰ-e-∅-ɹ Կը երգէր	kə-kɒɹtʰ-ɒ-∅-ɹ Կը կարդար
1PL	kə-jeɹkʰ-e-ŋkʰ Կը երգենք	kə-kɒɹtʰ-ɒ-ŋkʰ Կը կարդանք	kə-jeɹkʰ-∅-i-ŋkʰ Կը երգինք	kə-kɒɹtʰ-ɒj-i-ŋkʰ Կը կարդայինք
2PL	kə-jeɹkʰ-e-kʰ Կը երգեք	kə-kɒɹtʰ-ɒ-kʰ Կը կարդաք	kə-jeɹkʰ-∅-i-kʰ Կը երգիք	kə-kɒɹtʰ-ɒj-i-kʰ Կը կարդայիք
3PL	kə-jeɹkʰ-e-n Կը երգեն	kə-kɒɹtʰ-ɒ-n Կը կարդան	kə-jeɹkʰ-∅-i-n Կը երգին	kə-kɒɹtʰ-ɒj-i-n Կը կարդային
	FUT-√-AGR		FUT-√-PST-AGR	

Table 6.40: Connegative converbs for the E-Class and A-Class

	E-Class 'to sing'	A-Class 'to read'	
Infinitive	jeɹkʰ-e-l երգել	kɒɹtʰ-ɒ-l կարդալ	√-TH-INF
Connegative Possible analysis:	jeɹkʰ-i jeɹkʰ-i-∅ երգի	kɒɹtʰ-ɒ kɒɹtʰ-ɒ-∅ կարդայ	√-TH-CN.CVB

The above focused on the synthetic future and conditional when the verb is positive. When the verb is negative, then an entirely different periphrastic construction is used. Tense and agreement are placed on a negative auxiliary (§6.2). The verb is in the connegative form (Table 6.40), also called the negative participle (Dum-Tragut 2009: 214). The converb is called [ʒəχtakan deɾbaj] ժխտական դերբայ in Standard Eastern Armenian. The converb is constructed differently for the two classes. The converb suffix is a zero morph in the A-Class. In the E-Class, the theme vowel is replaced by /i/.

In terms of segmentation, we treat the connegative converb as a zero suffix in the A-Class. In the E-Class, we assume the connegative is a floating [+HIGH] feature that docks onto the /e/ theme vowel, thus changing /e/ to [i] (Rule 19). This is the same analytical strategy that we used for the subjunctive present 3SG (Rule 17). The alternatives in Rule 16 would also work.

Rule 19: Rule for the connegative converb

$$
\text{CN.CVB} \quad \leftrightarrow \quad
\begin{array}{ll}
[\text{+HIGH}] & / \text{ e \_} \qquad \text{(where /e/ is theme)} \\
-\varnothing & / \text{ elsewhere}
\end{array}
$$

We show the negative paradigm in Table 6.41. Note that because we are defining the future constructions in terms of their morphology, then the negative paradigm is actually "the negative periphrastic of the synthetic future".

We do not show Standard Eastern Armenian because it displays the exact same patterns, factoring out the phonological differences in the low vowel and rhotic, i.e., the connegative of 'to read' in Iranian Armenian [kɒɹtʰ-ɒ] corresponds to [kaɾtʰ-a] in Standard Eastern. We do not provide full segmentation for the auxiliary; for that see §6.2.3.

6.6 Complex regular verb class

The previous section provided the synthetic and periphrastic inflection of simple regular verbs. This section describes the inflection of complex verbs. Complex verbs are divided into passives, causatives, and inchoatives. These differ from simple verbs by including additional verbal material, such as the passive suffix. Their inflections differ from simple verbs in some but not all paradigm cells.

Table 6.41: Paradigm of the negative periphrastic form of the synthetic future and of the conditional past in Iranian Armenian

	Future				Conditional past			
	E-Class		A-Class		E-Class		A-Class	
1SG	tʃʰ-em ʒeɫkʰ-i-∅ 'I will not sing' ʃɛʊ̆ ɛɾɋh		tʃʰ-em kɒɫtʰ-ɒ-∅ 'I will not read' ʃɛʊ̆ ʊɑɾɋɑj		tʃʰ-im ʒeɫkʰ-i-∅ 'I would not sing' ʃhʊ̆ ɛɾɋh		tʃʰ-im kɒɫtʰ-ɒ-∅ 'I would not read' ʃhʊ̆ ʊɑɾɋɑj	
2SG	tʃʰ-es ʒeɫkʰ-i-∅ ʃɛu ɛɾɋh		tʃʰ-es kɒɫtʰ-ɒ-∅ ʃɛu ʊɑɾɋɑj		tʃʰ-iɫ ʒeɫkʰ-i-∅ ʃhɾ ɛɾɋh		tʃʰ-i-ɫ kɒɫtʰ-ɒ-∅ ʃhɾ ʊɑɾɋɑj	
3SG	tʃʰ-i ʃh		tʃʰ-i kɒɫtʰ-ɒ-∅ ʃh ʊɑɾɋɑj		tʃʰ-eɫ ʒeɫkʰ-i-∅ ʃɛɾ ɛɾɋh		tʃʰ-eɫ kɒɫtʰ-ɒ-∅ ʃɛɾ ʊɑɾɋɑj	
1PL	tʃʰ-eŋkʰ ʒeɫkʰ-i-∅ ʃɛup ɛɾɋh		tʃʰ-eŋkʰ kɒɫtʰ-ɒ-∅ ʃɛup ʊɑɾɋɑj		tʃʰ-iŋkʰ ʒeɫkʰ-i-∅ ʃhup ɛɾɋh		tʃʰ-iŋkʰ kɒɫtʰ-ɒ-∅ ʃhup ʊɑɾɋɑj	
2PL	tʃʰ-ekʰ ʒeɫkʰ-i-∅ ʃɛp ɛɾɋh		tʃʰ-ekʰ kɒɫtʰ-ɒ-∅ ʃɛp ʊɑɾɋɑj		tʃʰ-ikʰ ʒeɫkʰ-i-∅ ʃhp ɛɾɋh		tʃʰ-ikʰ kɒɫtʰ-ɒ-∅ ʃhp ʊɑɾɋɑj	
3PL	tʃʰ-en ʒeɫkʰ-i-∅ ʃɛu ɛɾɋh		tʃʰ-en kɒɫtʰ-ɒ-∅ ʃɛu ʊɑɾɋɑj		tʃʰ-in ʒeɫkʰ-i-∅ ʃhu ɛɾɋh		tʃʰ-in kɒɫtʰ-ɒ-∅ ʃhu ʊɑɾɋɑj	
	NEG-AUX.PRS.AGR √-TH-CN.CVB				NEG-AUX.PST.AGR √-TH-CN.CVB			

6.6.1 Passives

Passive verbs are formed by adding the suffix -*v*- (Table 6.42). The suffix is added directly after the root of an E-Class verb. For an A-Class verb, the passive triggers the morphomic aorist -*ts͡ʰ*- (an aorist stem). Passive formation is the same in the two lects. We show the deleted theme vowel as a zero morph.

The name of the passive is [kəɾavoɾakan] կրավորական in Standard Eastern Armenian.

Semantically, the passive suffix demotes the object argument of the active verb. The passive can likewise trigger a host of other argument-reducing operations such as reflexivization, anticausativization, and so on (Haspelmath 1993, Dum-Tragut 2009: 175). However, there are some high-frequency intransitive verbs that have the passive suffix, like *skəs-v-e-l* 'to begin', but do not really have passive semantics, just intransitive semantics. For consistency, we gloss all instances of the passive suffix -*v*- as just PASS even though its semantics can vary for some verbs.

Morphologically, the passive takes its own theme vowel -*e*-. We list some passives in Table 6.43.

Table 6.42: Passive verbs in Standard Eastern and Iranian Armenian

	E-Class		A-Class	
	SEA	IA	SEA	IA
Infinitive	jeɾkʰ-e-l	jeɹkʰ-e-l	kaɾtʰ-a-l	kɒɹtʰ-ɒ-l
	√-TH-INF		√-TH-INF	
	'to sing'		'to read'	
	երգել	երգել	կարդալ	կարդալ
Passive	jeɾkʰ-∅-v-e-l	jeɹkʰ-∅-v-e-l	kaɾtʰ-ɒ-t͡sʰ-v-e-l	kɒɹtʰ-ɒ-t͡sʰ-v-e-l
	√-TH-PASS-TH-INF		√-TH-AOR-PASS-TH-INF	
	'to be sung'		'to be read'	
	երգվել	երգուիլ	կարդացվել	կարդացուիլ

Table 6.43: Example passive verbs in Iranian Armenian

Active			Passive		
bərn-e-l	'to catch'	բռնել	bərnə-v-e-l	'to be caught'	բռնուիլ
kotɹ-e-l	'to break'	կոտրել	kotəɹ-v-e-l	'to be broken'	կոտրուիլ
skəs-e-l	'to start (trans.)'	սկսել	skəs-v-e-l	'to begin'	սկսուիլ
ɒzɒt-e-l	'to free'	ազատել	ɒzɒt-v-e-l	'to be freed'	ազատուիլ
ɒvɒɹt-e-l	'to finish'	աւարտել	ɒvɒɹt-v-e-l	'to graduate (school)'	աւարտուիլ
kɒɹtʰ-ɒ-l	'to read'	կարդալ	kɒɹtʰ-ɒ-t͡sʰ-v-e-l	'to be read'	կարդացուիլ

Table 6.44: Past perfective of passive verbs in Iranian Armenian

Active			Passive		
bərnə-v-e-l	'to be caught'	բռնուիլ	bərnə-v-ɒ-m	'I was caught'	բռնուամ
kotəɹ-v-e-l	'to be broken'	կոտրուիլ	kotəɹ-v-ɒ-v	'it broke'	կոտրուաւ
ɒvɒɹt-v-e-l	'to graduate'	աւարտուիլ	ɒvɒɹtv-ɒ-v	'he graduated'	աւարտուաւ
ɒzɒt-v-e-l	'to be freed'	ազատուիլ	ɒzɒt-v-ɒ-n	'they were freed'	ազատուան

Passive verbs are inflected as simple E-Class verbs. For example, in the past perfective, they take the past morph /-ɒ/ (Table 6.44).

The passive triggers schwa epenthesis after a CC cluster that cannot form a licit word-medial complex coda. For example, we see a schwa in [bərnə-v-e-l] 'to be caught' but not in [jeɹkʰ-v-e-l] 'to be sung'.[14] For an analysis of this phenomenon in Standard Eastern and Standard Western Armenian, see Vaux (1998b: 29,82) and Dolatian (2023a).

6.6.2 Inchoatives

Inchoatives are productively formed by adding the sequence [-ɒ-n-ɒ-l] to a noun or adjective (Table 6.45). The nasal is the inchoative affix. It is followed by the /ɒ/ theme vowel. Depending on the lexeme, the pre-nasal vowel is either /ɒ/ or /e/. But the low vowel is more common. We assume this pre-nasal vowel is a meaningless linking vowel (LV) (Dolatian & Guekguezian 2022b).

Table 6.45: Inchoative constructions

LV is /ɒ/		LV is /e/	
Base	Inchoative	Base	Inchoative
t͡ʃʰoɹ	t͡ʃʰoɹ-ɒ-n-ɒ-l	vɒχ	vɒχ-e-n-ɒ-l
√	√-LV-INCH-TH-INF	√	√-LV-INCH-TH-INF
'dry'	'to become dry'	'fear'	'to fear'
չոր	չորանալ	վախ	վախենալ

The meaning of an inchoative can be loosely paraphrased as 'to become X'. Note the contrast below between using the adjective as a predicate vs. as an inchoativized verb (13).

(13) a. uɹɒχ el-n-e-l
happy be-VX-TH-INF
'to be happy'
ուրախ ելնել

b. uɹɒχ-ɒ-n-ɒ-l
happy-LV-INCH-TH-INF
'to become happy'
ուրախանալ

---

[14]It is not completely clear to us why [rn] cannot form a complex coda in the passive verb [bərnə-v-e-l] 'to be caught'. An open question is whether complex codas like [rn] are truly banned across the entire lexicon, or just passives. See discussion of complex codas in Armenian in Dolatian (2023c)

We list below various morphologically inchoative verbs that we have elicited (Table 6.46).[15]

Table 6.46: Example inchoative verbs

mɒh-ɒ-n-ɒ-l	'to die'	մահանալ
hɒsk-ɒ-n-ɒ-l	'to understand'	հասկանալ
goʁ-ɒ-n-ɒ-l	'to steal'	գողանալ
im-ɒ-n-ɒ-l	'to know'	իմանալ
ləv-ɒ-n-ɒ-l	'to wash'	լուանալ
ɒɾtʰn-ɒ-n-ɒ-l	'to awake'	արթնանալ
t͡sʰɒŋk-ɒ-n-ɒ-l	'to wish'	ցանկանալ
hɒŋgəst-ɒ-n-ɒ-l	'to relax'	հանգստանալ
un-e-n-ɒ-l	'to have/own'	ունենալ

Inchoatives are inflected similarly to A-Class verbs but with some deviations, such as the imperative 2SG (Table 6.47). Inchoatives use the morphomic aorist suffix (aorist stem) in more contexts than typical A-Class verbs. When the aorist is used, the inchoative affix and its theme vowel are deleted. We show a partial paradigm below, just for the Iranian Armenian forms. We show only the deviations between the inchoative and A-Class. All other paradigm cells are formed the same. We do not use zero morphs to show deleted theme vowels and deleted inchoatives.[16] We place an asterisk for those paradigm cells where the inchoative nasal is deleted, and where the aorist stem is used instead.

Prohibitives are formed by adding the proclitic *mi-* before the imperative forms. For the other paradigm cells, inchoatives are inflected like A-Class verbs. These cells are the other converbs, the subjunctive, the synthetic future, and the conditional past. Complete paradigms are provided in the online archive.

---

[15] Some of these verbs like *goʁ-ɒ-n-ɒ-l* 'to steal' have inchoative morphology, but are transitive in their semantics and argument structure. And for some verbs like 'to understand' /hɒsk-ɒ-n-ɒ-l/ or 'to know' /im-ɒ-n-ɒ-l/, the root is a bound, and not an independent adjective or noun.

[16] Inchoatives are inflected similarly in Standard Eastern. The main difference is that in Standard Eastern, inchoatives are exceptional because they are inflected with the past tense morph /a/. Iranian Armenian on the other hand uses the past tense morph /ɒ/ which is the default form for the past perfective. For an analysis and documentation of similar facts in Standard Western Armenian, see Dolatian & Guekguezian (2022b).

Table 6.47: Partial paradigm of inchoatives vs. A-Class verbs

	A-Class 'to read'	Inchoative 'to become happy'
Infinitive	kɒɹtʰ-ɒ-l √-TH-INF կարդալ	uɹɒχ-ɒ-n-ɒ-l √-LV-INCH-TH-INF ուրախանալ
Past. Pfv. 1SG *	kɒɹtʰ-ɒ-t͡sʰ-i-m √-TH-AOR-PST-1SG կարդացիմ	uɹɒχ-ɒ-t͡sʰ-ɒ-m √-LV-AOR-PST-1SG ուրախացամ
Imp. 2SG *	kɒɹtʰ-ɒ-∅ √-TH-IMP.2SG կարդալ	uɹɒχ-ɒ-t͡sʰ-i √-LV-AOR-IMP.2SG ուրախացի
Imp. 2PL *	kɒɹtʰ-ɒ-t͡sʰ-ekʰ √-TH-AOR-IMP.2PL կարդացէք	uɹɒχ-ɒ-t͡sʰ-ekʰ √-LV-AOR-IMP.2PL ուրախացէք
Subj. Ptcp. *	kɒɹtʰ-ɒ-t͡sʰ-oʁ √-TH-AOR-SPTCP կարդացող	uɹɒχ-ɒ-t͡sʰ-oʁ √-LV-AOR-SPTCP ուրախացող
Res. Ptcp. *	kɒɹtʰ-ɒ-t͡sʰ-ɒtsʰ կարդացած √-TH-AOR-RPTCP	uɹɒχ-ɒ-t͡sʰ-ɒtsʰ ուրախացած √-LV-AOR-RPTCP
Pfv. Cvb. *	kɒɹtʰ-ɒ-t͡sʰ-el kɒɹtʰ-ɒ-t͡sʰ-eɹ √-TH-AOR-PERF.CVB կարդացել, կարդացեր	uɹɒχ-ɒ-t͡sʰ-el uɹɒχ-ɒ-t͡sʰ-eɹ √-LV-AOR-PERF.CVB ուրախացել, ուրախացեր

6.6.3 Causatives

A causative infinitive consists of a stem plus the sequence $-\widehat{ts^h}n\text{-}e\text{-}l$ (Table 6.48). The causative suffix is $-\widehat{ts^h}n\text{-}$ and it takes the $-e-$ theme vowel. The stem of the causative can be the root of a simple verb and its theme vowel. Causatives can also be derived from non-verbs and from inchoative verbs. When a causative is derived from an inchoative, the inchoative suffix and its theme vowel are deleted.[17] The name of the causative is [pattʃarakan] պատճառական in Standard Eastern Armenian.

Table 6.48: Forming causatives

(a) Causatives from simple verbs

Simple verb	Causative
sovoɹ-e-l	sovoɹ-e-$\widehat{ts^h}$n-e-l
√-TH-INF	√-TH-CAUS-TH-INF
'to learn'	'teach'
սովորել	սովորեցնել

(b) Causatives from non-verbs or inchoatives

Non-verb	Inchoative verb	Causative
uɪɒχ	uɪɒχ-ɒ-n-ɒ-l	uɪɒχ-ɒ-$\widehat{ts^h}$n-e-l
√	√-LV-INCH-TH-INF	√-LV-CAUS-TH-INF
'happy'	'to become happy'	'to make happy'
ուրախ	ուրախանալ	ուրախացնել

Our consultants feel that deriving causatives from simple verbs is not very productive in Iranian Armenian.[18] In contrast, causativization is more productive in Standard Eastern and Western Armenian (Daniel & Khurshudian 2015, Dolatian & Guekguezian 2022b). Deriving causatives from inchoatives is productive in Iranian Armenian (Megerdoomian 2005).

In many cases when a causative is derived from a simple verb, the post-root theme vowel differs between the simple verb and causative in Iranian Armenian (Table 6.49).[19]

Some common causatives are listed in Table 6.50. It is common to find causative verbs without any pre-causative vowel.

---

[17]The causative suffix can sometimes surface with a schwa [-$\widehat{ts}$ən-] in Iranian Armenian. This is likewise reported for Standard Eastern (Աբեղյան 1933: 47, Ղարագյուլյան 1974: 163, 1979: 42, Մարգարյան 1997: 59).

[18]Don Stilo (p.c.) suggests that language contact with Persian may be the reason why our IA consultants disprefer such causatives. He reports that:

> There are very few causative verbs in Persian that are formed on transitive verbs and those transitive verbs that are causativized are not commonly used verbs. The causative verbs in Persian are for the most part cases of valency changing strategies, i.e., intransitive > transitive ('be afraid of' > 'scare'). (Stilo, p.c)

[19]Megerdoomian (2005) lists many more cases of causative verbs that are derived from simple verbs but utilize a theme-vowel change.

Table 6.49: Differing pre-causative theme vowels

Theme vowel changes		Theme vowel stays constant	
kʰən-e-l	kʰən-ɒ-t͡sʰn-e-l	kɒɹtʰ-ɒ-l	kɒɹtʰ-ɒ-t͡sʰn-e-l
√-TH-INF	√-TH-CAUS-TH-INF	√-TH-INF	√-TH-CAUS-TH-INF
'to sleep'	'to make sleep'	'to read'	'to make read'
քնել	քնացնել	կարդալ	կարդացնել

Table 6.50: Other common causative verbs in Iranian Armenian

hɒŋgəst-ɒ-t͡sʰn-e-l	'to calm down'	հանգստացնել
ve(ɹ)-t͡sʰn-e-l	'to take'	վերցնել
lə-t͡sʰn-e-l	'to fill/pour'	լցնել
dɒɹ-t͡sʰn-e-l	'to turn into'	դարձնել

√(-LV)-CAUS-TH-INF

In terms of inflection, causatives are inflected primarily as E-Class verbs but with some deviation (Table 6.51). In the past perfective, the causative suffix uses a special allomorph -t͡sʰɹ-. This allomorph is likewise used in disparate paradigm slots. These are slots which tend to show morphomic aorist stems in other verb classes. We show a partial paradigm below. We only show the causative paradigm cells which differ from simple E-Class verbs. We place an asterisk for those paradigm cells where the -t͡sʰɹ- allomorph is used, meaning where we see the aorist stem. The theme vowel is deleted in most of these cells.

Prohibitives are formed by adding the proclitic *mi-* before the imperative forms. For the other paradigm cells, causatives are inflected like E-Class verbs. These cells are the other converbs, the subjunctive, the synthetic future, and the conditional past. The Iranian Armenian forms do not significantly differ from Standard Eastern except for the past perfective. The Standard Eastern past perfective of causatives uses the past tense morph /i/ instead of /ɒ/: Iranian Armenian *sovoɹ-e-t͡sʰɹ-ɒ-n* vs. Standard Eastern *sovor-e-t͡sʰr-i-n* 'they taught'. Complete paradigms are provided in the online archive.

Table 6.51: Partial paradigm of causatives vs. E-Class verbs

	E-Class	Causative
Infinitive	sovoɹ-e-l	sovoɹ-e-t͡sʰn-e-l
	$\sqrt{}$-TH-INF	$\sqrt{}$-TH-CAUS-TH-INF
	սովորել	սովորեցնել
Past. Pfv. 1SG *	sovoɹ-ɒ-m	sovoɹ-e-t͡sʰɹ-ɒ-m
	$\sqrt{}$-PST-1SG	$\sqrt{}$-TH-CAUS-PST-1SG
	սովրամ	սովրեցրամ
Imp. 2SG *	sovoɹ-i	sovoɹ-e-t͡sʰɹ-u
	$\sqrt{}$-IMP.2SG	$\sqrt{}$-TH-CAUS-IMP.2SG
	սովրի	սովրեցրու
Imp. 2PL *	sovoɹ-ekʰ	sovoɹ-e-t͡sʰɹ-ekʰ
	$\sqrt{}$-IMP.2PL	$\sqrt{}$-TH-CAUS-IMP.2PL
	սովրէք	սովրեցրէք
Subj. Ptcp.	sovoɹ-oʁ	sovoɹ-e-t͡sʰn-oʁ
	$\sqrt{}$-SPTCP	$\sqrt{}$-TH-CAUS-SPTCP
	սովրող	սովրեցնող
Res. Ptcp. *	sovoɹ-ɒt͡sʰ	sovoɹ-e-t͡sʰɹ-ɒt͡sʰ
	$\sqrt{}$-RPTCP	$\sqrt{}$-TH-CAUS-RPTCP
	սովրած	սովրեցրած
Pfv. Cvb. *	sovoɹ-el	sovoɹ-e-t͡sʰɹ-el
	sovoɹ-eɹ	sovoɹ-e-t͡sʰɹ-eɹ
	$\sqrt{}$-PERF.CVB	$\sqrt{}$-TH-CAUS-PERF.CVB
	սովրել, սովրեր	սովրեցրել, սովրեցրեր

6.7 Irregular verbs

The regular verb classes were discussed in the previous section. These classes constitute the majority of verbs in the Iranian Armenian lexicon. This section goes over some irregular classes. These are all rather low-frequency in terms of types, but seem high-frequency in their tokens. These irregulars can be divided into different subclasses: infixed verbs, suppletive verbs, defective verbs, and other verbs.

This section focuses on providing paradigms just for Iranian Armenian. To contrast these irregular paradigms with Standard Eastern, see Dum-Tragut (2009: 277ff). Complete paradigms are provided in the online archive.

6.7.1 Infixed verbs

In the infinitive form, simple regular verbs consist of a root, theme vowel, and the infinitive suffix -l. Iranian Armenian likewise has a set of irregular verbs where a meaningless morph /-n-/ surfaces between the root and theme vowel (Table 6.52). We gloss this meaningless verbal stem-extender as vx.[20]

Table 6.52: Infixed irregular verbs in Standard Eastern and Iranian Armenian

IA		SEA		
mət-n-e-l	'to enter'	mət-n-e-l	'to enter'	մտնել
tes-n-e-l	'to see'	tes-n-e-l	'to see'	տեսնել
ɒr-n-e-l	'to buy'	ɑr-n-e-l	'to take'	առնել
el-n-e-l	'to be'	jel-n-e-l	'to get up'	ելնել
tʰoʁ-n-e-l	'to let/leave'	tʰoʁ-n-e-l	'to let/leave'	թողնել
əŋgə-n-e-l	'to fall'	əŋk-n-e-l	'to fall'	ընկնել
itʃʰ-n-e-l	'to descend'	itʃʰ-n-e-l	'to descend'	իջնել
√-VX-TH-INF		√-VX-TH-INF		

Across Armenian lects, this nasal morph /-n-/ is diachronically a reflex of the Proto-Indo-European nasal infix (Greppin 1973, Hamp 1975, Kocharov 2019). Standard Eastern Armenian has these same verbs. However, for some of these verbs, the meaningless morph is an affricate /tʃʰ/ in Standard Eastern Armenian.

---

[20]For the verb əŋgə-n-e-l 'to fall,' the second schwa is epenthetic. It is absent before a vowel: əŋg-ɒ-ŋkʰ 'we fell' [√-PST-1PL].

It seems that Iranian Armenian has lost the affricate morph, and now all the infixed verbs just use the nasal morph (Table 6.53).[21]

Table 6.53: Infixed irregular verbs with affricates in Standard Eastern, but nasals in Iranian Armenian

IA		SEA		
pʰɒχ-n-e-l	փախնել	pʰaχ-t͡ʃʰ-e-l	'to escape'	փախչել
tʰər-n-e-l	թռնել	tʰər-t͡ʃʰ-e-l	'to fly'	թռչել
√-VX-TH-INF		√-VX-TH-INF		

What is irregular about this class is that the nasal is dropped in some but not all paradigm cells (Table 6.54). Whenever the verb lacks this nasal, the verb is said to use its aorist stem. For example, the nasal surfaces in the subjunctive present and the subjunctive past. But the nasal is deleted in the past perfective. The surface morphs are just the root and T-Agr suffixes.

Table 6.54: Nasal deletion in infixed verbs vs. E-Class verbs in Iranian Armenian

	Irregular infixed verb		Regular E-Class	
Infinitive	mer-n-e-l 'to die' մեռնել	√-VX-TH-INF	je.ɭkʰ-e-l 'to sing' երգել	√-TH-INF
Sbjv. Present 1PL	mer-n-e-ŋkʰ մեռնենք	√-VX-TH-1PL	je.ɭkʰ-e-ŋkʰ երգենք	√-TH-1PL
Past Pfv. 1PL	mer-ɒ-ŋkʰ մեռանք	√-PST-1PL	je.ɭkʰ-ɒ-ŋkʰ երգանք	√-PST-1PL

The partial paradigm below shows the finite and non-finite forms of this irregular class (Table 6.55). An asterisk is placed next to each cell that shows the

---

[21]The replacement of the affricate infix with the nasal infix is likewise attested in Colloquial Eastern Armenian (Dum-Tragut 2009: 172), Khoy/Urmia (Ասատրյան 1962: 98), Salmast (Vaux 2022b: §3.2.7), and all of the Southeastern group of dialects, and Van (Աճառյան 1952: 165). We could also find it perhaps in Alashkert, Mush, Agulis, New Julfa and other dialects that often pattern with Salmast.

deletion of this nasal morph. This class is inflected the same as the regular E-Class; the only difference is the deletion of the nasal morph in certain slots.[22]

Table 6.55: Distribution of nasal deletion in Iranian Armenian with [mer-n-e-l] 'to die'

Cell	Form	Gloss	
Infinitive	mer-n-e-l	$\sqrt{}$-VX-TH-INF	մեռնել
Imperfective converb	mer-n-um	$\sqrt{}$-VX-IMPF.CVB	մեռնում
Future converb	mer-n-e-l-u	$\sqrt{}$-VX-TH-INF-FUT.CVB	մեռնելու
Perfective converb *	mer-el, mer-eɹ	$\sqrt{}$-PERF.CVB	մեռել, մեռեր
Connegative converb	mer-n-i	$\sqrt{}$-VX-CN.CVB	մեռնի
Subject participle	mer-n-oʁ	$\sqrt{}$-VX-SPTCP	մեռնող
Resultative participle *	mer-ɒtsʰ	$\sqrt{}$-RPTCP	մեռած
Sbjv. Present 1PL	mer-n-e-ŋkʰ	$\sqrt{}$-VX-TH-1PL	մեռնենք
Sbjv. Past 1PL	mer-n-i-ŋkʰ	$\sqrt{}$-VX-PST-1PL	մեռնինք
Past Pfv. 1PL *	mer-ɒ-ŋkʰ	$\sqrt{}$-PST-1PL	մեռանք
Imperative 2SG *	mer-i	$\sqrt{}$-IMP.2SG	մեռի
Imperative 2PL *	mer-ekʰ	$\sqrt{}$-IMP.2PL	մեռէք
Causative *	mer-tsʰn-e-l	$\sqrt{}$-CAUS-TH-INF	մեռցնել
Passive	N/A		

For brevity, the above paradigm omits zero morphs (theme vowels). For the finite forms, we only show the 1PL; the other agreement cells behave the same with respect to the nasal. We omit the following:

- The negatives that derive from simple prefixation of $\widehat{tʃ^h}$- onto a subjunctive or past perfective base.

- The positive synthetic future and conditional past that are derived by prefixing *k(ə)-* to the subjunctive.

- The prohibitives that are derived by adding the proclitic *mi* to the imperative base.

It is difficult to find a single infixed verb that can be both causativized and passivized (Table 6.56). Causativization generally deletes the nasal morph, as seen in Table 6.55. Passivization generally keeps the nasal morph.

---

[22]In Standard Eastern Armenian, the infixed verbs are irregular in the past perfective not only because they drop the nasal, but also because they use the past T marker /a/: [mer-a-v] 'he died' [$\sqrt{}$-PST-3SG]. But in Iranian Armenian, the use of the past T marker /ɒ/ is a regular feature.

Table 6.56: Passivization of infixed verbs

Active		Passive	
tes-n-e-l	√-VX-TH-INF	tes-nə-v-e-l	√-VX-PASS-TH-INF
'to see'		'to be seen'	
տեսնել		տեսնուել	

For a typical infixed verb like *mer-n-e-l* 'to die', the imperative 2SG is formed by dropping the nasal and using the imperative 2SG suffix -*i*. A subset of these infixed verbs have an irregular imperative 2SG. This set is listed in Table 6.57. The prohibitive 2SG is derived from this imperative by adding the proclitic *mi*.

Table 6.57: Irregular imperative 2SG within irregular infixed verbs

	'to see'	'to buy'	'to let/leave'	
Infinitive	tes-n-e-l	ɒr-n-e-l	tʰoʁ-n-e-l	√-VX-TH-INF
	տեսնել	առնել	թողնել	
Imperative 2SG	tes	ɒr	tʰoʁ	√
	տես	առ	թող	

There is no semantic or morphosyntactic correlation that unites the various cells which show the deletion of the nasal. The distribution is morphomic, and is traditionally described as utilizing an aorist stem. The distribution of nasal dropping is the same in Standard Eastern Armenian, and essentially in Standard Western Armenian as well. Dolatian & Guekguezian (2022a) analyze the cognate infixed verbs of Standard Western Armenian as morphomic and provide an analysis of aorist stems.

For the infixed verb 'to let' [tʰoʁ-n-e-l] թողնել, AS reports that the fricative /ʁ/ can be optionally deleted in some of the inflected forms, such as the imperfective converb [tʰoʁ-n-um] or [tʰo-n-um]. We have not systematically studied this deletion, but it is likely just grammaticalized lenition in a highly-frequent verb. Similar deletion is attested in function words like [əste(ʁ)] 'here' (§5.2).

6.7.2 Suppletive verbs

A small class of irregular verbs are suppletive. These inflect as E-Class verbs in many parts of the paradigm. But in other parts, they use a different root allomorph and irregular imperative suffixes. Suppletive verbs can be categorized into three groups or subclasses, which we catalog below.

The first group of verbs is listed in Table 6.58. For a suppletive verb like 'to eat' *ut-e-l*, the root maintains a constant form *ut-* in many paradigm cells. In some other cells, the root uses a morphologically-conditioned allomorph *keɭ-*. We call *keɭ-* the restricted allomorph, while *ut-* is the elsewhere allomorph.[23] In the traditional literature, the restricted morph is also called the aorist stem.

Table 6.58: Suppletive verbs in Iranian Armenian - Group 1

	'to eat'	'to do'	'to take to'	'to put'	
Elsewhere allomorph:	ut-	ɒn-	tɒn-	dən-	
Infinitive	ut-e-l	ɒn-e-l	tɒn-e-l	dən-e-l	√-TH-INF
	ուտել	անել	տանել	դնել	
Sbjv. present 1PL	ut-e-ŋkʰ	ɒn-e-ŋkʰ	tɒn-e-ŋkʰ	dən-e-ŋkʰ	√-TH-1PL
	ուտենք	անենք	տանենք	դնենք	
Restricted allomorph:	keɭ-	ɒɭ-	tɒɭ-	dəɭ-	
Past Pfv. 1PL	keɭ-ɒ-ŋkʰ	ɒɭ-ɒ-ŋkʰ	tɒɭ-ɒ-ŋkʰ	dəɭ-ɒ-ŋkʰ	√-PST-1PL
	կերանք	արանք	տարանք	դրանք	
Imperative 2SG	keɭ	ɒɭ-ɒ	tɒɭ	diɭ	√-(IMP.2SG)
	կեր	արա	տար	դիր	

For the verb 'to eat', the imperative 2SG is formed by just using the restricted allomorph without further suffixation. In contrast, some suppletive verbs like 'to do' use an additional suffix. Some verbs like 'to put' use a special additional root allomorph that is only found in the imperative 2SG. We list the imperative 2SG of the suppletive verbs in Table 6.58. The prohibitive 2SG is derived from this imperative by adding the proclitic *mi*.

The above suppletive verbs all use the *-e-* theme vowel in their infinitive form. Outside of the imperative 2SG, they pattern the same in the distribution of their root allomorphs.

---

[23]For some of our speakers like NK, the suppletive verb *dən-e-l* 'to put' is pronounced with an initial voiceless stop [t] in all its allomorphs. In contrast, AS and KM report [d], just as in Standard Eastern Armenian.

The partial paradigm in Table 6.59 lists the distribution of the root allomorphs for Group 1 verbs. An asterisk is placed next to each cell that shows the restricted allomorph.[24] The subjunctive forms pattern like E-Class verbs.

Table 6.59: Distribution of root allomorphs in Iranian Armenian for [ut-e-l] 'to eat'

Cell	Form	Gloss	
Infinitive	ut-e-l	$\sqrt{}$-TH-INF	ուտել
Imperfective converb	ut-um	$\sqrt{}$-IMPF.CVB	ուտում
Future converb	ut-e-l-u	$\sqrt{}$-TH-INF-FUT.CVB	ուտելու
Perfective converb *	keɹ-el, keɹ-eɹ	$\sqrt{}$-PERF.CVB	կերել, կերեր
Connegative converb	ut-i	$\sqrt{}$-CN.CVB	ուտի
Subject participle	ut-oʁ	$\sqrt{}$-SPTCP	ուտող
Resultative participle *	keɹ-ɒtsʰ	$\sqrt{}$-RPTCP	կերած
Sbjv. Present 1PL	ut-e-ŋkʰ	$\sqrt{}$-TH-1PL	ուտենք
Sbjv. Past 1PL	ut-i-ŋkʰ	$\sqrt{}$-PST-1PL	ուտինք
Past Pfv. 1PL *	keɹ-ɒ-ŋkʰ	$\sqrt{}$-PST-1PL	կերանք
Imperative 2SG *	keɹ	$\sqrt{}$	կեր
Imperative 2PL *	keɹ-ekʰ	$\sqrt{}$-IMP.2PL	կերեք

The paradigm in Table 6.59 omits zero morphs (theme vowels). For the finite forms, we only show the 1PL; the other agreement cells behave the same with respect to the root allomorphy. We omit the following:

- The negatives that derive from simple prefixation of *tʃʰ*- onto a subjunctive or past perfective base.

- The positive synthetic future and conditional past that are derived by prefixing *k*- to the subjunctive.

- The prohibitives that are derived by adding the proclitic *mi* to the imperative base.

---

[24]As with the infixed verbs, in Standard Eastern Armenian, many of the suppletive verbs are irregular in the past perfective not only because they use a different root allomorph, but also because they use the past T marker /ɑ/: [ker-ɑ-v] 'he ate' [$\sqrt{}$-PST-3SG]. But in Iranian Armenian, the use of the past T marker /ɒ/ is a regular feature for verbs.

The second group of suppletive verbs consists of only the verb [etʰ-ɒ-l] 'to go'. It acts as an A-Class verb in terms of the distribution of theme vowels, the aorist suffix, and the past marker /i/. Its irregularity is that some of its paradigm cells utilize a restricted root allomorph *gən-*. We show a partial paradigm in Table 6.60. The asterisk is used to mark the cells that utilize the restricted allomorph.[25]

Table 6.60: Distribution of root allomorphs in Iranian Armenian for [etʰ-ɒ-l] 'to go'

Cell	Form	Gloss	
Infinitive	etʰ-ɒ-l	√-TH-INF	էթալ
Imperfective converb	etʰ-um	√-IMPF.CVB	էթում
Future converb	etʰ-ɒ-l-u	√-TH-INF-FUT.CVB	էթալու
Perfective converb *	gən-ɒ-t͡sʰ-el	√-TH-AOR-PERF.CVB	գնացել
	gən-ɒ-t͡sʰ-eɹ		գնացեր
Connegative converb	etʰ-ɒ	√-TH	էթայ
Subject participle *	gən-ɒ-t͡sʰ-oʁ	√-TH-AOR-SPTCP	գնացող
Resultative participle *	gən-ɒ-t͡sʰ-ɒtsʰ	√-TH-AOR-RPTCP	գնացած
Sbjv. Present 1PL	etʰ-ɒ-ŋkʰ	√-TH-1PL	էթանք
Sbjv. Past 1PL	etʰ-ɒj-i-ŋkʰ	√-TH-PST-1PL	էթայինք
Past Pfv. 1PL *	gən-ɒ-t͡sʰ-i-ŋkʰ	√-TH-AOR-PST-1PL	գնացինք
Imperative 2SG *	gən-ɒ	√-TH	գնա
Imperative 2PL *	gən-ɒ-t͡sʰ-ekʰ	√-TH-AOR-IMP.2PL	գնացեք

Finally, there is a third group of suppletive verbs (Table 6.61), made up of two members: [t-ɒ-l] 'to give' and [g-ɒ-l] 'to come'. These verbs use the -ɒ- theme vowel, and the elsewhere root allomorph is a single consonant. These two verbs have restricted allomorphs in the past perfective. Each has a separate allomorph used in the imperative 2SG.

---

[25] Some speakers pronounce the elsewhere root allomorph as *eɹtʰ-* instead of *etʰ-*. Some speakers can make the sbjv. past utilize the restricted root *gən-*, e.g. the 1PL form [gən-ɒj-i-ŋkʰ]. Some speakers use the restricted allomorph in the connegative converb: [gən-ɒ] instead of [etʰ-ɒ]. But others have told us that using *gən-* root in these contexts sounds more "Eastern" instead of Iranian Armenian. In Standard Eastern Armenian, the root *gən-* is used to form a regular non-suppletive A-Class verb *gən-a-l* 'to go'. Some of our speakers use this separate verb as well.

Table 6.61: Suppletive verbs with mono-consonantal root

	'to give'	'to come'	
Elsewhere allomorph	t-	g-	
Infinitive	t-ɒ-l	g-ɒ-l	√-TH-INF
	տալ	գալ	
Sbjv. Present 1PL	t-ɒ-ŋkʰ	g-ɒ-ŋkʰ	√-TH-1PL
	տանք	գանք	
Restricted allomorph	təv-	ek-	
Past Pfv. 1PL	təv-ɒ-ŋkʰ	ek-ɒ-ŋkʰ	√-PST-1PL
	տուանք	էկանք	
Imperative 2SG	tuɹ	ɒɹi	√
	տուր	արի	

These two verbs also use a special construction for forming the imperfective converb (Table 6.62). Whereas A-Class verbs use the template √-um, these two verbs use the template √-ɒ-l-is. The suffix *-is* is an irregular imperfective converb suffix. The final fricative is a latent segment, meaning this segment is deleted when the auxiliary has moved such as in negation. This segment's distribution parallels that of the perfective converb's latent segment; see §3.3.4.

Table 6.62: Imperfective converb for suppletive mono-consonantal root

	'to give'	'to come'	
Infinitive	t-ɒ-l	g-ɒ-l	√-TH-INF
	տալ	գալ	
Impf. converb	t-ɒ-l-is	g-ɒ-l-is	√-TH-INF-IMPF.CVB
	տալիս	գալիս	
Indc. Pres. 1PL	t-ɒ-l-is e-ŋkʰ	g-ɒ-l-is e-ŋkʰ	√-TH-INF-IMPF.CVB AUX-1PL
	տալիս ենք	գալիս ենք	
Neg. indc. Pres. 1PL	tʃʰ-e-ŋkʰ t-ɒ-l-i	tʃʰ-e-ŋkʰ g-ɒ-l-i	NEG-AUX-1PL √-TH-INF-IMPF.CVB
	չենք տալիս	չենք գալիս	

The partial paradigm of the verb 'to give' is shown in Table 6.63. The verb 'to come' is inflected similarly.[26] These verbs further differ from the previous set of

---

[26]The subject participle of 'to come' [g-ɒ-l] is typically [ek-oʁ] '√-SPTCP' եկող, but NK says the word [ek-ɒ-t͡sʰ-oʁ] '√-TH-AOR-SPTCP' եկացող is also attested, especially in the phrase [ek-ɒ-t͡sʰ-oʁ t͡ʃʰ-i] meaning 'he's not coming' with the negative 3SG auxiliary. The participle here is used to mean something like 'he's not the type of person to come', such as to a party.

suppletive verbs in that their subject participles utilize the restricted allomorph. Their subjunctive forms pattern like A-Class verbs.

Table 6.63: Distribution of root allomorphs in Iranian Armenian for [t-ɒ-l] 'to give'

Cell	Form	Gloss	
Infinitive	t-ɒ-l	√-TH-INF	տալ
Imperfective converb	t-ɒ-l-is	√-TH-INF-IMPF.CVB	տալիս
Future converb	t-ɒ-l-u	√-TH-INF-FUT.CVB	տալու
Perfective converb *	təv-el, təv-eɹ	√-PERF.CVB	տուել, տուեր
Connegative converb	t-ɒ	√-TH	տայ
Subject participle *	təv-oʁ	√-SPTCP	տուող
Resultative participle *	təv-ɒt͡sʰ	√-RPTCP	տուած
Sbjv. Present 1PL	t-ɒ-ŋkʰ	√-TH-1PL	տանք
Sbjv. Past 1PL	t-ɒj-i-ŋkʰ	√-TH-PST-1PL	տայինք
Past Pfv. 1PL *	təv-ɒ-ŋkʰ	√-PST-1PL	տուանք
Imperative 2SG *	tuɹ	√	տուր
Imperative 2PL *	təv-ekʰ	√-IMP.2PL	տուէք

It is difficult to make generalizations when it comes to causativizing or passivizing suppletive verbs. We have come across causatives of [ut-e-l] 'to eat' that use the elsewhere root allomorph: [ut-e-t͡sʰn-e-l] 'to feed' ուտեցնել. But we have also come across speakers who prefer not causativizing this verb at all. For passivization, Standard Eastern Armenian uses the restricted root allomorph to passivize 'to take to', 'to put', and 'to give'. Some (more literate) Iranian Armenian speakers do this as well: [tɒɹ-v-e-l] տարուել 'to be taken to', [dəɹ-v-e-l] դրուել 'to be put', [təɹ-v-e-l] տրուել 'to be given'. Some Iranian Armenian speakers prefer not passivizing these at all.

6.7.3 Defective verbs

There is a small set of defective verbs in Iranian Armenian. These verbs are defective in not having all possible types of finite and non-finite forms.

One defective verb is the copula, which only appears in the present tense and the past tense. We discussed the copula in §6.2 under the guise of the auxiliary.

Two other defective verbs are the verbs 'to exist' [k-ɒ-m] and 'to have' [un-e-m].[27] The verb 'to exist' is used to mark existential sentences like 'there is X'. The verb 'to have' is more accurately translated as 'to own'. This verb only marks possession and is not an auxiliary.

We show a partial paradigm in Table 6.64 with just the 1SG. Both of these verbs are used only in the indicative present and past, along with the corresponding negated forms. Unlike regular verbs, the indicative of these verbs is formed synthetically. The two verbs use the same T-Agr morphs as the subjunctive of the regular A-Class and E-Class respectively.

Table 6.64: Defective verbs 'to exist' and 'to own'

	'to exist'	'to have'	
Infinitive	N/A	N/A	
Indc. pres. 1SG	k-ɒ-m	un-e-m	$\sqrt{}$-TH-1SG
	կամ	ունեմ	
Neg. indc. pres. 1SG	tʃʰə-k-ɒ-m	tʃʰ-un-e-m	NEG-$\sqrt{}$-TH-1SG
	չկամ	չունեմ	
Indc. past 1SG	k-ɒj-i-m	un-∅-i-m	$\sqrt{}$-TH-PST-1SG
	կայիմ	ունիմ	
Neg. indc. past 1SG	tʃʰə-k-ɒj-i-m	tʃʰ-un-∅-i-m	NEG-$\sqrt{}$-TH-PST-1SG
	չկայիմ	չունիմ	

Note that the past markers are the ones used for the subjunctive past. But for these defective verbs, the meaning can be perfective as in the following examples (14).

(14)   a.   kɒtu un-∅-i-m
         cat   have-TH-PST-1SG
         'I had a cat.'   (NK)
         Կատու ունիմ:
   b.   t͡ʃɒʃ k-ɒ-∅-ɹ
         food exist-TH-PST-3SG
         'There was food.'   (NK)
         Ճաշ կար:

---

[27]For the verb 'to exist', the initial stop is usually voiceless *k-ɒ-m*, but some speakers voice it: *g-ɒ-m*.

For the verb 'to have', all other tenses are expressed by using the regular inchoative verb [un-e-n-ɒ-l] 'to have; own'. For the verb 'to exist', other tenses are
expressed by using the verb 'to be' (15).

(15) a. t͡ʃɒʃ k-el-n-i-∅
         food FUT-be-vx-TH-3SG
         'There will be food.'
         Ճաշ կելնի:

      b. t͡ʃɒʃ piti el-n-i-∅
         food must be-vx-TH-3SG
         'There will be food.'
         Ճաշ պիտի էլնի:

Another defective verb is the word for 'to be worth', but it is quite restricted in
use (16). It has two main functions: to say how much some item is worth or costs,
and as part of a social phrase. For Standard Eastern Armenian, it is restricted
to the indicative present and past imperfective, but synthetically. It is usable for
any person-number combination. However for Iranian Armenian, it seems to be
mainly used for the third person, and we have not been able to successfully elicit
it for other persons. Our online paradigms show all the possible persons (as they
would hypothetically be constructed), but it is possible there there are paradigm
gaps.

(16) a. hiŋg dolɒɹ ɒɹʒ-i-∅
         five dollar worth-TH-3SG
         'It's worth five dollars.'
         Հինգ դոլար արժի:

      b. t͡ʃʰ-ɒɹʒ-i-∅
         NEG-worth-TH-3SG
         Literal translation: 'It's not worth it.'
         Functional translation: 'You're welcome.'
         չարժի

Standard Eastern Armenian has a few additional defective verbs (Table 6.65).
But in Iranian Armenian, these have either been replaced or are not used in general.[28]

---

[28]It is difficult to be sure if these verbs truly do not exist in IA because of diglossia between IA
and SEA.

Table 6.65: Loss of defective verbs from Standard Eastern to Iranian
Armenian

Defective in Standard Eastern			Status in Iranian Armenian
$\sqrt{\text{-TH-1SG}}$			
hus-ɑ-m	'I hope'	հուսամ	does not exist
git-e-m	'I know'	գիտեմ	replaced by inchoative [im-ɒ-n-ɒ-l] իմանալ

6.7.4 Other irregular verbs

This section discusses verbs that have some irregularity in their conjugation, but
do not neatly fit into the previous categories.

Two irregular verbs in Table 6.66 are conjugated as regular E-Class verbs in
most of the paradigm except for the imperative 2SG (and prohibitive 2SG).

Table 6.66: E-Class verbs that are irregular in only the imperative 2SG

	'to say'	'to bring'	
Infinitive	ɒs-e-l	beɹ-e-l	$\sqrt{\text{-TH-INF}}$
	ասել	բերել	
Imperative	ɒs-ɒ	beɹ	$\sqrt{(\text{-IMP.2SG})}$
	ասա	բեր	

The verb 'to bring' has an irregular imperative 2SG also in SEA *ber* and in
SWA *pʰeɾ*. The verb 'to say' has an irregular imperative 2SG in SEA *as-a* but not
in SWA *əs-e* $\sqrt{\text{-TH}}$.

Among inchoative verbs (Table 6.67), the verb [dɒr-n-ɒ-l] has some irregularities. Before the nasal inchoative suffix, the rhotic surfaces as a trill /r/. But before
the aorist suffix, the rhotic is a retroflex approximant /ɹ/.[29] The inchoative 'to
wash' is irregular because it uses the past T marker /i/ in the past perfective. Its

---

[29]We have gotten some contradictory information from some informants. It is possible that some
more innovative speakers use a retroflex /ɹ/ throughout this verb's paradigm, while other more
conservative speakers have the /r/-/ɹ/ change as we describe above. Note that this verb has an
irregular imperative 2SG in Standard Eastern Armenian: [dɑrtsʰ]. In Iranian Armenian, the
imperative 2SG is regular.

imperative 2SG is likewise irregular.[30] One can argue this verb is actually heteroclitic (= mixed) with the A-Class because its past perfective and imperative pattern with the A-Class instead of with inchoatives.

Table 6.67: Two irregular inchoatives against the regular inchoative 'to become happy'

	Infinitive	Past Pfv. 1PL	Imperative 2SG
'to become happy'	aɫɒχ-ɒ-n-ɒ-l	aɫɒχ-ɒ-t͡sʰ-ɒ-ŋkʰ	aɫɒχ-ɒ-t͡sʰ-i
	√-LV-INCH-TH-INF	√-LV-AOR-PST-1PL	√-LV-AOR-IMP.2SG
	ուրախանալ	ուրախացանք	ուրախացիր
'to turn into'	dɒɾ-n-ɒ-l	dɒɟ-t͡sʰ-ɒ-ŋkʰ	dɒɟ-t͡sʰ-i
	√-INCH-TH-INF	√-AOR-PST-1PL	√-AOR-IMP.2SG
	դառնալ	դարձանք	դարձիր
'to wash'	ləv-ɒ-n-ɒ-l	ləv-ɒ-t͡sʰ-i-ŋkʰ	ləv-ɒ
	√-LV-INCH-TH-INF	√-LV-AOR-PST-1PL	√-LV
	լուանալ	լուացինք	լուա

There is evidence that Iranian Armenian has leveled out some irregularities in verbal inflection (Table 6.68). The following verbs are irregular in Standard Eastern Armenian but they either a) are regular verbs in Iranian Armenian, or b) have been replaced by regular verbs in Iranian Armenian.

Table 6.68: Loss of irregulars in Iranian Armenian, relative to Standard Eastern

Irregular in SEA		Status in IA		
zaɾk-e-l	'to hit'	replaced by E-Class	χəpʰ-e-l	'to hit'
զարկել			խփել	
l-ɑ-l	'to cry'	replaced by E-Class	lɒt͡sʰ-e-l	'to cry'
լալ			լացել	
bɑt͡sʰ-e-l	'to open'	regularized E-Class		
բացել				
ken-ɑ-l	'to stand'	replaced by E-Class	kɒŋg(ə)n-e-l	'to stand'
կենալ			կանգնել	

---

[30]The origin of the imperative 2SG of 'to wash' is likely from the synonymous A-Class verb [ləv-ɑ-l] which exists in Standard Eastern Armenian but not Iranian Armenian.

One convoluted case involves the Standard Eastern words [lin-e-l] 'to be' and [jel-n-e-l] 'to get up' or 'to go up' (Table 6.69). The first is suppletive; the second is an infixed verb. In Iranian Armenian, the form of the second verb is used as the verb 'to be', without an initial glide: [el-n-e-l]. The meaning of 'to get up' or 'to go up' is periphrastic with another verb.

Table 6.69: Lexical shift from Standard Eastern to Iranian Armenian

	SEA		IA	
	'to be'	'to get up'	'to be'	'to get up'
Infinitive	lin-e-l	jel-n-e-l	el-n-e-l	etʰ-ɒ-l veɹev
	$\sqrt{}$-TH-INF	$\sqrt{}$-VX-TH-INF	$\sqrt{}$-VX-TH-INF	$\sqrt{}$-TH-INF up
	լինել	ելնել	էլնել	էթալ վերև
Past Pfv. 1PL	jeʁ-a-ŋkʰ	jel-a-ŋkʰ	el-a-ŋkʰ	gən-ɒ-tsʰ-i-ŋkʰ veɹev
	$\sqrt{}$-PST-1PL	$\sqrt{}$-PST-1PL	$\sqrt{}$-PST-1PL	$\sqrt{}$-TH-AOR-PST-1PL up
	եղանք	ելանք	էլանք	գնացինք վերև

We have noted some degree of optional heteroclisis (Stump 2006), meaning that a verb changes its conjugation class in some paradigm cells (Table 6.70). Consider the common verb *siɹ-e-l* 'to like'. This verb is primarily a regular E-Class verb and is inflected as such. But in the past perfective, some speakers conjugate the verb as E-Class and some as A-Class. NK sometimes produced perfective converbs with the aorist stem, following the A-Class pattern.

Table 6.70: Variable aorist stem as a form of heteroclisis

	'to like'		
Infinitive	sir-e-l	$\sqrt{}$-TH-INF	սիրել
Past Pfv. 1SG	siɹ-ɒ-m	$\sqrt{}$-PST-1SG	սիրամ
	siɹ-ɒ-tsʰ-i-m	$\sqrt{}$-TH-AOR-PST-1SG	սիրացիմ
Pfv. converb	siɹ-el, siɹ-eɹ	$\sqrt{}$-PERF.CVB	սիրել, սիրեր
	siɹ-ɒ-tsʰ-el, siɹ-ɒ-tsʰ-eɹ	$\sqrt{}$-TH-AOR-PERF.CVB	սիրացել, սիրացեր

Some speakers consider the A-Class forms to be normal, but others perceive them as "done in jest." It is difficult to tell if this is genuine inter-speaker variation, or if it is due to hyper-correction from Standard Eastern Armenian.

Another possible case of heteroclisis that we found was for the A-Class verb [χos-ɒ-l] 'to speak'. NK inflects this as an A-Class almost always, but sometimes she produced an imperative 2PL that followed the E-Class pattern [χos-ekʰ] √-IMP.2PL instead of the A-Class pattern [χos-ɒ-t͡sʰ-ekʰ] √-TH-AOR-IMP.2PL. She likewise once produced an E-Class infinitive [χos-e-l] instead of [χos-ɒ-l]. Obviously, more data is needed to see the extent of lexical or speaker variation in such mixing of conjugation classes. It is possible that such class changes are a form of dialect-mixing between Iranian Armenian and Standard Eastern Armenian.

7 Syntax

In terms of its syntax, Iranian Armenian is largely identical to Standard Eastern Armenian. As such, we do not go over the syntax of Iranian Armenian in depth. In terms of general typological features, Iranian Armenian is SOV (1a), has optional post-verbal objects (1b), uses pro-drop (1c), and contextually-implied objects can drop too (1d).

(1) a. d͡ʒɒn-ə   ind͡z   mɒkʰɫ-ɒ-v
     John-DEF I.DAT clean-PST-3SG

     'John cleaned me.'   (NK)

     Ջոնը ինձ մաքրաւ:

   b. d͡ʒɒn-ə   mɒkʰɫ-ɒ-v   ind͡z
     John-DEF clean-PST-3SG I.DAT

     'John cleaned me.'   (NK)

     Ջոնը ինձ մաքրաւ:

   c. mɒkʰuɫ e-m
     clean   AUX-1SG

     'I am clean.'   (NK)

     Մաքուր եմ:

   d. i. d͡ʒuɫ-ə   χəm-ɒ-ɫ
          water-DEF drink-PST-2SG

          'Did you drink the water?'   (NK)

          Ջուրը խմա՞ր:

       ii. ɒjo, χəm-ɒ-m
          yes drink-PST-1SG

          'Yes, I drank it '   (NK)

          Այո, խմամ:

   More in-depth studies of Standard Eastern Armenian syntax exist (Dum-Tragut 2009, Yeghiazaryan 2010, Su 2012, Hodgson 2019b, Khurshudyan & Don-abédian 2021) and these descriptions largely apply to Iranian Armenian. Further-more, there are some studies of "Eastern Armenian", but these are actually done based on data from Iranian Armenian speakers who are bi-dialectal (Stevick 1955, Tamrazian 1994, Megerdoomian 2009).

This chapter focuses on describing those aspects of Iranian Armenian syntax that are innovative when compared to Standard Eastern. Some of these are grammaticalized from attested colloquial and optional properties of Standard Eastern Armenian. Some of these changes were likely encouraged by the use of similar structures in Persian (cf. other language-contact effects in the region: Donabédian & Sitaridou 2020). These changes are listed below.

- Using the second person possessive suffix as an object clitic (§7.1) → borrowed from Persian

- Preference for using resumptive pronouns over case-marked relativizers (§7.2) → language-internal but encouraged from Persian

- Preference for subjunctive marking in complement clauses (§7.3) → language-internal but encouraged from Persian

- Variation in expressing subject marking in participle clauses (§7.4) → language-internal

In previous sections of this grammar, we did briefly discuss some major aspects of Iranian Armenian syntax. These include auxiliary movement (§3.3.1) and interrogative questions (§5.3). Their syntax does not significantly differ from Standard Eastern Armenian.

Throughout this chapter, Persian sentences were elicited from Nazila Shafiei (NS), an Iranian syntactician. We use the glossing that she provided. The IPA transcriptions were double-checked with Koorosh Ariyaee, an Iranian phonologist.[1] The Standard Eastern Armenian sentences were judged by the consultants mentioned in §1.4.

7.1 Object clitic for second person

Due to contact with Persian, Iranian Armenian has extended the use of the 2SG possessive suffix /-(ə)t/ into an object clitic. Within Armenian dialectology, the use of /-(ə)t/ as an object clitic has been previously attested for Armenian dialects in Iran (Sayeed & Vaux 2017: 1159, citing Աճառեան 1911: 284, Սուրածյան et al.

---

[1]Ariyeae notes that what we transcribed as a Persian [ɒ] may be closer to [ɑ] for Iranian Persian speakers. See footnote 10 in §2.1.4 for discussion.

1977: item 675, Khurshudian 2020: 340, Hodgson 2022, Martirosyan 2018: 87, Vaux 2022b: §4.1).

For the Armenian community of Tehran and the diaspora, AS reports that this use of the clitic is "prevalent in generation Y's vernacular," where generation Y is anyone born in the 80's or 90's. The use of the clitic is stigmatized because it is part of a "very informal register." Speakers are aware of the register difference.

Most of our consultants could use the Armenian possessive as an object clitic. Some Iranian Armenians who were born and raised in the diaspora however said they had never heard of such constructions.

7.1.1 General use of the object clitic

In its typical uses, the morpheme /-(ə)t/ acts as a second person possessive suffix on nouns (2).

(2) senjɒk-ət
     room=POSS.2SG
     'your room'
     Սենեակդ:

But in Iranian Armenian, this morpheme also functions as an object clitic (3). As a clitic, this morpheme has some correlations with tense, mood, and valency. For example, many instances of the clitic are found for verbs with the synthetic future. The clitic is mostly used to replace the direct object of a transitive verb.

(3) a. kə-χəpʰ-e-m   kʰez
         FUT-hit-TH-1SG you.SG.DAT
         'I will hit you.'   (NK, AP, KM)
         Կը խփեմ քեզ:
     b. kə-χəpʰ-e-m=ət
         FUT-hit-TH-1SG=POSS.2SG
         'I will hit you.'   (NK, AP, KM)
         Կը խփեմդ:

Throughout this chapter, we gloss the /(ə)t/ morpheme consistently as a possessive, even when it is functioning as an object clitic /=(ə)t/.

Although the second person possessive /-(ə)t/ can function as an object clitic, the first person possessive /-(ə)s/ cannot (4).

(4) a. kə-χəpʰ-e-n   in͡dz
FUT-hit-TH-3PL I.DAT
'They will hit me.'   (NK)
Կը խփեն ինձ:

b. *kə-χəpʰ-e-n=əs
FUT-hit-TH-3PL=POSS.1SG
Intended: 'They will hit me.'   (*NK)

Similarly, the definite suffix is used for third person possessive marking, but it cannot be used as an object clitic (5).

(5) a. kə-χəpʰ-e-m   irɒn
FUT-hit-TH-1SG he.DAT
'I will hit him.'   (NK)
Կը խփեմ իրան:

b. *kə-χəpʰ-e-m=ə
FUT-hit-TH-1SG=DEF
Intended: 'I will hit him.'   (*NK)

There is no clitic option for plural objects.

The use of the possessive /-t/ as an object clitic likely developed by contact from Persian, which has an entire set of pronominal clitics that act as object clitics for every person-number combination (Mahootian 2002: 138, Samvelian & Tseng 2010). The object of a transitive verb can be either present (6a) or absent (6b). When the object is absent, Persian uses object clitics on the verb (6b).

(6)   Object cliticization in Persian
a. (mæn) to=ro   mi-zæn-æm
(I)   you=OM IMPF-hit-1SG
'I'm going to hit you.'   (NS)
من تو رو میزنم.

b. (mæn) mi-zæn-æm=et
(I)   IMPF-hit-1SG=2SG
'I'm going to hit you.'   (NS)
من میزنمت.

Although Persian allows object clitics for every person-number combination, Iranian Armenian has an object clitic /-t/ for only the 2SG. It is unclear why this restriction exists. Don Stilo (p.c.) suggests that the restriction might exist because of formality. To quote him:

It seems to me that this use of the possessive clitic as an object clitic only with the 2nd singular further emphasizes the 'informal' nature of this pattern. That is, since it is only used in the 2nd singular, this possibly shows that it is only used with friends. Otherwise, what would be the logic of using it only in the 2nd singular when Persian uses these clitics universally in all persons?

Furthermore, as we discuss in the following sections, the object clitic prefers certain tenses and moods; it is unclear to us if these restrictions were also copied from Persian.

7.1.2 Object clitic for direct objects in the synthetic future

As stated earlier, the most typical use of the object clitic is to replace the direct object of a verb in the synthetic future. The synthetic future is marked by the prefix /k-/.

The object clitic can be used for a range of verbs (7). These all seem to be verbs of physical action. More data is needed to determine if this is a general restriction or a tendency. For some cases, the use of the clitic carries an emphatic connotation, e.g., *kə-spɒn-e-m=ət* '(I am so mad that) I will kill you'.

(7) a. i. kə-spɒn-e-m   kʰez
         FUT-kill-TH-1SG you.SG.DAT
         'I will kill you.'   (NK)
         Կը սպանեմ քեզ:

     ii. kə-spɒn-e-m=ət
         FUT-kill-TH-1SG=POSS.2SG
         'I will kill you.'   (NK)
         Կը սպանեմդ:

     b. i. kə-χeχt-e-m   kʰez
         FUT-strangle-TH-1SG you.SG.DAT
         'I will strangle you.'   (NK)
         Կը խեղդեմ քեզ:

     ii. kə-χeχt-e-m=ət
         FUT-strangle-TH-1SG=POSS.2SG
         'I will strangle you.'   (NK)
         Կը խեղդեմդ:

c. i. kə-bərn-e-m   kʰez
   FUT-hold-TH-1SG you.SG.DAT
   'I will hold you.'   (NK)
   Կը բռնեմ քեզ:

ii. kə-bərn-e-m=ət.
   FUT-hold-TH-1SG=POSS.2SG
   'I will hold you.'   (NK)
   Կը բռնեմ քեզ:
   Կը բռնեմդ:

For some transitives, the clitic cannot be used by AP (8). Some of them can be used by KM.

(8) a. i. kə-tɒn-e-m   kʰez
      FUT-take-TH-1SG you.SG.DAT
      'I will take you.'   (AP).
      Կը տանեմ քեզ:

   ii. *kə-tɒn-e-m=ət
      FUT-take-TH-1SG=POSS.2SG
      'I will take you.'   (*AP, okay KM)
      Կը տանեմդ:

   b. i. kə-pʰəntr-e-m   kʰez
      FUT-take-TH-1SG you.SG.DAT
      'I will look for you.'   (AP)
      Կը փնտռեմ քեզ:

   ii. *kə-pʰəntr-e-m=ət
      FUT-take-TH-1SG=POSS.2SG
      Intended: 'I will look for you.'   (*AP)

The verb [mɒt͡ʃʰel] 'to kiss' cannot take the clitic for NK (9).

(9) a. kə-mɒt͡ʃʰ-e-m   kʰez
      FUT-kiss-TH-1SG you.SG.DAT
      'I will like you.'   (NK)
      Կը մաչեմ քեզ:

   b. *kə-mɒt͡ʃʰ-e-m=ət
      FUT-kiss-TH-1SG=POSS.2SG
      Intended: 'I will kiss you.'   (*NK)

In the domain of verbs of speech, the transitive verbs [kɒnt͡ʃʰel] 'to call' and [zɒŋgel] 'to phone' can take the clitic for some speakers (10).

(10) a. i. kə-kɒnt͡ʃʰ-e-m   kʰez
            FUT-call-TH-1SG you.SG.DAT
            'I will call you.'   (AP)
            Կը կանչեմ քեզ:

      ii. kə-kɒnt͡ʃʰ-e-m=ət
            FUT-call-TH-1SG=POSS.2SG
            'I will call you.'   (AP)
            Կը կանչեմդ:

  b. i. kə-zɒŋg-e-m   kʰez
            FUT-phone-TH-1SG you.SG.DAT
            'I will phone you.'   (AS)
            Կը զանգեմ քեզ:

      ii. kə-zɒŋg-e-m=ət
            FUT-call-TH-1SG=POSS.2SG
            'I will phone you.'   (AS)
            Կը զանգեմդ:

AS provides a common example with the verb 'to see'. He reports that this is a social expression and a calque from Persian (11).

(11) kə-g-ɒ-s   kə-tesn-e-m=ət
      FUT-come-TH-2SG FUT-see-TH-1SG=POSS.2SG
      'Come, let me see you.'   (AS)
      Կը գաս, կը տեսնեմդ.

Some verbs like [siɹel] 'to like' cannot take the clitic for some speakers (12). It is unclear if this is idiosyncratic, or if it reflects a restriction against verbs of non-physical action.

(12) a. kə-siɹ-e-m   kʰez
            FUT-like-TH-1SG you.SG.DAT
            'I will like you.'   (NK)
            Կը սիրեմ քեզ:

  b. *kə-siɹ-e-m=ət
            FUT-like-TH-1SG=POSS.2SG
            'Intended: 'I will like you.'   (*NK)
            Կը սիրեմդ:

173

7.1.3 Object clitic for other tenses and moods

The previous section focused on examples of the object clitic when the verb is in the synthetic future. It is rather difficult to find cases where the clitic is added for other tenses and moods for some of our consultants.

In other synthetic tenses, NK expressed uncertainty about using the clitic in the subjunctive (13).

(13) a. uz-um   e-m   kʰez   χəpʰ-e-m
      want-IMPF.CVB AUX-1SG you.SG.DAT hit-TH-1SG
      'I want to hit you.'   (NK)
      Ուզում եմ քեզ խփեմ:

     b. ?uz-um   e-m   χəpʰ-e-m=ət
      want-IMPF.CVB AUX-1SG hit-TH-1SG=POSS.2SG
      Intended: 'I want to hit you.'   (?NK)

AS however provides an example in the subjunctive. The phrase is a social expression (14).

(14) ɒɹi   tes-n-e-m=ət
     come.IMP.2SG see-VX-TH-1SG=POSS.2SG
     'Come, let me see you.'   (AS)
     Արի, տեսնեմդ:

For the past perfective, NK reports that she cannot use the object clitic (15).

(15) a. χəpʰ-ɒ-m   kʰez
      hit-PST-1SG you.SG.DAT
      'I hit (past) you.'   (NK)
      Խփամ քեզ:

     b. *χəpʰ-ɒ-m=ət
      hit-PST-1SG=POSS.2SG
      Intended: 'I hit (past) you.'   (*NK)

For periphrastic tenses, AS reports that the object clitic can be used (16). In such cases, the clitic would cliticize onto the auxiliary. Such cliticization is also reported in the Armenian dialect of Urmia in Iran (Ղարիբյան 1941: 282).

(16) a. i. nɒj-um   e-m   kʰez
        look-IMPF.CVB AUX-1SG you.SG.DAT
        'I am looking at you.'   (AS)
        Նայում եմ քեզ:

ii. nɒj-um e-m=ət
look-IMPF.CVB AUX-1SG=POSS.2SG

'I am looking at you.' (AS)

Նայում եմդ:

b. i. spɒs-um e-m kʰez
wait-IMPF.CVB AUX-1SG you.SG.DAT

'I am waiting for you.' (AS)

Սպասում եմ քեզ:

ii. spɒs-um e-m=ət
wait-IMPF.CVB AUX-1SG=POSS.2SG

'I am waiting for you.' (AS)

Սպասում եմդ:

c. i. kɒɹot-el e-m kʰez
miss-IMPF.CVB AUX-1SG you.SG.DAT

'I've missed you.' (AS)

Կարոտել եմ քեզ:

ii. kɒɹot-el e-m=ət
miss-IMPF.CVB AUX-1SG=POSS.2SG

'I've missed you.' (AS)

Կարոտել եմդ:

Don Stilo (p.c.) informs us that Persian can also add the object clitic to some periphrastic tenses, such as the present perfect (17).

(17) Persian (formal register)

di-d-e æm=æt
IMPF-look-PTCP AUX.1SG=2SG

'I have looked at you.' (NS, Don Stilo)

دیده‌امت

More common colloquial version with reduction: [di-d-æm-et]

7.1.4 Cliticizing other verbal arguments

All previous examples were cases where the object clitic replaced the direct object of a transitive verb. For other types of verbal arguments, we have found mixed judgments. We go through these other possible arguments.

The clitic has varying grammaticality when used to replace an indirect object (18). NK felt that use of the clitic was possible but sounded "silly." KM cannot say these.

(18) a. k-ɒs-e-m   kʰez
    FUT-say–TH-1SG you.SG.DAT
    'I will tell you.'   (NK)
    Կասեմ քեզ:

   b. k-ɒs-e-m=ət
    FUT-say-TH-1SG=POSS.2SG
    'I will tell you.'   (NK, *KM)
    Կասեմդ:

AS reports an example of an indirect object in the subjunctive (19).

(19) me bɒn ɒs-e-m=ət
   INDF thing tell-TH-1SG=POSS.2SG
   'Let me tell you something'.   (AS)
   Մի բան ասեմդ

As before, the indirect object clitic is not used in the past perfective (20).

(20) a. ɒs-ɒ-m   kʰez
    say-PST-1SG you.SG.DAT
    'I told you.'   (NK)
    Ասամ քեզ:

   b. *ɒs-ɒ-m=ət   .
    say-PST-1SG=POSS.2SG
    Intended: 'I told you.'   (*NK)

So far, it seems there is significant speaker variation for using the object clitic in place of an indirect object. Much stronger negative judgments are found for other possible arguments. For example, benefactive phrases cannot be replaced by the object clitic (21).

(21) a. jes kə-jeɹkʰ-e-m   kʰo   hɒmɒɹ
    I FUT-sing-TH-1SG you.SG.GEN for
    'I will sing for you.'   (NK)
    Ես կը երգեմ քո համար:

   b. *jes kə-jeɹkʰ-e-m=ət
    I FUT-sing-TH-1SG=POSS.2SG
    Intended: 'I will sing for you.'   (*NK)

However, AP reports that they can add the clitic onto the benefactive postposition (22).

(22) a. kʰo   hɒmɒɹ kə-jeɹkʰ-e-m
          you.SG.GEN for   FUT-sing-TH-1SG
          'I will sing for you.'   (AP)
          Քn համար կը երգեմ:
     b. hɒmɒɹ=ət   kə-jeɹkʰ-e-m
          for=POSS.2SG FUT-sing-TH-1SG
          'I will sing for you.'   (AP)
          Համարդ կը երգեմ:

Second-person substantives cannot be replaced by the object clitic (23).

(23) a. jes kʰo   jeɹkʰ-ə   kə-jeɹkʰ-e-m
          I   you.SG.GEN song-DEF FUT-sing-TH-1SG
          'I will sing your song.'   (NK)
          Ես քո երգը կը երգեմ:
     b. jes kʰon-ə   kə-jeɹkʰ-e-m
          I   yours-DEF FUT-sing-TH-1SG
          'I will sing yours.'   (NK)
          Ես քոնը կը երգեմ:
     c. *jes kə-jeɹkʰ-e-m-ət
          I   FUT-sing-TH-1SG=POSS.2SG
          Intended: 'I will sing yours'.   (*NK)

Nor can we turn the indirect object of the verb 'to speak' into an object clitic (24e). More accurately, the restriction could be against comitatives.

(24) a. kə-χos-ɒ-m
          FUT-speak-TH-1SG
          'I will speak.'   (NK)
          Կը խոսամ:
     b. jes es   lezu-n   kə-χos-ɒ-m
          I   this language-DEF FUT-speak-TH-1SG
          'I will speak this language.'   (NK)
          Ես էս լեզուն կը խոսամ:

c. jes es lezu-n   d͡ʒon-i   het kə-χos-ᴅ-m
   I   this language-ᴅᴇꜰ John-ɢᴇɴ with ꜰᴜᴛ-speak-ᴛʜ-1ꜱɢ
   'I will speak this language with John.'   (NK)
   Ես էս լեզուն Ջոնի հետ կը խոսամ:

d. jes es lezu-n   kʰo   het kə-χos-ᴅ-m
   I   this language-ᴅᴇꜰ you.ꜱɢ.ɢᴇɴ with ꜰᴜᴛ-speak-ᴛʜ-1ꜱɢ
   'I will speak this language with you.'   (NK)
   Ես էս լեզուն քո հետ կը խոսամ:

e. *jes es lezu-n   kə-χos-ᴅ-m=ət
   I   this language-ᴅᴇꜰ ꜰᴜᴛ-speak-ᴛʜ-1ꜱɢ=ᴘᴏꜱꜱ.2ꜱɢ
   Intended: 'I will speak this language with you'.   (*NK)

7.2 Resumptive pronouns in relative clauses

In Standard Eastern Armenian, relative clauses utilize case marking on the relativizer (relative pronoun *voɾ*: 25a). The use of a resumptive pronoun is judged
as ungrammatical, unnatural, or excessive for speakers (25b), and it is not even
mentioned in the Dum-Tragut grammar (2009: 478).

(25) Standard Eastern Armenian

a. ajn kin-ə   **voɾ-its**ʰ ajs giɾkʰ-ə   veɾ-t͡sʰɾ-e-t͡sʰ-i-∅
   that woman-ᴅᴇꜰ **that-ᴀʙʟ** this book-ᴅᴇꜰ buy-ᴄᴀᴜꜱ-ᴛʜ-ᴀᴏʀ-ᴘꜱᴛ-1ꜱɢ
   'that woman from whom I bought this book'   (MA, VK, VP)
   այն կինը որից այս գիրքը վերցրեցի

b. ajn kin-ə   **voɾ iɾen-its**ʰ ajs giɾkʰ-ə
   that woman-ᴅᴇꜰ **that she-ᴀʙʟ** this book-ᴅᴇꜰ
   veɾ-t͡sʰɾ-e-t͡sʰ-i-∅
   buy-ᴄᴀᴜꜱ-ᴛʜ-ᴀᴏʀ-ᴘꜱᴛ-1ꜱɢ
   'that woman from whom I bought this book'   (MA, ?VK, *VP)
   այն կինը որ իրենից այս գիրքը վերցրեցի

MA felt the use of a resumptive pronoun was grammatical but "includes complexity that we can avoid."

Similarly for Standard Western Armenian, HD's judgments are that using a
case-marked relativizer is the norm (26a). Using a separate resumptive pronoun
(26b) doesn't sound ungrammatical, but does sound "excessively clunky." It creates a sense that the relative clause is an after-thought.

(26) Standard Western Armenian

a. ajn gin-ə   **vor-m-e**   ajs kʰiɾkʰ-ə kʰənn-e-t͡sʰ-i-Ø
    that woman-DEF **that-NX-ABL** this book-DEF buy-TH-AOR-PST-1SG
    'that woman from whom I bought this book'   (HD)
    այն կինը որմէ այս գիրքը գնեցի

b. ?ajn gin-ə   **vor iɾ-m-e**   ajs kʰiɾkʰ-ə
    that woman-DEF **that she-NX-ABL** this book-DEF
    kʰənn-e-t͡sʰ-i-Ø
    buy-TH-AOR-PST-1SG
    'that woman from whom I bought this book'   (?HD)
    այն կինը որ իրմէ այս գիրքը գնեցի

However, resumptive pronouns are attested in some Colloquial Eastern Armenian registers (Polinsky 1995: 100, Hodgson 2020b: ex:5). Such resumptive pronouns are also attested and seem to be more common in Classical and Middle Armenian (Hewitt 1978, Hodgson 2020b: §3.3) and some other Armenian dialects (Aslanbeg: Vaux 2001: 53).

In contrast, in Iranian Armenian, both strategies are attested (27a), at least for clauses where the head noun acts as an ablative argument in the relative clause. For a bi-dialectal speaker like KM, both options were possible, while the resumptive pronoun feels more common (27b). For a mono-lectal speaker like NK, the resumptive pronoun strategy was the default, while using a case-marked complementizer felt odd.

(27) Iranian Armenian

a. en kin-ə   **voɾ-uts͡ʰ** es giɾkʰ-ə veɾ-t͡sʰɹ-ɒ-m
    that woman-DEF **that-ABL** this book-DEF take-CAUS-PST-1SG
    'that woman from whom I took this book'   (KM, ?NK)
    էն կինը որուց էս գիրքը վերցրամ

b. en kin-ə   **voɾ** jes **iɹɒn-its͡ʰ** es giɾkʰ-ə veɾ-t͡sʰɹ-ɒ-m
    that woman-DEF **that** I she-ABL this book–DEF take-CAUS-PST-1SG
    'that woman from whom I took this book'   (KM, NK)
    էն կինը որ ես իրանից էս գիրքը վերցրամ

It's unknown if the preference for resumptive pronouns is constant across all possible types of case-marking (nominative, accusative, genitive/dative, ablative, instrumental, and locative). However, as Katherine Hodgson reminds us, the Relativization Accessibility Hierarchy (Keenan & Comrie 1977) says that resumptives should be more common with lower roles like ablative than with higher ones like subject.

The preference for resumptive pronouns is likely due to contact with Persian (28). In Persian, if the head noun has oblique case in the relative clause, then the only strategy is to use a resumptive pronominal clitic (Mahootian 2002: 34, Abdollahnejad 2018: 2). The relativizer /ke/ cannot be case-marked.

(28) Persian
    un zæn-i   ke æz-æʃ in ketɒb-ro xærid-æm
    that woman-DEF that from-her this book-OM bought-1SG
    'the woman from whom I bought this book'   (NS)

اون زنی که ازش این کتاب رو خریدم

7.3 Subjunctive marking in complement clauses

In Standard Eastern Armenian, a modal verb like 'want' can select complement clauses where the verb is an infinitive (29a). The implicit subject of the complement clause is the subject of the main clause. An alternative strategy is to include a complementizer *vor*, and then change the verb into a finite subjunctive verb (29b). Both of these two options are judged as prescriptive norms. A third alternative however is to omit the complementizer but still use a subjunctive verb (29c). This third alternative is judged as quite colloquial (Dum-Tragut 2009: 425–427).

(29) Standard Eastern Armenian
    a. uz-um   e-n   indz gorts-i **dən-e-l**
        want-IMPF.CVB AUX-3PL I.DAT work-DAT put-TH-INF
        'They want to make me work.'   (MA, VK, VP)
        Ուզում են ինձ գործի դնել:
    b. uz-um   e-n   **vor** indz gorts-i **dən-e-n**
        want-IMPF.CVB AUX-3PL that I.DAT work-DAT put-TH-3PL
        'They want to make me work.'   (MA, VK, VP)
        Ուզում են որ ինձ գործի դնեն:
    c. uz-um   e-n   indz gorts-i **dən-e-n**
        want-IMPF.CVB AUX-3PL I.DAT work-DAT put-TH-3PL
        'They want to make me work.'   (MA, VK, VP)
        Ուզում են ինձ գործի դնեն:

Similar judgments apply for Standard Western Armenian. The norm is to use an infinitive (30a) or a complementizer (30b). Using a subjunctive (30c) is possible in colloquial speech. When the complement clause includes multiple items besides the verb, HD feels that using a subjunctive sounds more natural than using an infinitive.

(30) Standard Western Armenian

a. g-uz-e-n   ind͡z-i aʃχat-t͡sən-e-l
    IND-want-TH-3PL I-DAT work-CAUS-TH-INF
    'They want to make me work.'   (HD)
    Կ՚ուզեն ինծի աշխատցնել։

b. g-uz-e-n   vor ind͡z-i aʃχat-t͡sən-e-n
    IND-want-TH-3PL that I-DAT work-CAUS-TH-3PL
    'They want to make me work.'   (HD)
    Կ՚ուզեն որ ինծի աշխատցնեն։

c. g-uz-e-n   ind͡z-i aʃχat-t͡sən-e-n
    IND-want-TH-3PL I-DAT work-CAUS-TH-3PL
    'They want to make me work.'   (HD)
    Կ՚ուզեն ինծի աշխատցնեն։

In contrast, in Iranian Armenian, the use of a finite subjunctive verb is more common (31c). NK personally felt that using an infinitive was odd or ungrammatical (31a).

(31) Iranian Armenian

a. ʔuz-um   e-n   ind͡z-i go.t͡s-i   kʰɒʃ-e-l
    want-IMPF.CVB AUX-3PL I-DAT work-DAT drive-TH-INF
    'They want to make me work.'   (?NK)
    Ուզում են ինձի գործի քաշել։

b. uz-um   e-n   vor ind͡z-i go.t͡s-i   kʰɒʃ-e-n
    want-IMPF.CVB AUX-3PL that I-DAT work-DAT drive-TH-3PL
    'They want to make me work.'   (NK)
    Ուզում են որ ինձի գործի քաշեն։

c. uz-um   e-n   ind͡z-i go.t͡s-i   kʰɒʃ-e-n
    want-IMPF.CVB AUX-3PL I-DAT work-DAT drive-TH-3PL
    'They want to make me work.'   (KM, NK)
    Ուզում են ինձի գործի քաշեն։

AS reports more examples of embedded verbs where Standard Eastern Armenian would prefer an infinitive form, while Iranian Armenian prefers a subjunctive form (32).

(32) a. Iranian Armenian

   i. t͡ʃʰ-e-m   kɒɹ-oʁ   ɒs-e-m
       NEG-AUX-1SG can-SPTCP say-TH-1SG
       'I cannot say.'   (AS)
       Չեմ կարող ասեմ:

   ii. uz-um   ∅-i-m   ɒn-∅-i-m
        want-IMPF.CVB AUX-PST-1SG do-TH-PST-1SG
        'I wanted to do (it).'   (AS)
        Ուզում իմ անիմ:

   iii. int͡ʃʰ ∅-i-ɹ   uz-um   ɒs-∅-i-ɹ
        what AUX-PST-2SG want-IMPF.CVB say-TH-PST-2SG
        'What did you want to say?'   (AS)
        Ի՞նչ իր ուզում ասիր:

   b. Standard Eastern Armenian

   i. t͡ʃʰ-e-m   kɑɾ-oʁ   ɑs-e-l
       NEG-AUX-1SG can-SPTCP say-TH-INF
       'I cannot say.'   (AS)
       Չեմ կարող ասել:

   ii. uz-um   ej-i-∅   ɑn-e-l
        want-IMPF.CVB AUX-PST-1SG do-TH-INF
        'I wanted to do (it).'
        Ուզում էի անել:

   iii. int͡ʃʰ ej-i-ɾ   uz-um   ɑs-e-l
        what AUX-PST-2SG want-IMPF.CVB say-TH-INF
        'What did you want to say?'
        Ի՞նչ էիր ուզում ասել:

In Iran, the Salmast dialect of Armenian likewise prefers using subjunctive forms (Vaux 2022b: §4.5).

The preference for subjunctive forms is likely due to language-internal development that got encouraged by language contact with Persian (33). In Persian, verbs like 'want' select subjunctive verbs (Mahootian 2002: 29).

(33) Persian

    a. mi-tun-æm   be-ɾ-æm
       PROG-can-1SG SBJV-go-1SG
       'I can go.'   (NS)
       میتونم برم.

    b. ne-mi-tun-æm   be-g-æm
       NEG-PROG-can-1SG SBJV-say-1SG
       'I cannot say.'   (NS)
       نمیتونم بگم.

    c. mi-x-ænd   mæn be-ɾ-æm
       PROG-want-3PL I   SBJV-go-1SG
       'They want me to go.'   (NS)
       میخواند من برم.

7.4 Agreement-marking in nominalized relative clauses or participial clauses

A small area of microvariation concerns agreement marking on nominalized relative clauses. For a sentence like (34a), the relative clause is expressed as a post-nominal relative clause with a finite verb. In contrast, this sentence can be paraphrased as in (34b), but where the relative clause is now pre-nominal, and the finite verb is replaced by a participle.

(34) Standard Eastern Armenian

    a. giɾkʰ-ə   voɾ iŋkʰ-ə kaɾtʰ-a-t͡sʰ-Ø-Ø
       book-DEF that he-DEF read-TH-AOR-PST-3SG
       'the book that he read.'   (VP)
       գիրքը որ ինքը կարդաց

    b. (iɾ)   kaɾtʰ-a-t͡sʰ-ats   giɾkʰ-ə
       (he.GEN) read-TH-AOR-RPTCP book-DEF
       'the book that he read.'   (VP)
       (իր) կարդացած գիրքը

A special subcategory of such relative clause constructions is when the subject or 'doer' of the verb is either the first or second person singular (35a). We focus on the first person for illustration. When such a relative clause is converted to a participle clause (35b), the subject is expressed by the first person possessive suffix -(ə)s.

(35)   Standard Eastern Armenian

    a. girk^h-ə   vor kart^h-a-t͡s^h-i-∅
       book-DEF that read-TH-AOR-PST-1SG
       'the book that I read.'   (MA, VK, VP)
       գիրքը որ կարդացի

    b. kart^h-a-t͡s^h-at͡s-əs   girk^h-ə
       read-TH-AOR-RPTCP-POSS.1SG book-DEF
       'the book that I read.'   (MA, VK, VP)
       կարդացածս գիրքը

    c. **im**   kart^h-a-t͡s^h-at͡s-əs   girk^h-ə
       I.GEN read-TH-AOR-RPTCP-POSS.1SG book-DEF
       'the book that I read.'   (*MA, ?VK, *VP)
       իմ կարդացածս գիրքը

Our Standard Eastern Armenian consultants all felt that using an overt genitive pronoun alongside the possessive suffix on the participle (35c) was odd or ungrammatical.

For these participle clauses, there is dialectal variation in how the subject or doer of the action is marked for the first/second person singular. In Standard Eastern Armenian, the norm is (i) to not use an overt genitive pronoun, (ii) to place a subject-marking possessive suffix -əs on the participle, and (iii) to mark the head noun as definite (Dum-Tragut 2009: 508–509).

In contrast in Standard Western Armenian (36a), the norm is to (ii') make the participle unmarked, while (iii') the noun gets the possessive suffix. The pronoun is optional (i'). For more data, see Ackerman & Nikolaeva (1997), Ackerman (1998), Ackema & Neeleman (2004), and Ackerman & Nikolaeva (2013: 284ff). For Standard Eastern, such constructions are deemed "okay but not default" for VK and "not preferable" for VP (36b). Neither consultant approved of adding the pronoun.

(36)   a. Standard Western Armenian
      (im) gart^h-a-t͡s^h-ad͡z   k^{h}irk^h-əs
      I.GEN read-TH-AOR-RPTCP book-POSS.1SG
      'the book that I read'   (HD)
      (իմ) կարդացած գիրքս

b. Standard Eastern Armenian
(*im) kɑɾtʰ-ɑ-t͡sʰ-ɑts   giɾkʰ-əs
I.GEN read-TH-AOR-RPTCP book-POSS.1SG
'the book that I read'   (VK, ?VP)
(իմ) կարդացած գիրքս

Note that some speakers like MA feel that having the possessive on the noun
(36b) was grammatical but had a distinct meaning of 'I own the book and I read
it.' In contrast, when the possessive suffix is on the participle (35b), there is no
information concerning who the owner of the book is.

In contrast, in Iranian Armenian, it seems that there is optionality across these
parameters. We can either follow SEA and place the possessive on the participle
(37b), or we can follow SWA and place the possessive on the noun (37d). An
intermediate option is to not use a possessive suffix at all (37c).

(37)   Iranian Armenian
a. giɾkʰ-ə   voɾ kɒɾtʰ-ɒ-t͡sʰ-i-m
book-DEF that read-TH-AOR-PST-1SG
'the book that I read.'   (NK)
գիրքը որ կարդացիմ

b. (im)   kɒɾtʰ-ɒ-t͡sʰ-ɒts-əs   giɾkʰ-ə
(I.GEN) read-TH-AOR-RPTCP-POSS.1SG book-DEF
իմ կարդացածս գիրքը   (KM, ?NK)

c. im   kɒɾtʰ-ɒ-t͡sʰ-ɒts   giɾkʰ-ə
I.GEN read-TH-AOR-RPTCP   book-DEF
իմ կարդացած գիրքը   (KM, NK)

d. (im)   kɒɾtʰ-ɒ-t͡sʰ-ɒts   giɾkʰ-əs
(I.GEN) read-TH-AOR-RPTCP   book-POSS.1SG
'the book that I read'
(իմ) կարդացած գիրքս   (KM, ?NK)

For a bi-dialectal speaker like KM, all of the options were acceptable. For a
mono-lectal speaker like NK, the intermediate option (37c) was judged as the
best option, the SEA-style sentences were judged as odd (37b), while the SWA-
sentences (37d) were judged as better than the SEA-style ones, but not as good
as the intermediate.

This intermediate option (37c) was likewise accepted for SEA (38) by our consultants; VK and MA went as far to say this intermediate option is as good as

the norm (35b). Katherine Hodgson informs us that all this variation is likewise attested in Colloquial Eastern Armenian.

(38)   Standard Eastern Armenian
     im   kɑɾtʰ-ɑ-t͡sʰ-ɑt͡s   giɾkʰ-ə
     I.GEN read-TH-AOR-RPTCP book-DEF
     'the book that I read.'   (MA, VK, VP)
     իմ կարդացած գիրքը

Among these various options for Iranian Armenian, KM reports that the intermediate option is relatively more preferred (37c). The SWA-style option is attested but rather stigmatized (37d). The SEA-style option is prescriptively the rule but rather uncommon (37b). It seems that at some point, Standard Eastern Armenian developed this intermediate option as an acceptable colloquial alternative. Iranian Armenian then grammaticalized this intermediate option as the norm.

8 Text

Iranian Armenian is a spoken vernacular. Thus, it is difficult to find any written records of the language. What makes it more difficult is that, as AS informs us, Iranian Armenian is so stigmatized that he has not found any common Iranian Armenian songs or folk tales in his decade-long interaction with the community.

In recent years, however, there have been Iranian Armenians who have posted online comedic sketches. These are posted on various social media platforms like Twitter, Instagram, and Facebook. We examined and transcribed one such sketch which is a 9-minute-long scripted dialogue between six Iranian Armenian comedians (May 2021). The original video is available on Instagram as a publicly-accessible video with subtitles.[1] Ethically, although the video is public, we wanted to obtain the consent of the comedians so that they know we were using their sketch for our academic purposes. We managed to track down and get the consent of four out of the six participants. We did not hear back from the other two despite multiple attempts at contacting them.

The sketch is rather long with around 9 minutes of speech, and over 650 words. We transcribed the entire video using our IPA and glossing system with Praat Boersma 2001.[2] We demarcated borrowed words with <>. The Armenian orthography line uses romanization for Persian-based loanwords. Our English translation differs slightly from the subtitles. The entire transcript can be found in our online archive as a Praat TextGrid.[3] Because the video is long, we present only one dialog between Vahik and Anjel, both acted out by the same male speaker (Ryan Ebrahamian).

---

[1]https://www.instagram.com/tv/COWtIvUn4KA/

[2]We generally did not gloss zero morphs. We used zero morphs ∅ for the past morpheme and past auxiliary like [∅-i-m] 'AUX-PST-1SG' meaning 'I was'.

[3]https://github.com/jhdeov/iranian_armenian

(1) Vahik

  a. ɒndʒel ləs-el   e-s   es <væksin>-ə voɹ duɹs ɒ
     Anjel hear-PERF.CVB AUX-2SG this vaccine-DEF that out AUX
     g-ɒ-l-is
     COME-TH-INF-IMPF.CVB

     'Anjel, have you heard of this vaccine that's coming out?'[4]
     Անջել, լսե՞լ ես էս <vaccine>-ը որ դուրս ա գալիս:

  b. mæt   noɹ-ən   ɒ
     INDF.CLF new-DEF AUX

     'It's a new one.'
     Մի հատ նորն ա:

  c. <dʒɒnsən dʒɒnsən>-n ɒ   sɒɹkʰ-um
     Johnson Johnson-DEF AUX make-IMPF.CVB

     'Johnson and Johnson is making it.'
     <Johnson and Johnson>-ն ա սարքում:

  d. me ɒŋkʰɒm piti   χəpʰ-e-s   tʰev-i-t
     INDF time   should shoot-TH-2SG arm-DAT-POSS.2SG

     'You only take it once. (Lit: You should shoot it at your arm once)'
     Մի անգամ պիտի խփես թևիդ:

  e. himɒ ɒmen əŋkeɹ-neɹ-i-s   zɒŋg-e-l-uw   e-m
     now all   friend-PL-DAT-POSS.1SG ring-TH-INF-FUT.CVB AUX-1SG
     mæt   mek mek k-ɒs-e-m
     INDF.CLF one one FUT-say-TH-1SG

     'I'm gonna call all my friends to tell them one-by-one. (Lit: Now I will call all my friends, tell each one-by-one)'
     Հիմա ամէն ընկերներիս զանգելու եմ, մի հատ մէկ մէկ կասեմ:

(2) Anjel

  a. bɒbɒ dzer kʰɒʃ-i
     dude hand pull-IMP.2SG

     'Just leave it alone. (Lit. and idiomatic: Dude, pull your hand)'
     Բաբա ձեռ քաշի:

---

[4]Vahik does not drop the fricative /s/ of the imperfective converb suffix. It is more typical to drop the /s/. The fact that he does not, suggests that there is either more variation than we found (§3.3.4), or that he may be code switching or trying to sound more formal.

b. gəluχ kə-tɒn-e-s vɒhik d͡ʒɒn-ət
head FUT-take-TH-2SG Vahik dear-POSS.2SG

'You'll drive people crazy, Vahik, dear. (Lit and idiomatic: you shall take away heads?)'[5]

Գլուխս կը տանես, Վահիկ ջանդ:

c. ov vo.ɹ uz-um ɒ i.ɹɒ tʰev-ə χəpʰ-i int͡ʃʰ-i
who that want-IMPF.CVB AUX he.GEN arm-DEF shoot-TH what-GEN

het uz-um ɒ χəpʰ-i kə-χəpʰ-i
with want-IMPF.CVB AUX shoot-TH FUT-shoot-TH

'Whoever wants to stick themselves can stick themselves with whatever they'd like.'

Ով որ ուզում ա իրա թեւը խփխի, ինչի հետ ուզում ա խփխի կը խփխի:

d. kʰez int͡ʃʰ
you.SG.DAT what

'What's it to you?'

Քեզ ինչ:

(3) Vahik

a. <jæni> int͡ʃʰ indz int͡ʃʰ
meaning what I.DAT what

'What do you mean, "what's it to me"?'

<Yani> ի՞նչ «ինձ ինչ»:

Borrowed from Persian یعنی 'meaning'

b. jetʰe me ɒŋkʰɒm piti e.ɹt-ɒ-n χəpʰ-e-n i.ɹɒnt͡sʰ
if INDF time should go-TH-3PL strike-TH-3PL they.GEN

tʰev-e.ɹ-ə
arm-PL-DEF

'If they only need to stick themselves once,'

Եթէ մի անգամ պիտի էրթան խփեն իրանց թեւերը,

c. heto ɒrɒt͡ʃʰ t͡ʃʰ-i piti kʰəʃ-e-n vo.ɹ benzin e.ɹ-e-n
after before NEG-AUX should drive-TH-3PL that gasoline burn-TH-3PL

pʰoʁ t͡sɒχs-e-n
money spend-TH-3PL

'then they don't have to drive back and forth to burn gas, spend money.'

յետոյ առաջ չի պիտի քշեն, որ բենզին էրեն, փող ծախսեն:

---

[5]We find the use of the possessive suffx -t on [d͡ʒɒn-ət] 'your dear' puzzling. We're not sure if we're mishearing this [t], or if this is some novel construction for some speakers of IA.

d. <nɒtʰiŋg iz f̞ɹi> es ɒmeɹikɒ-ji metʃʰ ɒnd͡ʒel d͡ʒɒn
    nothing is free this America-GEN in   Anjel dear
    'Nothing is free in America, Anjel, dear.'
    <Nothing is free> էս Ամերիկայի մէջ, Անջել ջան:

e. lɒv me bɒn el   uz-um   e-m   ɒn-e-m
    good INDF thing also/even want-IMPF.CVB AUX-2SG do-TH-1SG
    tʰɒpʰ-um   e-s   gəlχ-i-s
    throw-IMPF.CVB AUX-2SG head-DAT-POSS.1SG
    'Even when I want do something good, you're still on top of me. (Lit:
    you throw at/on my head)'
    Լաւ մի բան էլ ուզում եմ անեմ թափում ես գլխիս:

f. bɒbɒ d͡zer kʰɒʃ-i   ind͡z-n-itsʰ
    dude hand pull-IMP.2SG me-NX-ABL
    'Dude, leave me alone! (Lit: pull away your hand from)'
    Բաբա, ձեռ քաշի ինծնից:

Since writing this grammar, we discovered that the UCLA Phonetics Lab
archive had recordings of Tehrani Armenians in Los Angeles (*The UCLA Phonetics Lab Archive* 2007).[6] We are currently in the process of transcribing their
material, with the goal of archiving more material.

---

[6]http://archive.phonetics.ucla.edu/Language/HYE/hye.html

References

Abdollahnejad, Elias. 2018. Competing grammars in language acquisition: The case of resumption in Persian relative clauses. In E. Abdollahnejad, D. Abu Amsha, K. Burkinshaw, A.D. Daniel & B.C. Nelson (eds.), *Calgary Working Papers in Linguistics*, vol. 30(Fall), 1–14.

Ackema, Pete & Ad Neeleman. 2003. Context-sensitive spell-out. *Natural Language & Linguistic Theory* 21(4). 681–735. DOI: 10.1023/A:1025502221221.

Ackema, Peter & Ad Neeleman. 2004. *Beyond morphology*. Oxford: Oxford University Press. DOI: 10.1093/acprof:oso/9780199267286.001.0001.

Ackerman, Farrell. 1998. Constructions and mixed categories: Determining the semantic interpretation of person/number marking. In Miriam Butt & Tracy Holloway-King (eds.), *Proceedings of the LFG98 Conference*. Stanford, CA: CSLI Publications.

Ackerman, Farrell & Irina Nikolaeva. 1997. Identity in form, difference in function: The person/number paradigm in W. Armenian and N. Ostyak. In Miriam Butt & Tracy Holloway-King (eds.), *Proceedings of the LFG97 Conference*. Stanford, CA: CSLI Publications.

Ackerman, Farrell & Irina Nikolaeva. 2013. *Descriptive typology and linguistic theory: A study in the morphosyntax of relative clauses* (CSLI Lecture Notes 212). Stanford, CA: CSLI Publications, Center for the Study of Language and Information.

Adjarian, Hrachia. 1909. *Classification des dialectes arméniens*. Paris: Librairie Honoré Champion. https://archive.org/details/bibliothquedel173ecol/page/n7/mode/2up.

Akinlabi, Akinbiyi. 2011. Featural affixes. In Marc van Oostendorp, Colin J. Ewen, Elizabeth Hume & Keren Rice (eds.), *The Blackwell companion to phonology*, vol. 4, 1945–1972. Cambridge, MA: John Wiley & Sons, Ltd. DOI: 10.1002/9781444335262.wbctp0082.

Allen, W. S. 1950. Notes on the phonetics of an Eastern Armenian speaker. *Transactions of the Philological Society* 49(1). 180–206. DOI: 10.1111/j.1467-968X.1950.tb00241.x.

References

Amirian, Beaina. 2017. ویژگیهای صوتشناختی همخوانهای انسدادی و انسایشی در زبان ارمنی شرقی *[A study of acoustic features of stops and affricates in Eastern Armenian]*. Department of Linguistics, Allameh Tabataba'i University. (MA thesis).

Amurian, A. & M. Kasheff. 1986. Armenians of modern Iran. In *Encyclopædia Iranica*, vol. II/5, 478–483. https://iranicaonline.org/articles/armenians-of-modern-iran.

Andonian, Hagop. 1999. *Beginner's Armenian*. New York: Hippocrene Books.

Ariyaee, Koorosh & Peter Jurgec. 2021. Variable hiatus in Persian is affected by suffix length. In *Proceedings of the Annual Meetings on Phonology*, vol. 9. DOI: 10.3765/amp.v9i0.4919.

Aronoff, Mark. 1994. *Morphology by itself: Stems and inflectional classes* (Linguistic Inquiry Monographs 22). London/Cambridge: The MIT Press.

Aronow, Robin, Brian D. McHugh & Tessa Molnar. 2017. A pilot acoustic study of Modern Persian vowels in colloquial speech. In *Proceedings of the Linguistic Society of America*, vol. 2, 17. DOI: 10.3765/plsa.v2i0.4059.

Arregi, Karlos, Neil Myler & Bert Vaux. 2013. Number marking in Western Armenian: A non-argument for outwardly-sensitive phonologically conditioned allomorphy. Unpublished manuscript. Talk given at the 87th Linguistic Society of America Annual Meeting, Boston.

Arsenault, Paul. 2018. Retroflexion in South Asia: Typological, genetic, and areal patterns. *Journal of South Asian Languages and Linguistics* 4(1). 1–53. DOI: 10.1515/jsall-2017-0001.

Bakalian, Anny. 2017. *Armenian Americans: From being to feeling Armenian*. London/New York: Routledge.

Bale, Alan & Hrayr Khanjian. 2008. Classifiers and number marking. *Semantics and Linguistic Theory* 18. 73. DOI: 10.3765/salt.v18i0.2478.

Bale, Alan & Hrayr Khanjian. 2014. Syntactic complexity and competition: the singular-plural distinction in Western Armenian. *Linguistic Inquiry* 45(1). 1–26. DOI: 10.1162/LING_a_00147.

Bardakjian, Kevork B. & Robert W Thomson. 1977. *A textbook of Modern Western Armenian*. Delmar, NY: Caravan Books.

Bardakjian, Kevork B. & Bert Vaux. 1999. *Eastern Armenian: A textbook*. Ann Arbor: Caravan Books.

Bardakjian, Kevork B. & Bert Vaux. 2001. *A textbook of Modern Western Armenian*. Delmar, NY: Caravan Books.

Baronian, Luc. 2017. Two problems in Armenian phonology. *Language and Linguistics Compass* 11(8). e12247. DOI: 10.1111/lnc3.12247.

Barry, James. 2017a. Monologue and authority in Iran: Ethnic and religious heteroglossia in the Islamic Republic. In Matt Tomlinson & Julian Millie (eds.), *The monologic imagination*, vol. 1, 143–158. New York: Oxford University Press. DOI: 10.1093/acprof:oso/9780190652807.003.0008.

Barry, James. 2017b. Re-Ghettoization: Armenian Christian neighborhoods in multicultural Tehran. *Iranian Studies* 50(4). 553–573. DOI: 10.1080/00210862.2017.1294528.

Barry, James. 2018. *Armenian Christians in Iran: Ethnicity, religion, and identity in the Islamic Republic.* Cambridge: Cambridge University Press. DOI: 10.1017/9781108684873.

Bezrukov, Nikita. 2016. *Number marking mismatches in Modern Armenian: A Distributed Morphology approach.* University of Chicago. (MA thesis).

Bezrukov, Nikita. 2022. *Caucasus in motion: Dynamic wordhood and morpheme positioning in Armenian and beyond.* University of Pennsylvania. (Doctoral dissertation).

Boersma, Paul. 2001. Praat, a system for doing phonetics by computer. *Glot International* 5(9/10). 341–345.

Boyacioglu, Nisan. 2010. *Hay-Pay: Les verbs de l'arménien occidental.* Paris: L'Asiathèque.

Boyacioglu, Nisan & Hossep Dolatian. 2020. *Armenian verbs: Paradigms and verb lists of Western Armenian conjugation classes.* Zenodo. DOI: 10.5281/ZENODO.4397423.

Chabot, Alex. 2019. What's wrong with being a rhotic? *Glossa* 4(1). DOI: 10.5334/gjgl.618.

Comrie, Bernard. 1984. Some formal properties of focus in Modern Eastern Armenian. *Annual of Armenian Linguistics* 5. 1–21.

Cosroe Chaqueri (ed.). 1998. *The Armenians of Iran: The paradoxical role of a minority in a dominant culture; Articles and documents* (Harvard University Center for Middle East Studies Monograph Series 30). Cambridge: Harvard University Press.

Côté, Marie-Hélène. 2011. French liaison. In Marc van Oostendorp, Colin J. Ewen, Elizabeth Hume & Keren Rice (eds.), *The Blackwell companion to phonology*, vol. 5, 2685–2710. Cambridge, MA: John Wiley & Sons, Ltd. DOI: 10.1002/9781444335262.wbctp0112.

Crum, Jonathan. 2020. Eastern Armenian pseudo-incorporation. Unpublished manuscript.

Curtis, Glenn E & Eric Hooglund. 2008. *Iran: A country study.* 5th edition. Federal Research Division. Library of Congress. https://lccn.loc.gov/2008011784.

References

Dąbkowski, Maksymilian & Hannah Sande. 2021. Phonology-syntax interleaving in Guébie focus fronting. Paper presented at the 14th Brussels Conference on Generative Linguistics (BCGL14), Brussels, Belgium.

Daniel, Michael & Victoria Khurshudian. 2015. Valency classes in Eastern Armenian. In Andrej Malchukov & Bernard Comrie (eds.), *Valency classes in the world's languages*, 483–540. Berlin & Boston: De Gruyter. DOI: 10.1515/9783110338812-018.

Dehghan, Masoud & Aliyeh Kord-e Zafaranlu Kambuziya. 2012. A short analysis of insertion in Persian. *Theory and Practice in Language Studies* 2(1). 14–23. DOI: 10.4304/tpls.2.1.14-23.

Dekmejian, Hrair. 1997. The Armenian diaspora. In Richard G. Hovannisian (ed.), *The Armenian people from ancient to modern times*, vol. 2, 413–445. Houndsmill/London: Macmillan Press.

Der-Martirosian, Claudia. 2021. Economic and social integration of Armenian Iranians in Southern California. In Richard G. Hovhannisian (ed.), *Armenian communities of Persia/Iran*, 545–560. Costa Mesa, California: Mazda Publishers.

DiCanio, Christian. 2020. *Sound file subdivision*. Praat script. https://www.acsu.buffalo.edu/~cdicanio/scripts/Sound_file_division.praat (15 April, 2022).

Dolatian, Hossep. 2020. *Computational locality of cyclic phonology in Armenian*. Stony Brook University. (Doctoral dissertation).

Dolatian, Hossep. 2021a. Cyclicity and prosodic misalignment in Armenian stems: Interaction of morphological and prosodic cophonologies. *Natural Language & Linguistic Theory* 39(3). 843–886. DOI: 10.1007/s11049-020-09487-7.

Dolatian, Hossep. 2021b. The role of heads and cyclicity in bracketing paradoxes in Armenian compounds. *Morphology* 31(1). 1–43. DOI: 10.1007/s11525-020-09368-0.

Dolatian, Hossep. 2022a. An apparent case of outwardly-sensitive allomorphy in the Armenian definite. *Glossa* 7(1). DOI: 10.16995/glossa.6406.

Dolatian, Hossep. 2022b. Interface constraints for nuclear stress assignment under broad focus in Western Armenian vs. Turkish and Persian. In Öner Özçelik & Amber Kennedy (eds.), *Proceedings of the 4th Conference on Central Asian Languages and Linguistics (ConCALL-4)*, 59–80.

Dolatian, Hossep. 2022c. Variation in a bracketing paradox: A case study in Armenian compounds. In Öner Özçelik & Amber Kennedy (eds.), *Proceedings of the 4th Conference on Central Asian Languages and Linguistics (ConCALL)*, 95–108.

Dolatian, Hossep. 2023a. Cyclic residues of affix deletion in Armenian passive stems. *Natural Language & Linguistic Theory*. DOI: 10.1007/s11049-023-09586-1.

Dolatian, Hossep. 2023b. Fluctuations in allomorphy domains: Applying Stump 2010 to Armenian ordinal numerals. *Journal of Linguistics*. 1–35. DOI: 10.1017/S0022226723000099.

Dolatian, Hossep. 2023c. Isomorphism between orthography and underlying forms in the syllabification of the Armenian schwa. *Phonological Data and Analysis* 5(4). DOI: 10.3765/pda.v5art4.68.

Dolatian, Hossep. 2023d. Output-conditioned and non-local allomorphy in Armenian theme vowels. *The Linguistic Review* 40. 1–42. DOI: 10.1515/tlr-2022-2104.

Dolatian, Hossep. Submitted. Translation and commentary on Adjarian 1911 'Armenian dialectology'. Unpublished manuscript. https://github.com/jhdeov/adjarian1911/.

Dolatian, Hossep & Peter Guekguezian. 2022a. Derivational timing of morphomes: Canonicity and rule ordering in the Armenian aorist stem. *Morphology* 32(3). 317–357. DOI: 10.1007/s11525-022-09397-x.

Dolatian, Hossep & Peter Guekguezian. 2022b. Relativized locality: Phases and tiers in long-distance allomorphy in Armenian. *Linguistic Inquiry*. 1–41. DOI: 10.1162/ling_a_00456.

Donabédian, Anaïd. 1997. Neutralisation de la diathèse des participes en -*ac* de l'arménien moderne occidental. *Studi italiani di linguistica teorica ed applicata* 26(2). 327–339.

Donabédian, Anaïd. 2016. The aorist in Modern Armenian: Core values and contextual meanings. In Zlatka Guentchéva (ed.), *Aspectuality and temporality: Descriptive and theoretical issues*, 375–412. Amsterdam: John Benjamins. DOI: 10.1075/slcs.172.12don.

Donabédian, Anaïd. 2018. Middle East and beyond - Western Armenian at the crossroads: A sociolinguistic and typological sketch. In Christiane Bulut (ed.), *Linguistic minorities in Turkey and Turkic-speaking minorities of the periphery*, 89–148. Wiesbaden: Harrassowitz Verlag. DOI: 10.2307/j.ctvckq4v1.

Donabédian, Anaïd & Ioanna Sitaridou. 2020. Anatolia. In Adamou Evangelia & Yaron Matras (eds.), *The Routledge handbook of language contact*, 404–433. London: Routledge.

Donabédian-Demopoulos, Anaïd. 2007. A la recherche de la logophoricité en arménien moderne. In Jocelyne Fernandez-Vest (ed.), *Combat pour les langues du monde/Fighting for the world's languages, hommage à Claude Hagège*, 165–176. Paris: Editions L'Harmattan.

Dum-Tragut, Jasmine. 2009. *Armenian: Modern Eastern Armenian* (London Oriental and African Language Library 14). Amsterdam: John Benjamins. DOI: 10.1075/loall.14.

References

Embick, David & Kobey Shwayder. 2018. Deriving morphophonological (mis)applications. In Roberto Petrosino, Pietro Cerrone & Harry van der Hulst (eds.), *From sounds to structures: Beyond the veil of Maya*, 193–248. Berlin: De Gruyter. DOI: 10.1515/9781501506734-007.

Erschler, David. 2018. Suspended affixation as morpheme ellipsis: Evidence from Ossetic alternative questions. *Glossa* 3(1). DOI: 10.5334/gjgl.501.

Esfandiari, Nasim, Batool Alinezhad & Adel Rafiei. 2015. Vowel classification and vowel space in Persian. *Theory and Practice in Language Studies* 5(2). 426–434. DOI: 10.17507/tpls.0502.26.

Fairbanks, Gordon H. 1948. *Phonology and morphology of modern spoken West Armenian*. University of Wisconsin-Madison. (Doctoral dissertation).

Fairbanks, Gordon H. 1958. *Spoken West Armenian*. New York: American Council of Learned Societies.

Fairbanks, Gordon H. & Earl W. Stevick. 1975. *Spoken East Armenian*. New York: American Council of Learned Societies.

Falahati, Reza. 2020. The acquisition of segmental and suprasegmental features in second language Persian: A focus on prosodic parameters of politeness. In Pouneh Shabani-Jadidi (ed.), *The Routledge handbook of second language acquisition and pedagogy of Persian*, 9–35. New York: Routledge.

Fenger, Paula. 2020. *Words within words: The internal syntax of verbs*. University of Connecticut. (Doctoral dissertation).

Feydit, Frédéric. 1948. *Manuel de langue arménienne: Arménien occidental moderne*. Paris: Klincksieck.

Fittante, Daniel. 2017. But why Glendale? A history of Armenian immigration to Southern California. *California History* 94(3). 2–19. DOI: 10.1525/ch.2017.94.3.2.

Fittante, Daniel. 2018. The Armenians of Glendale: An ethnoburb in Los Angeles's San Fernando Valley. *City & Community* 17(4). 1231–1247. DOI: 10.1111/cico.12340.

Fittante, Daniel. 2019. Constructivist theories of political incorporation. *Ethnicities* 19(5). 809–829. DOI: 10.1177/1468796819833007.

Fleming, Harold C. 2000. Glottalization in Eastern Armenian. *Journal of Indo-European Studies* 28(1/2). 155–196.

Ghiasian, Maryam & Hakimeh Rezaei. 2014. بررسی نقش نماهای کلامی فارسی در مکالمات دوزبانههای ارمنی-فارسی [The study of Persian multifunctional discourse markers in Armenian-Persian bilinguals]. *Language Studies* 5(9). 125–147. https://languagestudy.ihcs.ac.ir/article_1438.html.

Ghiasian, Maryam Sadat & Hakimeh Rezayi. 2014. رمزگردانی با نگاهی بررسی پدیدۀ به گفتار دوزبانههای ارمنی- فارسی تهرانی [A study of code-switching according to

Armenian conversations of Armenian-Persian bilinguals]. *Language and Linguistics* 10(20). 103–120. https://lsi-linguistics.ihcs.ac.ir/article_1880.html.

Ghougassian, Vazken S. 2021. Armenian rural settlements and New Julfa (seventeenth-nineteenth century). In Richard G. Hovhannisian (ed.), *Armenian communities of Persia/Iran*, 311–350. Costa Mesa, California: Mazda Publishers.

Giorgi, Alessandra & Sona Haroutyunian. 2016. Word order and information structure in Modern Eastern Armenian. *Journal of the Society for Armenian Studies* 25. 185–200.

Greppin, John A. C. 1973. The origin of Armenian nasal suffix verbs. *Zeitschrift für vergleichende Sprachforschung* 87(2. H). 190–198.

Greppin, John A. C. & Amalya A. Khachaturian. 1986. *A handbook of Armenian dialectology*. Delmar, NY: Caravan Books.

Guekguezian, Peter & Hossep Dolatian. Forthcoming. Distributing theme vowels across roots, verbalizers, and voice in Western Armenian verbs. In *Proceedings of the 39th Meeting of the West Coast Conference on Formal Linguistics (WCCFL)*.

Gulian, Kevork H. 1902. *Elementary modern Armenian grammar*. Heidelberg: Julius Groos.

Hacopian, Narineh. 2003. A three-way VOT contrast in final position: Data from Armenian. *Journal of the International Phonetic Association* 33(1). 51–80. DOI: 10.1017/S0025100303001154.

Hagopian, Gayané. 2005. *Armenian for everyone: Western and Eastern Armenian in parallel lessons*. Ann Arbor, MI: Caravan Books.

Hamp, Eric P. 1975. On the nasal presents of Armenian. *Zeitschrift für vergleichende Sprachforschung* 89(1. H). 100–109.

Haspelmath, Martin. 1993. More on the typology of inchoative/causative verb alternations. In Bernard Comrie & Maria Polinsky (eds.), *Causatives and transitivity* (Studies in Language 23), 87–121. Amsterdam: John Benjamins. DOI: 10.1075/slcs.23.05has.

Haspelmath, Martin. 2020. The morph as a minimal linguistic form. *Morphology* 30(2). 117–134. DOI: 10.1007/s11525-020-09355-5.

Haugen, Jason D. 2016. Readjustment: Rejected? In Daniel Siddiqi & Heidi Harley (eds.), *Morphological metatheory*, 303–342. Amsterdam: John Benjamins. DOI: 10.1075/la.229.11hau.

Haugen, Jason D. & Daniel Siddiqi. 2016. Towards a restricted realization theory: Multimorphemic monolistemicity, portmanteaux, and post-linearization spanning. In Daniel Siddiqi & Heidi Harley (eds.), *Morphological metatheory*, 343–386. Amsterdam: John Benjamins. DOI: 10.1075/la.229.12hau.

Hewitt, Brian George. 1978. The Armenian relative clause. *International Review of Slavic Linguistics* 3. 99–138.

Hockett, Charles F. 1942. A system of descriptive phonology. *Language* 18(1). 3–21. DOI: 10.2307/409073.

Hodgson, Katherine. 2019a. Information structure and word order in Armenian. Unpublished manuscript.

Hodgson, Katherine. 2019b. *Relative clauses in colloquial Armenian: Syntax and typology*. Université Sorbonne Paris. (Doctoral dissertation).

Hodgson, Katherine. 2020a. Discourse configurationality and the noun phrase in Eastern Armenian. *Faits de Langues* 50(2). 137–166. DOI: 10.1163/19589514-05002015.

Hodgson, Katherine. 2020b. Finite relative clauses in colloquial Armenian and the phenomenon of "inverse attraction". *Lingua* 246. 1029–50. DOI: 10.1016/j.lingua.2020.102950.

Hodgson, Katherine. 2022. Grammaticalization of the definite article in Armenian. *Armeniaca* 1. 125–150. DOI: 10.30687/arm/9372-8175/2022/01/008.

Hovakimyan, Knar. 2016. *Eastern Armenian consonant clusters*. Reed College. (Bachelor's Thesis).

Hovhannisian, Richard G. 2021. Armenian communities of Persia/Iran: An introduction. In Richard G. Hovhannisian (ed.), *Armenian communities of Persia/Iran*, 1–16. Costa Mesa, California: Mazda Publishers.

Iskandaryan, Gohar. 2019. The Armenian community in Iran: Issues and emigration. *Global Campus Human Rights Journal* 3. 127–140.

Johnson, Emma Wintler. 1954. *Studies in East Armenian grammar*. University of California, Berkeley. (Doctoral dissertation).

Jones, Taylor. 2019. A corpus phonetic study of contemporary Persian vowels in casual speech. In *University of Pennsylvania Working Papers in Linguistics*, vol. 25, 15.

Jun, Sun-Ah. 2005. *Prosodic typology: The phonology of intonation and phrasing*. Oxford: Oxford University Press. DOI: 10.1093/acprof:oso/9780199249633.001.0001.

Kabak, Bariş. 2007. Turkish suspended affixation. *Linguistics* 45(2). 311–347. DOI: 10.1515/LING.2007.010.

Kahnemuyipour, Arsalan. 2009. *The syntax of sentential stress*. Oxford: Oxford University Press. DOI: 10.1093/acprof:oso/9780199219230.001.0001.

Kahnemuyipour, Arsalan & Karine Megerdoomian. 2011. Second-position clitics in the vP phase: The case of the Armenian auxiliary. *Linguistic Inquiry* 42(1). 152–162. DOI: 10.1162/LING_a_00033.

Kahnemuyipour, Arsalan & Karine Megerdoomian. 2017. On the positional distribution of an Armenian auxiliary: Second-position clisis, focus, and phases. *Syntax* 20(1). 77–97. DOI: 10.1111/synt.12129.

Kaisse, Ellen M. 1985. *Connected speech: The interaction of syntax and phonology.* Orlando, FL: Academic Press.

Kalomoiros, Alexandros. 2022. Bare singulars and pseudo-incorporation in Western Armenian. *Semantics and Linguistic Theory* 31. 365–384. DOI: 10.3765/salt.v31i0.5087.

Karakaş, Ayla, Hossep Dolatian & Peter Guekguezian. 2021. Effects of zero morphology on syncretism and allomorphy in Western Armenian verbs. In *Proceedings of the Workshop on Turkic and Languages in Contact with Turkic*, vol. 6, 5056. DOI: 10.3765/ptu.v6i1.5056.

Karapetian, Shushan. 2014. *"How do I teach my kids my broken Armenian?": A study of Eastern Armenian heritage language speakers in Los Angeles.* University of California, Los Angeles. (Doctoral dissertation).

Keenan, Edward L. & Bernard Comrie. 1977. Noun phrase accessibility and Universal Grammar. *Linguistic Inquiry* 8(1). 63–99.

Khanjian, Hrayr. 2009. Stress dependent vowel reduction. In Iksoo Kwon, Hannah Pritchett & Justin Spence (eds.), *Annual Meeting of the Berkeley Linguistics Society*, vol. 35, 178–189. Berkeley, CA: Berkeley Linguistics Society. DOI: 10.3765/bls.v35i1.3609.

Khanjian, Hrayr. 2013. *(Negative) concord and head directionality in Western Armenian.* Massachusetts Institute of Technology. (Doctoral dissertation).

Khurshudian, Victoria. 2020. Some aspects of possessive markers in Modern Armenian. In A. Kibrik, K. Semenova, D. Sichinava, S. Tatevosov & A. Urmanchieva (eds.), *Вапросы языкознания [Voprosy Jazykoznanija]. Collection of articles dedicated to the anniversary of V. A. Plungyan*, 337–343. Moscow: Russian Academy of Sciences.

Khurshudyan, Victoria & Anaïd Donabédian. 2021. Cleft constructions and focus strategies in Modern Armenian. *Faits de Langues* 52(1). 89–116. DOI: 10.1163/19589514-05201005.

Kocharov, Petr. 2019. *Old Armenian nasal verbs. Archaisms and innovations.* Leiden University. (Doctoral dissertation).

Kogian, Sahak L. 1949. *Armenian grammar (West dialect).* Vienna: Mechitharist Press.

Kontovas, Nicholas. 2012. *Lubunca: The historical development of Istanbul's queer slang and a social-functional approach to diachronic processes in language.* Indiana University. (MA thesis).

Kornfilt, Jaklin. 2012. Revisiting "suspended affixation" and other coordinate mysteries. In Laura Brugé, Anna Cardinaletti, Giuliana Giusti, Nicola Munaro & Cecilia Poletto (eds.), *Functional heads: The cartography of syntactic struc-*

tures, 181–196. Oxford/NY: Oxford University Press. DOI: 10.1093/acprof:oso/9780199746736.003.0014.

Kouymjian, Dickran. 1997. Armenia from the fall of the Cilician Kingdom (1375) to the forced emigration under Shah Abbas (1604). In Richard G. Hovannisian (ed.), *The Armenian people from ancient to modern times*, vol. 2, 1–50. Houndsmill/London: Macmillan Press.

Kozintseva, Natalia. 1995. *Modern Eastern Armenian*. München: Lincom Europa.

Ladd, D. Robert. 1986. Intonational phrasing: The case for recursive prosodic structure. *Phonology Yearbook* 3. 311–340. DOI: 10.1017/S0952675700000671.

Ladefoged, Peter & Ian Maddieson. 1996. *The sounds of the world's languages*. Malden, MA: Blackwell Publishing.

Macak, Martin. 2017. The phonology of Classical Armenian. In Jared Klein, Brian Joseph & Matthias Fritz (eds.), *Handbook of comparative and historical Indo-European linguistics*, 1037–1079. Berlin/Munich/Boston: Walter de Gruyter. DOI: 10.1515/9783110523874-016.

Maddieson, Ian & Kristin Hanson. 1990. Updating UPSID. In *UCLA Working Papers in Phonetics*, vol. 74, 104–111.

Mahjani, Behzad. 2003. *An instrumental study of prosodic features and intonation in Modern Farsi*. University of Edinburgh. (MA thesis).

Mahootian, Shahrzad. 2002. *Persian*. Abingdon & New York: Routledge.

Majidi, Mohammad-Reza & Elmar Ternes. 1991. Persian (Farsi). *Journal of the International Phonetic Association* 21(2). 96–98. DOI: 10.1017/S0025100300004461.

Martirosyan, Hrach. 2018. The Armenian dialects. In Geoffrey Haig & Geoffrey Khan (eds.), *The languages and linguistics of Western Asia*, 46–105. Berlin/Boston: De Gruyter. DOI: 10.1515/9783110421682-003.

Martirosyan, Hrach. 2019. The Armenian dialects: Archaisms and innovations; description of individual dialects. *Bulletin of Armenian Studies / Армянский гуманитарный вестник* 5. 164–258.

Martirosyan, Hrach. Submitted. Lingo-cultural studies on Persian Armenia. Unpublished manuscript.

Megerdoomian, Karine. 2005. Transitivity alternation verbs and causative constructions in Eastern Armenian. *Annual of Armenian Linguistics* 24. 13–33.

Megerdoomian, Karine. 2009. *Beyond words and phrases: A unified theory of predicate composition*. Berlin: VDM, Verlag Dr. Müller.

Mesropyan, Haykanush. 2022. *The linguistic geographical characteristics of the dialects of the Armenians in Persia and the migration of the dialect speakers*. http://eng.aybuben.com/the-linguistic-geographical-characteristics-of-the-dialects-of-the-armenians-in-persia-and-the-migration-of-the-dialect-speakers/ (1 March, 2022).

Meyer, Robin. 2017. *Iranian-Armenian language contact in and before the 5th century CE: An investigation into pattern replication and societal multilingualism.* University of Oxford. (Doctoral dissertation).

Minassian, Martiros. 1980. *Grammaire d'arménien oriental.* Delmar, NY: Caravan Books.

Mokari, Payam Ghaffarvand, Stefan Werner & Ali Talebi. 2017. An acoustic description of Farsi vowels produced by native speakers of Tehrani dialect. *The Phonetican Journal of the International Society of Phonetic Sciences* 114. 6–23.

Moran, Steven & Daniel McCloy. 2019. *PHOIBLE 2.0.* Jena: Max Planck Institute for the Science of Human History. https://phoible.org/.

Nercissians, Emilia. 1988. Bilingualism with diglossia: Status and solidarity dimensions. In J. Normann Jørgensen, Elisabeth Hansen, Anne Holmen & Jørgen Gimbe (eds.), *Bilingualism in society and school*, 55–68. Clevedon: Multilingual Matters.

Nercissians, Emilia. 2001. Bilingualism and diglossia: Patterns of language use by ethnic minorities in Tehran. *International Journal of the Sociology of Language* 148. 59–70. DOI: 10.1515/ijsl.2001.014.

Nercissians, Emilia. 2012. Life and culture of Armenians in Iran. *Language Discourse & Society* 2. 31–54.

Nichols, Stephen. 2016. *An acoustic study of the Turkish rhotic.* Poster. 5th International Workshop on Phonetic, Phonological, Acquisitional, Sociolinguistic and Dialect-Geographic Aspects of Rhotics, 18–20 May, Leeuwarden, Netherlands.

Nikolaian, Varand. 2016. Dialects of the Armenian of the Iranian diaspora: A study of the hierarchical interaction of the Iranian-Armenian dialects. Unpublished manuscript.

Paster, Mary. 2006. *Phonological conditions on affixation.* University of California, Berkeley. (Doctoral dissertation).

Pater, Joe. 2007. The locus of exceptionality: Morpheme-specific phonology as constraint indexation. In Leah Bateman, Michael O'Keefe, Ehren Reilly & Adam Werle (eds.), *University of Massachusetts Occasional Papers in Linguistics 32: Papers in Optimality Theory III*, 187–207. Amherst, MA: Graduate Linguistics Student Association, University of Massachusetts. DOI: 10.7282/T38C9TB6.

Pierrehumbert, Janet Breckenridge. 1980. *The phonology and phonetics of English intonation.* Massachusetts Institute of Technology. (Doctoral dissertation).

Plungian, Vladimir. 2018. Notes on Eastern Armenian verbal paradigms. In Daniël Olmen, Tanja Mortelmans & Frank Brisard (eds.), *Aspects of linguistic variation*, 233–246. Berlin: De Gruyter. DOI: 10.1515/9783110607963-009.

References

Polinsky, Maria. 1995. Cross-linguistic parallels in language loss. *Southwest Journal of Linguistics* 14(1-2). 88–123.

Rafat, Yasaman. 2010. A socio-phonetic investigation of rhotics in Persian. *Iranian Studies* 43(5). 667–682. DOI: 10.1080/00210862.2010.518030.

Rezaei, Saeed & Maryam Farnia. 2023. Armenian language and identity in Iran: The case of Iranian Armenians of Isfahan. In Anousha Sedighi (ed.), *Iranian and minority languages at home and in diaspora*, 249–270. Berlin/Boston: Walter de Gruyter. DOI: 10.1515/9783110694277-010.

Rezaei, Saeed & Maedeh Tadayyon. 2018. Linguistic landscape in the city of Isfahan in Iran: The representation of languages and identities in Julfa. *Multilingua* 37(6). 701–720. DOI: 10.1515/multi-2017-0031.

Riggs, Elias. 1856. *A grammar of the modern Armenian language as spoken in Constantinople and Asia Minor*. Constantinople: AB Churchill.

Sadat-Tehrani, Nima. 2007. *The intonational grammar of Persian*. University of Manitoba. (Doctoral dissertation).

Sadat-Tehrani, Nima. 2011. The intonation patterns of interrogatives in Persian. *Linguistic Discovery* 9(1). 105–136. DOI: 10.1349/PS1.1537-0852.A.389.

Sağ, Yağmur. 2019. *The semantics of number marking: Reference to kinds, counting, and optional classifiers*. Rutgers University. (Doctoral dissertation).

Sakayan, Dora. 2000. *Modern Western Armenian for the English-speaking world: A contrastive approach*. Montreal: Arod Books.

Sakayan, Dora. 2007. *Eastern Armenian for the English-speaking world: A contrastive approach*. Yerevan: Yerevan State University Press.

Sampson, Rodney. 2016. Sandhi phenomena. In Adam Ledgeway & Martin Maiden (eds.), *The Oxford guide to the Romance languages*, 669–680. Oxford: Oxford University Press. DOI: 10.1093/acprof:oso/9780199677108.003.0040.

Samvelian, Pollet & Jesse Tseng. 2010. Persian object clitics and the syntax-morphology interface. In Stefan Müller (ed.), *Proceedings of the 17th International Conference on Head-Driven Phrase Structure Grammar*, 212–232. Paris: CSLI Publications.

Sanasarian, Eliz. 2000. *Religious minorities in Iran*. Cambridge: Cambridge University Press. DOI: 10.1017/CBO9780511492259.

Sanjian, Avedis K. 1996. The Armenian alphabet. In Peter T. Daniels & William Bright (eds.), *The world's writing systems*, 356–363. New York and Oxford: Oxford University Press.

Sanker, Chelsea, Sarah Babinski, Roslyn Burns, Marisha Evans, Jeremy Johns, Juhyae Kim, Slater Smith, Natalie Weber & Claire Bowern. 2021. (Don't) try this at home! The effects of recording devices and software on phonetic analysis. *Language* 97(4). e360–e382. DOI: 10.1353/lan.2021.0075.

Sargsyan, Hasmik. 2022. The forms of the indefinite article in Eastern Armenian: Pre-modern, early and colloquial Eastern Armenian sources. *Armeniaca* 1. 151–170. DOI: 10.30687/arm/9372-8175/2022/01/009.

Sayeed, Ollie & Bert Vaux. 2017. The evolution of Armenian. In Jared Klein, Brian Joseph & Matthias Fritz (eds.), *Handbook of comparative and historical Indo-European linguistics*, 1146–1167. Berlin/Munich/Boston: Walter de Gruyter. DOI: 10.1515/9783110523874-021.

Scala, Andrea. 2011. Differential object marking in Eastern Armenian: Some remarks. In Vittorio Springfield Tomelleri, Manana Topadze & Anna Lukianowicz (eds.), *Current advances in Caucasian studies*, 363–372. Munich: Otto Sagner.

Schirru, Giancarlo. 2012. Laryngeal features of Armenian dialects. In Benedicte Nielsen Whitehead, Thomas Olander, Birgit Olsen & Jens Elmegard Rasmussen (eds.), *The sound of Indo-European: Phonetics, phonemics, and morphophonemics*, 435–457. Copenhagen: Museum Tusculanum Press.

Selkirk, Elisabeth. 1986. On derived domains in sentence phonology. *Phonology Yearbook* 3(1). 371–405. DOI: 10.1017/S0952675700000695.

Seyfarth, Scott, Hossep Dolatian, Peter Guekguezian, Niamh Kelly & Tabita Toparlak. Forthcoming. Armenian (Yerevan Eastern and Beirut Western varieties). *Journal of the International Phonetic Association*.

Seyfarth, Scott & Marc Garellek. 2018. Plosive voicing acoustics and voice quality in Yerevan Armenian. *Journal of Phonetics* 71. 425–450. DOI: 10.1016/j.wocn. 2018.09.001.

Shakibi, Jami Gilani & Hermik Bonyadi. 1995. *A short survey of the Armenian language: Tehrani dialect*. Nashville, TN: Babylonia Language and Translation Center.

Sharifzadeh, Afsheen. 2015. *On "Parskahayeren", or the language of Iranian Armenians*. https : / / borderlessblogger . wordpress . com / 2015 / 08 / 25 / on -parskahayeren-or-the-language-of-iranian-armenians/ (1 March, 2022).

Siddiqi, Daniel. 2009. *Syntax within the word: Economy, allomorphy, and argument selection in Distributed Morphology*. Amsterdam: John Benjamins. DOI: 10.1075/la.138.

Sigler, Michele. 1997. *Specificity and agreement in Standard Western Armenian*. Massachusetts Institute of Technology. (Doctoral dissertation).

Sigler, Michele. 2001. A logophoric pronoun in Western Armenian. *Annual of Armenian Linguistics* 21. 13–30.

Sigler, Michele. 2003. A note on the classifier in Western Armenian: Had. *Annual of Armenian Linguistics* 22. 41–53.

Silvestri, Giuseppina. 2022. Italian dialects at the phonology-syntax interface: The case of propagination. *Proceedings of the Linguistic Society of America* 7(1). 5256. DOI: 10.3765/plsa.v7i1.5256.

Stevick, Earl W. 1955. *Syntax of Colloquial East Armenian*. Cornell University. (Doctoral dissertation).

Stump, Gregory T. 2006. Heteroclisis and paradigm linkage. *Language* 82(2). 279–322. DOI: 10.1353/lan.2006.0110.

Stump, Gregory T. 2010. The derivation of compound ordinal numerals: Implications for morphological theory. *Word Structure* 3(2). 205–233. DOI: 10.3366/word.2010.0005.

Su, Yu-Ying Julia. 2012. *The syntax of functional projections in the vP periphery*. University of Toronto. (Doctoral dissertation).

Sy, Mariame. 2005. Ultra Long-Distance ATR Agreement in Wolof. *Annual Meeting of the Berkeley Linguistics Society* 31(2). 95–106. DOI: 10.3765/bls.v31i2.824.

Tahtadjian, Talia. 2020. *Western Armenian rhotics: A differential phonetic study*. Carleton University. (Bachelor's Thesis).

Tamrazian, Armine. 1994. *The syntax of Armenian: Chains and the auxiliary*. University College London. (Doctoral dissertation).

The UCLA Phonetics Lab Archive. 2007. UCLA Department of Linguistics. Los Angeles, CA. http://archive.phonetics.ucla.edu/ (20 May, 2022).

Thomson, Robert W. 1989. *An introduction to Classical Armenian*. Delmar, NY: Caravan Books.

Tıraş, Melda Nisan. 2021. */r/ sesinin uzamsal özelliklerinin ultrason yöntemiyle incelenmesi [Investigation of the spatial properties of the /r/ sound using speech ultrasound]*. İstanbul Medipol Üniversitesi. (MA thesis).

Toparlak, Tabita. 2017. *Etude phonétique des consonnes occlusives de l'arménien oriental*. Université Paris 3 - Sorbonne Nouvelle. (MA thesis).

Toparlak, Tabita. 2019. *Etudes phonétiques en arménien*. Université Paris 3 - Sorbonne Nouvelle. (MA thesis).

Toparlak, Tabita & Hossep Dolatian. 2022. Intonation and focus marking in Western Armenian. In Öner Özçelik & Amber Kennedy (eds.), *Proceedings of the 4th Conference on Central Asian Languages and Linguistics (ConCALL)*, 81–94.

Toparlak, Tabita & Hossep Dolatian. 2023. Aerodynamics and articulation of word-final ejectives in Eastern Armenian. In Radek Skarnitzl & Jan Volín (eds.), *Proceedings of the 20th International Congress of Phonetic Sciences*, 3246–3251. Guarant International.

Tranel, Bernard. 1996. French liaison and elision revisited: A unified account within Optimality Theory. In Claudia Parodi, Carlos Quicoli, Mario Saltarelli &

Maria Luisa Zubizarreta (eds.), *Aspects of Romance linguistics*, 433–455. Washington, D.C.: Georgetown University Press.

United States Census Bureau. 2015. *Place of birth for the foreign-born population in the United States.* https://data.census.gov/cedsci/table?q=armenian&g=0400000US06&tid=ACSDT5YSPT2015.B05006.

van der Wal Anonby, Christina. 2015. *A grammar of Kumzari: A mixed Perso-Arabian language of Oman.* Leiden University. (Doctoral dissertation).

Vaux, Bert. 1995. A problem in diachronic Armenian verbal morphology. In Jos Weitenberg (ed.), *New approaches to medieval Armenian language and literature*, 135–148. Amsterdam: Rodopi.

Vaux, Bert. 1997. The phonology of voiced aspirates in the Armenian dialect of New Julfa. In Nicholas Awde (ed.), *Armenian perspectives. 10th anniversary conference of the Association Internationale des Études Arméniennes*, 231–248. Richmond, Surrey: Curzon.

Vaux, Bert. 1998a. The laryngeal specifications of fricatives. *Linguistic Inquiry* 29(3). 497–511. DOI: 10.1162/002438998553833.

Vaux, Bert. 1998b. *The phonology of Armenian.* Oxford: Clarendon Press.

Vaux, Bert. 2001. The Armenian dialect of Aslanbeg. *Annual of Armenian Linguistics* 21. 31–64.

Vaux, Bert. 2003. Syllabification in Armenian, Universal Grammar, and the lexicon. *Linguistic Inquiry* 34(1). 91–125. DOI: 10.1162/002438903763255931.

Vaux, Bert. 2007. Homshetsma: The language of the Armenians of Hamshen. In Hovann Simonian (ed.), *The Hemshin: History, society and identity in the highlands of northeast Turkey*, 257–278. London and New York: Routledge.

Vaux, Bert. 2022a. *Does Armenian have glottalized IOR ejective stops?* Talk. Cambridge Phonetics and Phonology Seminar, 8 November 2022. https://lingbuzz.net/lingbuzz/007165.

Vaux, Bert. 2022b. The Armenian dialect of Salmast. Unpublished manuscript. https://lingbuzz.net/lingbuzz/007166.

Vaux, Bert. In preparation. The Armenian dialect of New Julfa, Isfahan. Unpublished manuscript.

Vaux, Bert & Andrew Wolfe. 2009. The appendix. In Eric Raimy & Charles E. Cairns (eds.), *Contemporary views on architecture and representations in phonology*, 101–143. Cambridge, MA: The MIT Press. DOI: 10.7551/mitpress/9780262182706.003.0005.

Veselinova, Ljuba. 1997. Suppletion in the derivation of ordinal numerals: A case study. In Benjamin Bruening (ed.), *Proceedings of the 8th Student Conference in Linguistics*, 429–44. Cambridge, MA: MIT Working Papers in Linguistics.

References

Weisser, Philipp. 2019. Telling allomorphy from agreement. *Glossa* 4(1). DOI: 10. 5334/gjgl.803.

Weitenberg, Jos J.S. 2008. Diphthongization of initial E- and the development of initial Y- in Armenian. In Alexander Lubotsky, Jos Schaeken, Jeroen Wiedenhof, Rick Derksen & Sjoerd Siebinga (eds.), *Evidence and counterevidence: Essays in honour of Frederik Kortlandt, volume 1: Balto-Slavic and Indo-European linguistics*, 609–616. Amsterdam/New York: Rodopi. DOI: 10.1163/ 9789401206358.

Yeghiazaryan, Lusine. 2010. *Caso, definitude e os sintagmas nominais no armênio*. Universidade de São Paulo. (Doctoral dissertation).

Zamir, Jan Roshan. 1982. *Variation in Standard Persian: A sociolinguistic study*. University of Illinois at Urbana-Champaign. (Doctoral dissertation).

Zimmermann, Eva. 2019. Gradient symbolic representations and the typology of ghost segments. In *Proceedings of the Annual Meetings on Phonology*, vol. 7. DOI: 10.3765/amp.v7i0.4576.

Աբեղյան, Մանուկ. 1933. Հայոց Լեզվի Տաղաչափություն: Մետրիկա *[Metrics of the Armenian language]*. Երևան: Հայկական ՍՍՌ Գիտությունների Ակադեմիա Հրատարակչություն.

Ախվերդեան, Գէորգեայ. 1852. Սայեաթ-Նովայ. Լուս Գցած Աշխատասիրութէնով *[Sayat-Nova]*. Մոսկվը: Ի տպարանի Վլատիմիրայ Գատիե. https://www.google. co.uk/books/edition/Sajeath_N%5C%C3%5C%B4waj/-bg-AAAAcAAJ.

Աճառեան, Հրաչեայ. 1911. Հայ Բարբառագիտություն *[Armenian dialectology]*. Մոսկուա-Նոր-Նախիջեւան: Լազարեան ճեմարան Արեւելեան Լեզուաց.

Աճառեան, Հրաչեայ. 1925. Քննութիւն Նոր-Նախիջեւանի (Խրիմի) Բարբառի *[Examination of the New Nakhichevan (Crimea) dialect]*.

Աճառեան, Հրաչեայ. 1926. Հայերէն Արմատական Բառարան *[Armenian etymological dictionary]*. Երեւան: Երեւանի Համալսարանի Հրատարակչուհին.

Աճառյան, Հրաչյա. 1926. Քննություն Մարաղայի Բարբառի *[Examination of the Maragha dialect]*.

Աճառյան, Հրաչյա. 1940. Քննություն Նոր-Ջուղայի Բարբառի *[Examination of the New Julfa dialect]*.

Աճառյան, Հրաչյա. 1952. Քննություն Վանի Բարբառը *[Study of the the dialect of Van]*. Երևան: Երևանի Պետական Համալսարանի Հրատարակչություն.

Աճառյան, Հրաչյա. 1954. Լիակատար Քերականություն Հայոց Լեզվի *[Complete grammar of the Armenian language]*. Vol. 2. Երևան: Հայկական ՍՍՌ Գիտությունների Ակադեմիա Հրատարակչություն.

Աճառյան, Հրաչյա. 1961. Լիակատար Քերականություն Հայոց Լեզվի *[Complete grammar of the Armenian language]*. Vol. 4.2. Երևան: Հայկական ՍՍՌ Գիտությունների Ակադեմիա Հրատարակչություն.

Ասատրյան, Մանվել. 1962. Ուրմիայի (Խոյի) Բարբառը *[Dialect of Urmia or Khoy]*. Երևան: Երևանի Պետական Համալսարանի Հրատարակչություն.

Ավետյան, Սարգիս. 2020. Համաբանական Փոփոխությունների Երկու Միտում Արդի Արևելահայերենի Աորիստի Հարացույցում (Համաժամանակյա և Տարաժամանակյա Քննություն) [Two tendencies of analogical changes in the aorist paradigm of Modern Eastern Armenian (A synchronic and diachronic examination)]. Բանբեր Երևանի Համալսարանի. Բանասիրություն 31(1). 24–39.

Ավետյան, Սարգիս. 2022. Արդի Արևելահայերենի Կ(ը)- Ապառնիի և -Ու Ապառնիի Իմաստագործառնությային Փոխհարաբերություն Հարցի Շուրջ [On the question of the semantic-functional relationship between the Կ(ը)- future and the -Ու future in Modern Eastern Armenian]. Բանբեր Երևանի Համալսարանի. Բանասիրություն 13(2 (38)). 22–35.

Բաղրամյան, Ռ. Հ. 1985. Ղարադաղի Միջենթաբարբառը [The intermediate subdialect of Gharadagh]. Պատմա-բանասիրական հանդես 1. 185–194.

Գրիգորյան, Գայանե. 2018. Խոսակցական Լեզվում Վաղակատար Դերբայի L-ի Անկումը Շրջման Շարադասության Ժամանակ (Փորձառական Հետազոտություն) [The fall of the sound "L" of the past participle during the inversion in the spoken language]. In Վ. Լ. Կատվալյան (ed.), Ջահուկյանական Ընթերցումներ, 53–60. Երևան: ՀՀ ԳԱԱ Հրաչյա Աճառյանի անվան լեզվի ինստիտուտ.

Գրիգորյան, Գայանե. 2019. Խոսակցական Լեզվում Հրամայական Եղանակի Իր Վերջավորության Ր-ի Անկման Մասին [On the fall of "r" of the suffix "ir" of the imperative mood in the spoken language]. In Վ. Լ. Կատվալյան (ed.), Ջահուկյանական Ընթերցումներ, 180–88. Երևան: ՀՀ ԳԱԱ Հրաչյա Աճառյանի անվան լեզվի ինստիտուտ.

Եզեկյան, Լևոն. 2007. Հայոց Լեզու *[Armenian language]*. Երևան: Երևանի Պետական Համալսարանի Հրատարակչություն.

Զաքարյան, Հովհաննես. 1981. Հայերենի Հասարակական Տարբերակումը Երևանում [Social differentiation of Armenian in Yerevan]. In Էդուարդ Բագրատի Աղայան (ed.), Ժամանակակից Հայերենի Խոսակցական Լեզուն *[Modern colloquial Armenian]*, 120–278. Երևան: Հայկական ՍՍՀ Գիտությունների Ակադեմիա.

Խաչատրյան, Ամայա. 1988. Ժամանակակից Հայերենի Հնչյութաբանություն *[Phonetics of contemporary Armenian]*. Երևան: Հայկական ՍՍՀ Գիտությունների Ակադեմիա Հրատարակչություն.

Կատվալյան, Վիկտոր. 2018a. Հայաստանի Հանրապետության Բարբառային Համապատկեր, Գիրք 1: Գեղարքունիքի Մարզ *[Dialectal summary of the Republic of Armenian; Book 1, Gegharkunik Province]*. Երևան: Ասողիկ հրատարակչություն.

References

Կատվալյան, Վիկտոր. 2018b. Մակուի Խոսվածքը Գեղարքունիքի Մարզում [Maku speech in the region of Gegharkunik]. In Հայաստանի Հանրապետության Բարբառային Համապատկեր. Գիրք 1 Գեղարքունիքի Մարզ [Dialectal overview of the Republic of Armenia, volume 1, Region of Gegharkunik], 73–81. Երևան: Ասողիկ.

Կատվալյան, Վիկտոր. 2020. Հայաստանի Հանրապետության Բարբառային Համապատկեր, Գիրք 2: Կոտայքի Մարզ [Dialectal summary of the Republic of Armenian; Book 1, Kotayk Province]. Երևան: Ասողիկ հրատարակչություն.

Դամոյան, Լուսինե, Մերի Սարգսյան & Անահիտ Քարտաշյան. 2014. Երևանի Խոսակցական Լեզուն [The colloquial language of Yerevan]. ՀՀ ԳԱԱ Հրաչյա Աճառյանի անվան լեզվի ինստիտուտ.

Դարագյուլյան, Թերեզա. 1974. Ժամանակակից Հայերենի Ուղղախոսությունը [Modern Armenian orthoepy]. Երևան: Հայկական ՍՍՀ Գիտությունների Ակադեմիա Հրատարակչություն.

Դարագյուլյան, Թերեզա. 1979. Հայերենի Գաղտնավանկային Ը-ի Հնչման Հիմնական Առանձնահատկությունները [Primary characteristics of epenthetic schwas in Armenian]. Լրաբեր Հասարակական Գիտությունների 12. 35–45.

Դարագյուլյան, Թերեզա. 1981. Ակնարկներ Ժամանակակից Հայերեն Խոսակցական Լեզվի [Observations on modern colloquial Armenian]. In Էդուարդ Բագրատի Աղայան (ed.), Ժամանակակից Հայերենի Խոսակցական Լեզուն [Modern colloquial Armenian], 120–278. Երևան: Հայկական ՍՍՀ Գիտությունների Ակադեմիա.

Դարիբյան, Արարատ. 1941. Համառոտություն Հայ Բարբառագիտության [Summary of Armenian dialectology]. Երևան: Պետհամալսարանի տպ.. https://arar.sci.am/dlibra/publication/307074/.

Դուկասյան, Սևակ. 1990. Գրական Արևելահայերենի և Արևմտահայերենի Հնչերանգային Առանձնահատկությունները: Փորձառական-Զուգադրական Հետազոտություն [The intonational features of literary Eastern Armenian and Western Armenian: Experimental-comparative research]. Երևան: Հայկական ՍՍՀ Գիտությունների Ակադեմիա Հրատարակչություն.

Դուկասյան, Սևակ. 1999. Արևելահայերենի Այո-Ոչ Հարցման Հնչերանգը [Intonation of yes-no questions in Eastern Armenian]. Լրաբեր Հասարակական Գիտությունների 1. 125–134.

Մարգարյան, Ալեքսանդր. 1997. Ժամանակակից Հայոց Լեզու. Հնչյունաբանություն [Contemporary Armenian language: Phonology]. Երևան: Երևանի Պետական Համալսարանի Հրատարակչություն.

Մարգարյան, Ալեքսանդր Սիմոնի. 1975. Գորիսի Բարբառը [The dialect of Goris]. Երևան: Երևանի Համալսարնի Հրատարակչություն.

Մարկոսյան, Ռազմիկ Արարատի. 1989. Արարատյան Բարբառ [The dialect of Ararat]. Երևան: Լույս.

Մուրադյան, Հ. Դ., Դ. Մ. Կոստանդյան, Ա. Ն. Հանեյան, Մ. Հ. Մուրադյան & Ա. Վ. Գրիգորյան. 1977. Հայերենի Բարբառագիտական Ատլասի Նյութերի Հավաքման Ծրագիր *[Program for the collection of materials for an Armenian dialectological atlas]*. Երևան։ Հայկական ՍՍՀ Գիտությունների Ակադեմիա.

Ջահուկյան, Գևորգ Բեգլարի. 1972. Հայ Բարբառագիտության Ներածություն *[Introduction to Armenian dialectology]*. Երևան։ ՀՀ ԳԱԱ Հրաչյա Աճառյանի անվան լեզվի ինստիտուտ.

Սարգսյան, Ամայա. 1987. Գոյականական զուգաձևությունները ժամանակակից հայերենում [Noun doublets in contemporary Armenian]. Լեզվի և ոճի հարցեր 10. 123–230.

Սարգսյան, Արտեմ. 1985. Արևելահայ և Արևմտահայ Գրական Լեզուներ։ Զուգադրական-տիպաբանական Քննություն *[Literary languages of Western and Eastern: A comparative-typological examination]*. Երևան։ Հայկական ՍՍՀ ԳԱ Հրատարակչություն.

Սարգսյան, Արտեմ Եղիշեի, Լավրենտի Շահենի Հովհաննիսյան, Նվեր Սարգսյան, Ռոբերտ Թոխմախյան & Ռոբերտ Ուտուտյան (eds.). 2001. Հայոց Լեզվի Բարբառային Բառարան *[Dialectological dictionary of the Armenian language]*. Երևան։ Հրաչյա Աճառյանի Անվան Լեզվի Ինստիտուտ։ ՀՀ Գիտությունների Ազգային Ակադեմի.

Սաակ, Գուրգեն. 2009. Ժամանակակից Հայոց Լեզվի Դասընթաց *[Course in Modern Armenian]*. Երևան։ ԵՊՀ Հրատարակչություն.

Քամալյան, Արևիկ. 2015. Գրական և Խոսակցական Արևելահայերեն. Փոփոխություններ և Կանոնարկում [Literary and colloquial Eastern Armenian changes and standardization]. In Լիլիթ Գալստյան & Յուրի Ավետիսյան (eds.), Արդի Հայերենի Հիմնախնդիրներ, 162–172. Երևան.

Name index

Name index

Name index